BUILDING A NEW
AFGHANISTAN

BUILDING A NEW AFGHANISTAN

ROBERT I. ROTBERG

Editor

WORLD PEACE FOUNDATION
Cambridge, Massachusetts

BROOKINGS INSTITUTION PRESS
Washington, D.C.

 # 76864028

Building a New Afghanistan may be ordered from:
Brookings Institution Press, 1775 Massachusetts Avenue, N.W.
Washington, D.C. 20036
Telephone: 1-800/537-5487 or 410/516-6956
E-mail: hfscustserv@press.jhu.edu; www.brookings.edu

Library of Congress Cataloging-in-Publication data
Building a new Afghanistan / Robert I. Rotberg, editor.
    p.   cm.
    Summary: "Discusses what Afghanistan and the international community should do to resolve dangerous issues and bolster a still fragile state. Offers a blueprint for moving toward greater democracy and prosperity while arguing that the future success of state building in Afghanistan depends on diversifying the economy and enhancing its economic status"— Provided by publisher.
    Includes bibliographical references and index.
    ISBN-13: 978-0-8157-7568-3 (cloth : alk. paper)
    ISBN-10: 0-8157-7568-7 (cloth : alk. paper)
    ISBN-13: 978-0-8157-7569-0 (pbk. : alk. paper)
    ISBN-10: 0-8157-7569-5 (pbk. : alk. paper)
    1. Nation-building—Afghanistan.   2. Postwar reconstruction—Afghanistan.   3. Democratization—Afghanistan.   4. National security—Afganistan.   5. Afghanistan—Politics and government—2001– I. Rotberg, Robert I.
    DS371.4.B83 2007
    958.104'7—dc22   2006038563

9 8 7 6 5 4 3 2 1

The paper used in this publication meets minimum requirements of the American National Standard for Information Sciences—Permanence of Paper for Printed Library Materials: ANSI Z39.48-1992.

Typeset in Adobe Garamond

Composition by R. Lynn Rivenbark
Macon, Georgia

Printed by R. R. Donnelley
Harrisonburg, Virginia

Contents

Preface

Afghanistan has made a remarkable recovery in five years from a war-convulsed, rubble-strewn, and shell-shocked postconflict trauma case to an economically active emerging democracy. Afghans have voted for president, elected a parliament, and embraced a new constitution. Parliament has flexed its muscles, too, refusing to be intimidated by executive prerogatives. Young women are in school, and older women hold national office. Millions of refugees have come home and been resettled. In 2005 double-digit economic growth occurred, and 2006 should show similar results. Roads have been restored and new ones reconstructed. Cell phones are in almost every urban dweller's hand. Kabul, the capital, displays unavoidable symbols of progress: skyscrapers, housing shortages, soaring rentals, and traffic jams. Overall, Afghanistan is no longer battered, fettered, and regimented.

Nevertheless, as the argument throughout this book demonstrates, the Afghan state is not yet fully rebuilt. The necessary institutional scaffolding is in place, but the institutions themselves are still very embryonic. The struggle between the new state, with its democratic ethos and its participatory framework of governing, and the authority structure of the old Afghanistan, with its fiefs and regional and local sources of strength, persists and may not be resolved for a decade or more. The opium trade, narcotrafficking, and rampant corruption are pervasive. That unholy triad motivates and fuels traditional Afghan bases of power and undermines the writ of the central government. Similarly, it undercuts the moral and fiscal foundations of the new state at a decisive time when the central government struggles to deliver improved services—political goods—to the nation for which and to which it is responsible.

These concerns would be sufficient to overwhelm any new state. But the undoubted progress in so many Afghan spheres in 2006 was dramatically threatened by worsened security. No state can build well when it is under siege from within, and in 2006 that was the Afghan condition. State building, much less the larger, long-term project of nation building, can hardly succeed if assaults on the very architecture of the developing state grow more frequent and more destabilizing. Throughout 2006 several thousand regrouped and rearmed Taliban forces were battling NATO legions in southern Afghanistan, and provinces in the eastern part of the country also harbored militant insurgents being hunted by American detachments. If the Taliban cannot be contained and the zones of instability reduced severely by 2007, building the Afghan state could lose momentum and the project to introduce democracy fail. Those and other overriding dilemmas, and their fundamental perils, are examined in detail in this book. Security, institution building, growth and prosperity, and the realities of the drug economy are all analyzed critically by experienced and expert Afghan, American, and British contributors.

This book is the latest in a series of collective studies of developing world nations under severe stress prepared by the Program on Intrastate Conflict and Conflict Resolution of the Kennedy School of Government's Belfer Center, Harvard University, and the World Peace Foundation. Previous books in this series focused on Burma, Nigeria, Sri Lanka, the Sudan, and Zimbabwe, and paralleled the joint efforts of the Program and the Foundation to understand such phenomena as nation-state weakness, failure, and collapse; the functioning of repressive nation-states; combating terrorism in the Horn of Africa; and the nature of good and bad governance in nation-states.[1] Each book and report attempted, as this book does, to offer policy diagnoses founded on a clear and realistic appraisal of the key internal and international obstacles to peace and peaceful development within the nation being dispassionately examined.

This book emerged from discussions that began, for nearly all of its contributors, at a three-day meeting held at the Kennedy School of Government in late 2005. Many senior Afghan officials, in addition to those who
have written chapters for this book, participated in those deliberations, as
did officials from European and American governments, representatives of
nongovernmental organizations, journalists, and scholars. Sham Bathija's
initiative inspired the meeting and persuaded many of his Afghan colleagues to attend. Elisa Pepe, then program manager of the Program on
Intrastate Conflict, brought them from near and far with unusual skill.
The organizers are also grateful to everyone who took part so vigorously in
those discussions, and to Graham Allison, director of the Belfer Center of
Science and International Affairs, Kennedy School, and Philip Khoury,
chair, and to the Trustees of the World Peace Foundation, for their support
of the meeting and of the subsequent writing of this volume, the editing of
which was skillfully accomplished by Deborah L. West.

ROBERT I. ROTBERG
January 2007

Note

1. *Burma: Prospects for a Democratic Future* (1998), *Creating Peace in Sri Lanka: Civil
War and Reconciliation* (1999), *Zimbabwe Before and After the Elections: A Concerned Assessment* (2001), *State Failure and State Weakness in a Time of Terror* (2003), *Crafting the New
Nigeria: Confronting the Challenges* (2004), *When States Fail: Causes and Consequences*
(2004), *The Good Governance Problem: Doing Something About It* (2004), *Battling Terrorism in the Horn of Africa* (2005), *Worst of the Worst: Dealing with Repressive and Rogue
Nations* (forthcoming, 2007).

BUILDING A NEW
AFGHANISTAN

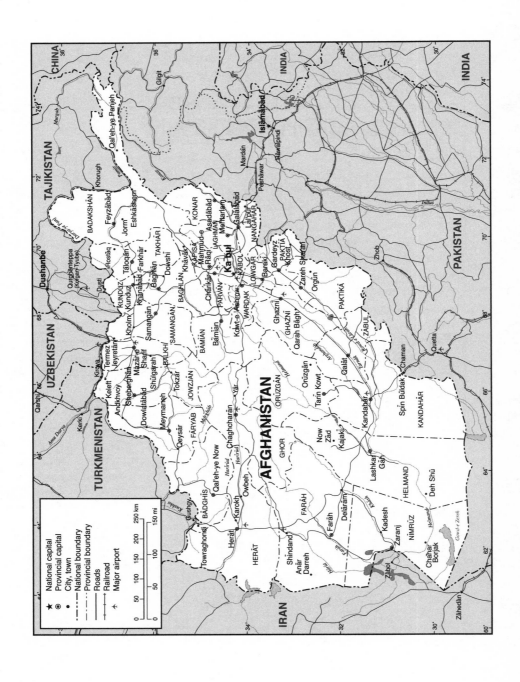

1 | Renewing the Afghan State

Robert I. Rotberg

State building anywhere in the war-torn developing world is hard and exacting. Land-locked Afghanistan represents an extreme level of difficulty, not least because of the destruction of national political institutions during the Russian occupation and the Taliban hegemony. Today's Afghanistan is only very slowly learning how to build upon the wreckage of those years—how to create a government that succeeds for all Afghans. Establishing a nation in the full sense will continue to be a work in progress for many years. For now, it will be enough to establish a framework for good governance and for the administration of President Hamid Karzai to begin consistently to deliver a high order of political goods—security, rule of law, political freedom, and economic opportunity.[1]

Return of the Taliban

As the chapters in this book and the daily news reports from Kandahar, Kabul, and elsewhere in Afghanistan make abundantly clear, the political good of security is only very slowly, very painfully, being realized in parts of the country. Throughout the country, especially in the strongholds of the newly

1

revived Taliban, the writ of the Karzai government runs intermittently and only when enforced stringently by NATO and U.S. forces. In Helmand beginning in May 2006, there were major bursts of Taliban-instigated violence, causing many casualties. Throughout the rest of that spring and summer, attacks and firefights continued, testing recently arrived soldiers from Canada and Britain and undercutting the legitimacy of the Karzai government. As the head of the U.S. Defense Intelligence Agency told Congress as early as February 2006, well before the major battles of the summer, the renewed Taliban insurgency presented a threat to the authority of the Karzai government more severe than any since 2001. "Something has gone alarmingly wrong in Afghanistan," the *New York Times* editorialized in June.[2]

At least four southern Pashtun-dominated provinces—Helmand, Uruzgan, Zabul, and Kandahar—were deeply penetrated by the Taliban by May and June 2006. A villager told the *Boston Globe* in June that he had no choice but to help the Taliban. "They come in groups of five, ten, or twenty. Some are local, others are speaking Urdu . . . and Arabic. . . . They ask for food, but you can't refuse. You can't argue with men with guns." Clearly, villagers in these unsafe provinces feel caught between the Taliban and the weakened government. "To be honest," one said, "we cannot fight anyone. We don't like either side."[3]

The villager's dilemma is the national one. As the chapters by Ali A. Jalali, Hekmat Karzai, and Paula R. Newberg express at some length, in 2006 security in Afghanistan became increasingly elusive. Despite major initiatives to transform the Afghan National Army into a capable and strong military force, in 2006 it possessed insufficient firepower, hardly any indigenous air support, and no secure operational budget. Insecurity vitiated both the state-building and nation-building projects, undermined every conceivable recovery initiative, and made the four years from 2002 to 2006 seem like a bubble of opportunity that had been burst by the U.S. failure to extirpate Taliban remnants and locate Osama bin Laden and his protectors and by the Karzai government's refusal or inability fully to take charge and appear credible to villagers and warlords alike. On the positive side, as Newberg makes clear, reasonably free and fair national elections had been held in 2005, and a legitimized parliament had emerged that effectively challenged Karzai's executive prerogatives.[4] Kabul had grown in size and wealth, and NATO or U.S., and sometimes Afghan, troops had managed now and then to push back Taliban and other insurgents. New roads had been constructed. Communications within the country were much improved. But villagers and inhabitants of several of the more significant regional centers, with their own overlords, hardly believed that the Karzai government was anything more than a distant, quasi-foreign implant.

The security situation continued to deteriorate throughout 2006. Each week brought renewed confrontations. Although NATO contingents in the Pashtun provinces of the south inflicted many casualties on the Taliban, they also lost surprising numbers of their own British, Canadian, Australian, and Dutch troops. The British commander of the NATO force admitted that the task of pacification was much more difficult than he had anticipated; the Taliban were much tougher and better equipped than he had been led to believe. He and the American commander of NATO called for substantial reinforcements from Europe.[5]

The violence in southern Afghanistan also prevented NATO from winning local hearts and minds. Arguably, most Afghans were less secure in 2006 than they were under Taliban rule. No greater number of Afghans had access to electric power than they had in Taliban times. NATO, with money to spend, was not able to build bridges and market stalls, drill wells, construct schools, and otherwise enable villagers to go peacefully about their daily lives. In fact, as several chapters in this book hint, by mid-2006 it was clear that the Taliban, with rear bases in Pakistan, had seized the initiative from the United States and NATO. Whole rural areas became no-go areas for foreign troops. There had been a Taliban resurgence that persisted throughout the remaining months of the year.

Given these ominous developments in the southern countryside, suicide bombings in Kabul, the failure to find either Osama bin Laden or Mullah Omar, and the massive income from narcotics trafficking and the resultant flow of arms into Taliban areas, it is no wonder that Secretary of State Condoleezza Rice said that Afghanistan could become a failed state. She argued strongly against abandoning the war against the Taliban in Afghanistan.[6] Indeed, toward the end of 2006, it was clear that Afghanistan had never really recovered from its early convalescence as a failed nation-state.

Without the ability to project state power beyond Kabul, and without a monopoly of force, the new state is bound to continue weak and troubled. If its writ fails to run very far, if the state seems more and more unable to protect villagers from the Taliban and from criminal gangs, and if the moral authority of the state seems weaker rather than stronger, state building becomes a much tougher project than ever before. Security at the personal level is critical and among the fundamental determinants of nation-state effectiveness. So far, personal security throughout the proto-nation remains a rhetorical aspiration. Consequently, nearly every other item on the state-building agenda will continue to be held hostage to security weaknesses and failures. Other political goods—together the germ of state building—are capable of being delivered best when a state is thoroughly secure.

There are many remedies. More foreign boots on the ground is one; in 2006 the NATO force battling the Taliban in four key southern provinces reached 20,000, plus another 12,000 American troops transferred to it from anti–al Qaeda duties, when at least double that first number were needed. Another answer was for the NATO and American troops on the ground to fight "smarter," engaging the local stakeholders more fully and providing realistic alternatives to whatever is being supplied by the Taliban. Villagers will back winners, as well as whichever party can offer them security and a proper economic future.

Rule of Law

The rule of law is in part what an effective national government promises. Otherwise the guns of the steppe govern, and the ability of Afghanistan's central administration to act with authority becomes more and more questionable. In any new state, and especially in a traditionally rough and dangerous area such as Afghanistan, creating a robust rule of law practice and atmosphere is critical. Doing so is essential if Afghanistan seeks to revive its economy and provide hope and opportunity to its long-battered constituents. Alastair J. McKechnie offers a diagram that expresses these interrelationships—what he terms "the informal equilibrium," with rule of law at the center and macroinstability and a poor regulatory framework on the periphery.[7]

Afghans understand and appreciate both the common law and the sharia approaches to jurisprudence. Parts of Karzai's modern-tending state want desperately to follow a fully Western-based system that embraces individual rights and thus human rights. It also wants to strengthen a Western-style method of contract that is well adapted to international commerce. But Karzai's new Afghanistan also acknowledges the cultural vitality of traditional forms of lawmaking and adjudication. In domestic matters and in other large swathes of life, the clan-based notions of right and wrong are still potent. These inherent contradictions and ambiguities are reflected in the composition of the revived judicial system and are also intrinsic to the shifting manner in which justice is accomplished in a country that needs consistency and clear focus if it is to begin to create the institutions of a modern state.

Religiously conservative countries will always have difficulty establishing Western style democratic institutions and believing fully in them. Or, as Barnett Rubin writes, "The lack of judicial reform has become a bottleneck for security, governance, and economic development."[8] The justice system is corrupt and ineffective, whether in the cities or in the villages, where customary, Islamic law still prevails despite the fine words of the new national constitution. The latter promises freedom of speech and sexual equality, but mullahs prefer to base their decisions on the constitutional article that says that no law can contradict the beliefs and provisions of Islam.

In the commercial arena, as Hedayat Amin Arsala discusses, a 1955 commercial code establishes dispute resolution procedures for businesses, side by side with sharia law and traditional systems of informal justice.[9] Commercial entities, especially foreign ones, prefer greater predictability and certainty, and a much reduced expectation of corrupt practice. Arsala relates the government's anticorruption strategy, which includes a strengthening of public sector management and the legal system.

Judges are poorly paid, and most are clerics with little knowledge of or interest in the secular laws now being promulgated by the executive and legislative branches of the Afghan government. Some of the judges are barely literate, and prosecutors and police investigators are no more thoroughly trained or capable. Lengthy new legal codes may therefore be difficult to administer, much less translate into practice. Italy has been in charge of Western efforts to assist the Afghan judicial system, and some new judges and prosecutors have been trained, but the prevailing political culture of jurisprudence has not yet begun to alter significantly. Ali Jalali suggests that the court structure is outdated, personnel are unqualified, and corruption is deep-rooted.[10]

In other words, any attempt by the Karzai government to deliver a high order of political goods across Afghanistan's critical sectors will be hindered—possibly fatally—by the regime's seeming need to placate or neutralize traditionalists, Islamists, and quasi-Islamists, and every leader whose base of support is rural and antimodern. Carlotta Gall called Karzai "a consummate tribal politician."[11] But Karzai's administration also needs traditional and Islamist associations to help counter renewed appeal to Afghans by the Taliban. That is presumably why President Karzai attempted in 2006 to reappoint Fazel Hadi Shinwari as chief justice of the Afghan Supreme Court. Shinwari heads the Ulema Shura, or Council of Clerics, a group of 100 religious clerics from across Afghanistan. It meets monthly and approves President Karzai's decisions on many issues. Ultimately, the new parliament rejected Shinwari because of his lack of education, compelling Karzai to choose again. He then appointed and parliament approved a strong group of new jurists who were professionals and reformers, and included well-respected legal theorists. Abdul Salam Azimi, a moderate Islamic scholar and constitution framer, became chief justice.[12]

Engines of Growth

Postconflict transitional polities need urgently to jump-start their economies—to revive a sense of purpose and give people reasons to think positively about the new or growing state. That is exactly what foreign donors sought to do in postconflict Timor Leste. With foreign capital, roads and schools were rebuilt and hospitals were refurbished and reequipped. Radio stations and newspaper presses were repaired and turned over to new employees. With a renewed infrastructure, Timor could begin to function after its severe trauma. Most of all, with wages growing, money began to circulate, and a virtuous cycle of development commenced.

In Afghanistan the arteries of commerce still need to be refurbished—urgently. Communications facilities remain rudimentary, especially for a reviving economy. But an equally significant obstacle to jump-starting the Afghan economy is its human capital deficit. Fifty-seven percent of Afghans are under eighteen years of age, and that cohort and the young adult cohort (ages eighteen to thirty-five) have very little opportunity for employment. How to create jobs for indigenous Afghans, and not for the better trained Iranians and Pakistanis who now provide a part of the low-skilled national labor force, is a major issue with severe consequences. Capacity building is an immediate as well as a critical medium- and long-term imperative.

Afghanistan is also among the poorest countries on the globe. Most of its inhabitants subsist on less than $1 a day. In 2005 the average annual per capita GDP was estimated to be about $300. Taking poverty and other social indicators together, in 2004 Afghanistan ranked 173rd of 178 countries on the UN Human Development Index.[13]

Yet in 2007 the biggest problem for Afghans and for the Afghan state is how to transform its primary export commodity and its dominant source of both foreign exchange and internal prosperity—opium, raw and processed—into an engine of growth. In 2005 opium earnings constituted about 50 percent of the country's export earnings (47 percent came from foreign assistance and 32 percent from nonopium agriculture) and approximately 35 percent of national GDP.[14] Afghanistan supplied about 92 percent of the world's heroin and 90 percent of that consumed in Europe. Inside Afghanistan opium also contributed significantly to the country's rampant levels of corruption as well a rising internal consumption problem. Transparency International rates Afghanistan among the most corrupt of the world's countries (117 of 159 in 2005). It was unrated in 2006, presumably because of troubled conditions in the country.[15] Narcotrafficking always corrodes a country's moral fiber and distorts its economy and trade.

Achieving Legitimacy

For the Afghan state to attain legitimacy, many reforms are essential in addition to those focusing on substitutes for the poppy crop and opium processing. Narcotrafficking envelops the state; it also adds measurably to existing corrupt practices. If and when the Karzai government can curb corruption, it will immensely boost its legitimacy as a governing entity. But every anticorruption maneuver creates problems for a fragile regime. Ostensible political allies are liable to be implicated; all of the warlords who support the balance of interests on which Karzai's fragile leadership rests are capable of being compromised. As a leaked UN report suggests, all of the key power brokers of modern Afghanistan are implicated in one or more ways in past or current attacks on persons, groups, and the state. Many have looted the state as well as committed atrocities.[16] Serving the interests of the emerging nation-state and its constituents often clashes with maintaining the interests of powerful political and military brokers. A central problem for President Karzai is how to achieve a workable balance and legitimacy for himself and his government. Otherwise, state building cannot succeed, and the once promising Afghan state will crumble as destructively as its predecessors.

Is President Karzai making the best or the right choices? For example, it was reported in mid-2006 that European diplomats in Kabul were outraged that President Karzai had appointed thirteen former regional militia commanders with links to drug smuggling and organized crime (the country's twin plagues) to senior police positions. The new chief of police in Kabul has been tied to theft and extortion rings. As Declan Walsh commented wisely, these appointments and the controversy over them were "indicative of the dilemma facing the Karzai government: how to balance the demands of international donors who seek accountability for past crimes and merit-based appointments for government jobs [against] the ethnic and political demands of powerful interest groups such as the former mujahideen fighters."[17]

The International Crisis Group (ICG) sagely asks if the Karzai administration has learned the lessons of its country's past.[18] It accuses the administration of wanting a weak, fragmented legislative assembly in order to keep power to itself. The ICG further suggests that Karzai is minimizing the formation and development of political parties instead of using the assembly and parties to reduce the influence of warlords. Moderation and democracy, the ICG proposes, will only grow in Afghanistan if the Karzai government empowers the assembly and strengthens nontraditional—that is, modern—methods of participation at every conceivable level. The chapter by Sarah Lister and Hamish Nixon shows how this same result can be realized at the provincial and local levels in Afghanistan.[19] Jalali comments on the reintegration of local elected and traditional bodies into the country's governance.[20] Newberg, in turn, wonders whether unfinished plans for local level redevelopment are the responsibility of faltering international donors or local actors.[21]

If the nascent Afghanistan is going to build a state successfully, much less a nation, doing so will depend on a healthy provision of security, rule of law, and economic opportunity. Participation, political freedom, accountability, and civil society will all have to be strengthened as well. Afghanistan has already had elections, but now the new nation-state needs to enhance free expression through radio, television, and the press, and shift gradually to a regime that safeguards human rights.[22] In states such as Afghanistan, these are always critical questions of creative statecraft and dedicated, bold leadership. The state further needs to empower civil society outside as well as inside Kabul. Doing so may threaten the power of regional authorities, but if the Karzai government is successfully going to make the transition from a tentative postconflict proto–nation-state to an effective growing democracy, it will need to develop a base of popular support that can trump the satrapies of the warlords. A national government needs a national constituency if it is gradually to democratize Afghanistan. It also needs a lively supportive media and, through appeals to participatory principles, a way to counter the attractions of the traditional mullahs. Whether or not these are realistic projects in contemporary Afghanistan depends on leadership strategies and instincts, and on a precariously and imaginatively balanced government's fundamental appetite for trading short-term political risk for sustainable political security.

Afghanistan is a donor project, too. If the country, with foreign assistance and attention, can begin to win the renewed battles against the Taliban, and if donors can embolden the government that they support to provide greater political freedom, economic opportunity, and a much stronger rule of law, then the donors and the government can together uplift the educational and medical services of the entire country—winning hearts and minds along the way. Critics of the level of foreign assistance to Afghanistan point out that American and other donors have provided barely 5 percent of the per capita level of assistance that has been lavished (to what effect?) on Iraq. In 2006, Washington even reduced its help. Two of the keys to unlocking the potential of inner Afghanistan and also winning support for the Karzai regime are better schooling and better health provisioning. Without advances on these fronts, the overall Afghan project, and state building in general, becomes more problematic. All impoverished constituencies in the developing world seek results. It is from those returns that legitimacy can be enhanced. So far, the program of modernization of which these advances are a part is embryonic. Letting Afghanistan relapse back into state failure may be a dreaded option, but unless the Afghanistan nation-building project soon shows results, the centripetal forces of decay may well prevail.

Creating a Secure Nation

Jalali, in the next chapter, underscores the aforementioned point: the operational exigencies of military action to repress insurgent activity in the towns and villages of the countryside continue "to cast a long shadow" on long-term development. Moreover, inadequate investment in post-conflict reconstruction "continues to haunt the process of recovery." Jalali, the Afghan interim government's minister of the interior, castigates the donor community's "restrained" rehabilitation efforts. He carefully reviews his country's turbulent past before epitomizing the impact on it of the cold war struggle and Soviet occupation. In a compassionate and nuanced analysis, he blames the international community (and Iran) for abandoning the Afghan people after the ouster of the Soviets and for permitting the triumph of the Taliban (with Pakistani connivance). Hekmat Karzai, in a succeeding chapter, takes care to explain the appeal of the Taliban to other Afghans and elaborates on Pakistani influence.[23] He also alludes to Arab financial support and to the Taliban's consummate ability to profit from the opium trade.

The successful American intervention ousted the Taliban and empowered the Northern Alliance, its main ally in the reconquest. That altered the national power configuration in a manner that was confirmed in Bonn in late 2001 and again by the Loya Jirga (grand tribal council) in mid-2002. It has, Jalali asserts, influenced all subsequent political and economic developments and led to the constitutional "defragmentation" of the country. Moreover, he says, a crude ethnic-factional integration into state structures has been substituted for a truly national unification. Thus Afghanistan's renewed instability in part still reflects overweening Tajik and Uzbek (Northern Alliance) influence, the continuation of private sources of income and private armies, and consequent distrust by the more numerous Pashtun speakers of the south (who have become fodder for the Taliban). Despite urgent and determined efforts to integrate private armies into the national force and to reduce regional autonomies, more should be done if national unification is to be achieved.

In order to improve security, especially given the resurgence of the Taliban in 2006, Jalali calls for urgent attention to the training and equipping of proper police detachments. As of 2006, he says, despite well-intended local and international efforts, the national police were "ill trained, poorly paid, underequipped, and inadequately armed." In other words, they are patently unequal to Afghanistan's security challenges and needs. In one regional center in the south in late 2006, leading Afghans returning from exile were astonished to find that of 3,000 policemen, only 1,000 were trained. The remainder were former guerrilla fighters who "punished members of other tribes and turned a blind eye toward rogues of their own."[24] Hekmat Karzai suggests, too, that the concept of policing and a national police is new to much of Afghanistan, so there are cultural as well as logistical and capacity-building obstacles to the deployment of an effective police mechanism.

Jalali further calls for the creation of effective joint mechanisms—a combined command—between the International Security Force for Afghanistan and NATO and local commanders to plan and coordinate the battle for national stability. He reports that there has been too little connection between local and international operations and too little attention to considerations of local culture. That has led to unnecessary collateral damage, intense local anger, and more ammunition for Taliban-inspired antagonism to the Karzai government and to foreign "invaders." It has also weakened the central administration's attempt to hold regional warlords accountable and reduce their power. "Unless the government lives up to public expectations for providing security and services," Jalali warns, "local patronage networks will not only survive but will use their power to influence national programs" and to subvert the reform agenda.

Hekmat Karzai explains the reasons behind the reemergence of the Taliban in 2005 and 2006: the return of foreign fighters (some after training in Iraq), better tactics, new outside support, sanctuaries in Pakistan, and financial leverage based on vast profits from narcotics trafficking. He says that the Taliban are more decentralized than before and are organized into small cells capable of gaining village support and attacking national and international forces in guerrilla fashion. But recognizing their inherent weaknesses, they now attack soft, civilian targets rather than taking on international forces directly. They have used suicide bombers for the first time. They are employing the media to disseminate propaganda and to indoctrinate cadres. Depriving rural Afghans of essential services (health clinics, schools, and roads) is fundamental to their strategy in addition to creating as much chaos and fear as possible. Spreading terror is basic to the tactics of small, tightly organized insurgent groupings like the reconfigured Taliban.

Combating the Taliban has been difficult because of weaknesses in the Afghan army and police but also because the indigenous intelligence services have not traditionally been used to infiltrate and learn about dissident groups such as the Taliban. Another factor that Karzai emphasizes is the continued meddling of Pakistan. There is a suspicion that Taliban camps in Pakistan remain open thanks to official support. Pakistan has a long-term interest in destabilizing Afghanistan and thus reasserting its influence there. But, in addition to a new military strategy, Karzai also puts substantial emphasis on those developmental, political, and social measures that should be capable of undermining any appeal of the Taliban. The battle against the Taliban must, he insists, be joined on both broad fronts.[25]

Newberg echoes the concern of all the other contributors to this book: "Despite the enormous strides that have been made since the anarchy of the late 1990s, efforts firmly to establish representative government will . . . falter on the twin grounds of external aggression and internal war." Democratic development and recovery thus must remain—until the nation-state is secured—tantalizing and elusive goals.

Newberg, like Arsala and other contributors, also recognizes how much has been accomplished since 2001: successful elections, the empowerment of a legislative assembly that has exerted its will, disarmament of many militiamen, the return to school of 5 million children, the much strengthened role of women in politics and society, and a postconflict economic boom in the cities. The miracle of Afghanistan post-2001 is that it has "moved forward at all." Yet international assistance has not kept pace with the needs of recovery, most monies having been devoted to security. Outside efforts have not been able to overcome the absence of an effective national infrastructure or the regional power complications already mentioned.

Discontent in 2006, reports Newberg, is based on old frustrations. The rural poor remain economic outcasts and the urban poor are hardly embraced by the new engines of growth. Even so, poverty has not displaced a yearning for peace. The problem, as she and other contributors say, is that peace is coming hard. A durable recovery is increasingly problematic rather than increasingly successful, thanks to insecurity and a standoff between a sustainable delivery of political goods and the swirling eddies of frustration and conflict. Reconstruction, she fears, may never be completed. Political progress is also slow, impeded by the constant trade-off between expediency and objectives. Newberg suggests that whether or not Afghanistan recovers fully may depend first on an end to conflict and second on whether or not the internationally assisted experiment of reconstruction is or is not fully joined to a locally determined democratic outcome.

The Emerging Economy

The available statistics, provided by the World Bank and discussed in McKechnie's evaluation of all aspects of Afghanistan's economic performance, offer a positive perspective on Afghanistan's economy.[26] They show that the country has made remarkable advances since vanquishing the Taliban in 2001. Legal real GDP has grown by 80 percent, the equivalent of about $180 a head at current prices.

Aid funds are reaching many of the rural areas, tunnels and roads have been constructed, with more to come, and there is at least the germ of significant development everywhere. Yet, McKechnie reports, recovery is inherently fragile, especially if (as in 2006 seemed likely) foreign assistance flows diminished and fell behind promises. Moreover, progress in institution building is slow, hardly affecting the nation's reliance on Soviet bureaucratic methods and traditions of organization and response.

Arsala, senior advisor to President Karzai and former minister of commerce, is convinced that Afghanistan requires a strong private sector–led economy to provide employment, support a representative democratic government, and destroy the opium trade. Fortunately, he believes that Afghanistan's assets are equal to the need for a radical, national transformation. Afghans are ready and able, especially after being tested in the twin crucibles of Soviet and Taliban occupation. Both Arsala and McKechnie acknowledge, however, that the productivity of Afghan workers is low; median output per worker is $333 in Afghanistan versus $10,000 in Pakistan and $20,000 in China.[27] McKechnie, however, says that Afghan workers have a higher output than those in Uzbekistan and Tajikistan. Progress in this area is hampered by low levels of adult literacy, which are probably only about 36 percent.

The national development strategy of 2005 depends on integrating what is now a highly fragmented economy. Furthermore, the informal sector is much too large, reflecting a powerful antibusiness environment that has prevailed for almost three decades. The government therefore needs to connect existing commercial centers electronically and by road.[28] If and when these commercial arteries are refurbished, then intraregional trade can be developed, taking advantage of the country's strategic location linking Central and South Asia.

Providing power is another major infrastructural need. Afghan firms overwhelmingly declare that the lack of electricity from a grid is their most important constraint. Most rely on costly and inefficient private diesel-fueled generators. McKechnie reports that 76 percent of Afghan firms depend on a generator, as compared to 42 percent in Pakistan and 2 percent or less in Central Asia. Soon, Arsala hopes, his country will generate more of its own power from natural gas transported from Central Asia by pipeline. S. Frederick Starr's chapter provides a useful, speculative blueprint indicating how such an expansion could be realized.

Access to land is another major constraint, and a World Bank report indicates how the formal system for recording land ownership and resolving disputes over land no longer functions.[29] With private armies enforcing the fiat of regional strongmen, and populations having greatly shifted because of war and its aftermath, land rights have become precious and almost impossible to secure.

Arsala advocates bringing leading "firms" in the informal economy into the formal economy so that they pay taxes, can engage easily in international trade, are subject to national laws, and have access to bank credit. McKechnie provides a comprehensive analysis of the informal sector, with manufacturing listed as the largest component (9 percent of GDP) after opium (35 percent of GDP). The latter employs as many as 2 million Afghans. McKechnie also suggests that beyond narcotrafficking there is a shadowy, also illicit, economy that traffics in persons and body organs, enslaves, deals in stolen archaeological artifacts, trades lethal weapons, and seizes land and property by force.

The World Bank and Arsala recognize that the banking sector is weak, if much improved since 2002 when three variants of the Afghani circulated and no central bank existed. Even the state-owned banks cannot effectively analyze business plans; they also have no reliable protection against defaults. For those reasons Arsala says that the banking system lends only 20 percent of the capital nominally available.

If the commercial sector can come to embrace the formal economy, if the energies and avarice that fuel the narcotics trade can be directed into legal channels, and if Afghanistan can begin to grow at 9 percent or more a year for at least a decade—the goal of the national strategy—then jobs can be created to lower the country's staggering rates of unemployment. Doing so will greatly assist the battle for stability and undermine the appeal of insurgents.

So will finding a way to reduce corruption, liberalizing trade in a part of the world where statist modalities have long been preferred, and expanding regional economic cooperation. Afghanistan's new preferential trade pact with India should help, as will its trade agreement with Pakistan and its membership in the South Asia regional cooperation association.

McKechnie warns, however, that so many reforms of the Afghan economy need to be implemented rapidly that there is a danger that it will take too long to accomplish any or many of them. Then the country's ambitious growth targets will prove hard to attain. Sequencing of reform is essential, but little has been done in this regard, and informal arrangements and corrupt practices almost preclude accomplishing the reforms in time, or ever.

Starr joins Arsala and McKechnie in envisaging the new Afghanistan as a regional trade hub, the economic pivot of Central Asia. Starr makes this case with great optimism and verve, envisaging increased cooperation with and the transport of natural gas from Turkmenistan as one of the essential ways in which Afghanistan can move to the center of a revived Silk Road or a Greater Central Asia. Additionally, there was once a flourishing trade with India, which should be resurrected to move energy rather than just fruit and nuts.

Starr suggests that since neither manufacturing nor agriculture promises great returns to Afghans (if poppy growing is somehow diminished), Afghan's future lies assuredly in facilitating regional trade. The old Silk Road can be revived, with Afghanistan at its center. But in order to do so, borders to the north, to the old Soviet states, need to be opened, and trade to Iran and further to Turkey must be encouraged.

Starr urges a U.S. role in making these connections across Central Asia, and even South Asia, work for Afghanistan. To date, however, he sees little awareness in Washington that thinking of Afghanistan as a regional fulcrum might help strengthen the country's security as well as its economic sustainability in a dangerous and largely autarkic region.

Few of these laudable goals can be accomplished without foreign investment. Arsala advocates wholesale reform of existing governmental procedures in order to eliminate red tape and modify existing business registration procedures, land regulations, and capital repatriation rules. There are new laws in these areas, as well as new customs regulations. But the process of bringing capital into the country and taking it out again still needs to be streamlined. And, as mentioned earlier, rampant and growing corruption must be reduced if for no other reason than to boost investor confidence.

The Drug Economy

As McKechnie indicates, despite massive urbanization since 2002, Afghanistan is still predominantly rural. Over 85 percent of the population inhabits villages. Range pasture accounts for 45 percent of the total land area and pastoral activities produce significant food and income. Only 12 percent of the country's total land is arable. Two-thirds of that arable acreage is usually covered in wheat, the nation's primary cereal crop. The bulk of wheat production comes from irrigated growing areas. Even so, wheat yields are low and substantially less than in neighboring countries. Yields in Pakistan, Iran, and Uzbekistan are almost double the best Afghan results. There is abundant room, in other words, for significant improvement in Afghan yields. Together, grazing, wheat growing, and horticulture (fruit and nuts were 40 percent of export earnings in the 1970s) employ about 59 percent of the national labor force. Another 8 percent was engaged in 2004 in growing poppies on less than 3 percent of the cultivated area. Two years on, presumably both numbers have grown substantially.

Cindy Fazey carefully reviews the different proposals that have been advanced to reduce or eliminate the opium trade.[30] Paying farmers not to grow poppies has not worked in Afghanistan recently or in the 1970s. In some cases farmers who ceased poppy cultivation did not receive the promised cash, thus fatally undercutting the integrity of the program. Britain has targeted heroin-processing laboratories, but those centers are easily moveable, difficult to find, and operate intermittently. Restricting the supply of chemicals required for laboratory processing is another idea, but the most prevalent chemical, acetic anhydride, is easily transported across porous borders.

Turning illicit growing of opium into licit production for medical use, via a licensing scheme, is another suggestion. But it presupposes an unmet demand for painkillers such as morphine and a global shortage of legal opiates. Fazey shows that both assumptions are incorrect. She also suggests that converting Afghan farmers from illicit to licit growers would produce an explosion in the amount of land cultivated, thus making no sense of the proposal.

Regular crop substitution programs all have their inherent flaws: the returns are neither steady nor attractive. For example, that is the case with apricots, once widely grown in Afghanistan. Anyway, most of the older apricot trees have been chopped down to make way for poppies, and they take seven years to bear. To be effective any crop substitution incentive will have to have its price guaranteed for a full decade.

Official national policy was aligned with the U.S. approach to narcotics everywhere—the eradication of the poppy plants and prosecution of traffickers. But Afghanistan does not yet have robust markets for alternative crops. Nor are the traffickers the usual riffraff of the criminal underworld. In Afghanistan, most big-time traffickers are associated with or protected by the key regional warlords who are integral to the political success of the Karzai presidency. They profit mightily from opium exports, and their patronage networks require continued flows of cash. Likewise, the stability of the Karzai regime depends on a satisfactory balancing of central power against regional power. If eradication were really to take hold, the evolution of the central government as the key wielder of predominant power in the emerging state might be crippled. Similarly, if eradication were to succeed before alternative farming livelihoods were introduced, the economy of Afghanistan might plunge backwards instead of moving hesitantly and erratically from its postwar nadir toward greater promise. Impoverishing villagers in this manner will only strengthen the impress of the Taliban, especially in remote provinces like Uruzgan and Helmand.

Eradication is the tool of choice favored by the United States and the United Kingdom and, until recently, embraced by President Karzai and other leading Afghans. The poppy crop can theoretically be destroyed on the ground with a fungus or by spraying with herbicides. Both methods damage other crops and can injure humans. In any event, despite partial successes against coca in the Andes, there is little evidence that eradication is more than marginally effective there or elsewhere. Given the Afghan terrain, eradication is a questionable (and costly) remedy.

In 2006, President Karzai admitted that eradication had failed; Afghanistan's poppy production had increased by 49 percent over 2005. He said that he was therefore launching a new national strategy to disrupt the opium trade by targeting traffickers, providing alternative employment for farmers, and strengthening weak state institutions.[31] However, Karzai did not say how he intended to target traffickers, much less provide alternative employment.

Other than strong incentives, only draconian police methods work to reduce poppy growing. The Taliban accomplished this feat briefly, before they were overthrown, and the Syrians were successful in Lebanon in the early 1990s. In today's Afghanistan, with a weak central government and so much power on the periphery that is based on profiteering from drugs, it is unlikely that similar methods would work, much less be tried.

From a commonsense point of view, eradication is foolish as well as wasteful and costly.[32] Why not wean Afghans away from the profits of poppy growing—now mostly enjoyed by traffickers and warlords but still valuable to peasant farmers—by providing realistic incentives to grow crops as rewarding to the farmers if not the traffickers? Saffron and other proposed fanciful substitute agricultural crops cannot command ready markets of sufficient size. Nor, in Afghanistan's drought-dominated terrain, can peasants grow such crops as easily as they can comparatively drought-resistant poppy plants.

A reasonable answer will be to use eradication monies to subsidize the growing of another crop on a long-term (ten-year) basis. Only by offering enduring incentives will it be possible to persuade or induce conservative and rational farmers to switch from the comparatively easy money of poppies to another crop. That crop has to be one that can be consumed locally as well as exported, so it needs to be valued by villagers as well as by consumers in the international neighborhood.

Afghans eat wheat. They have grown wheat for centuries, and the nearby Punjab is a center of South Asian wheat growing. Why not encourage Afghan farmers to grow more wheat by promising them enduring rewards equal to or better than what they receive for their poppies in local markets? Surpluses could be stored, as years of plenty are bound to be followed by dearth (rains frequently fail). As long as there is a central buying mechanism and prices guaranteed for at least a decade, farmers would switch. But they will also distrust and test such promises for the first years, so local markets and a national market will have to be organized by the state and secured by donors—spending funds otherwise wasted on eradication.

Even if the shift from poppies to wheat is but an interim measure as Afghanistan moves away from primary crop production to light industry, servicing Turkmenistan gas pipelines, or developing vegetable and tree crops for the Indian and world markets, wheat profits would provide a cash crop to cushion the transition. Otherwise, Afghanistan cannot easily evolve from its parlous economic present (as described in detail in the chapter by McKechnie) to the prosperous future imagined so well in the chapters by Arsala and Starr.

According to the UN Office on Drugs and Crime, in 2004 poppy production per hectare was valued at $4,600 versus $390 for wheat.[33] Thus to provide incentives to farmers to grow wheat instead of poppies, a long-term fair price for wheat would have to be set well above current world and local prices. Attention would have to be paid to improving irrigation systems and to providing preferential treatment to current poppy growers (especially smallholders) who choose to switch. As McKechnie suggests in a different context, to make enhanced wheat growing and selling practical, more rural credit and better access roads will need to be supplied. Furthermore, at national borders and within each wheat-producing region, a mechanism would need to be instituted to prevent wheat from elsewhere being smuggled into Afghanistan and sold as locally grown. If the wheat piles up, it can be exported by the proposed special marketing board or consumed locally.

Generating the social and economic upheaval necessary to switch farmers from producing opium poppies to growing wheat and other crops is daunting and conceivably unrealistic. As Fazey says in her chapter, "Opium poppies are the best cash crop there is: cultivation is easy, prices are usually excellent, and there is a ready market." In 2004, cultivation of opium poppies had spread for the first time into all of Afghanistan's thirty-two provinces. It became firmly established as the country's main engine for economic growth. Moreover, many millions of Afghans—from smallholders and village chiefs to a string of "protectors" and, finally, big-time traffickers and warlords—profit from the growing, gathering, processing, transporting, and selling of raw and processed opium. The UN Office on Drugs and Crime estimates, however, that less than 30 percent of the enormous profits from this trade accrue to farmers.[34] Fazey reports that the farm gate value in 2005 was a mere $560 million. But its export value was about $2.7 billion.

There are many conceivable objections to this alternative crop proposal. Impracticality is one. Utopianism is another. But eradication provides no lasting answer to Afghanistan's twin overriding concerns: how to provide jobs and income (and alleviate poverty) and how to achieve a workable balance between the power of regional and central authorities. Nor is eradication likely to reduce the corrosive hold of corruption on the national body politic. Of all of the potential substitute crops and livelihoods, wheat holds the surest advantage.

What Is to Be Done?

As the chapters in this book show so well, a new government in Afghanistan, backed by coalition troops and supported by massive amounts of outside assistance, has brought democratic stirrings to a country long ruled much more autocratically. It has begun supplying essential services and political goods in the form of educational opportunity and a new infrastructure. It understands the need for a stronger rule of law regime and is proceeding steadily to improve the delivery of justice. It has produced more political freedom, particularly through elections, and it appreciates the desire for greater accountability. There is a reasonably thriving civil society. The economy is booming, even if that boom depends fundamentally on aid flows and opium profits and has not significantly alleviated poverty. But greater GDP growth has been accompanied by an escalation of corruption and corrupt practices. The moral authority and political legitimacy of the Karzai government are threatened by corruption and equally by wholesale narcotrafficking. Most of all, Afghanistan has become less rather than more safe. The failure of the government to unify the country and substitute the promised future progress for the tough reality of day-to-day rural living has emboldened the defeated Taliban and other insurgents. Until Afghanistan is secured and Afghans can work, travel, and sleep without fear, achievement of the splendid twenty-first-century Afghanistan project—no less than the construction of an entirely new state on the rubble of old compromises and fractured models—will elude Afghans and their coalition partners.

Notes

1. For "political goods" and an extended argument on what constitutes governance, see Robert I. Rotberg, "The Failure and Collapse of Nation-States: Breakdown, Prevention, and

Repair," in Rotberg (ed.), *When States Fail: Causes and Consequences* (Princeton, 2004), 3–44; Robert I. Rotberg and Deborah L. West, "The Good Governance Problem: Doing Something about It," WPF Report 39 (Cambridge, Mass., 2004).

2. *New York Times,* June 1, 2006, as quoted in the *Economist* (June 10, 2006).

3. See Declan Walsh, "Afghan Civilians Accuse U.S.-Led Soldiers of Abuse," *Boston Globe* (June 25, 2006).

4. See chapter 4 in this volume.

5. BBC News (October 6, 2006); Judy Dempsey, "NATO Seeks Afghan Reinforcements," *International Herald Tribune* (September 7, 2006).

6. Condoleezza Rice, quoted in BBC News (October 6, 2006).

7. See chapter 5, figure 5-3, in this volume.

8. Barnett R. Rubin, *Afghanistan's Uncertain Transition from Turmoil to Normalcy* (New York, 2006), 24.

9. See chapter 6 in this volume.

10. See chapter 2 in this volume.

11. Carlotta Gall, "Nation Faltering, Afghan Leader Draws Criticism," *New York Times* (August 23, 2006).

12. See J. Alexander Thier, "Order in the Courts," *New York Times* (August 28, 2006).

13. United Nations Development Program–Afghanistan, "Overview of UNDP in Afghanistan" (Kabul, 2005),www.undp.org.af/about_us/overview_undp_afg/default.htm.

14. All statistics for Afghanistan are problematic. The World Bank offers the 35 percent figure for the contribution of opium and opium products to national GDP (2005). The UN Office of Drug Control calculates that contribution at 52 percent, and Fazey puts it at 60 percent. For a further discussion of these numbers, see McKechnie, chapter 5 in this volume. For late 2006 released numbers (including the 92 percent figure), see UN Office of Drugs and Crime and World Bank, *Afghanistan's Drug Industry: Structure, Functioning, Dynamics and Implications for Counter-Narcotics Policy* (Washington, D.C., 2006).

15. Transparency International, "Corruption Perceptions Index 2005" (Berlin, 2006), www.transparansi.or.id/cpi/2005/media_pack_en.pdf.

16. UN High Commissioner for Human Rights, 2005 draft report, leaked in 2006. See Declan Walsh, "Dark Pasts of Afghans Are Kept Quiet," *Boston Globe* (June 16, 2006).

17. Walsh, "Dark Pasts." See also Jalali, chapter 2 in this volume.

18. International Crisis Group, "Afghanistan's New Legislature: Making Democracy Work," Asia Report 116 (Brussels, May 15, 2006).

19. See chapter 9 in this volume.

20. See chapter 2.

21. See chapter 4.

22. Ibid., for comments on lapses in these areas.

23. See chapter 3 in this volume.

24. David Rohde, "Afghan Symbol for Change Becomes a Symbol of Failure," *New York Times* (September 5, 2006). In late 2006, a joint report prepared by the inspectors general of the U.S. Departments of State and Defense decided that "the American trained police

force in Afghanistan [was] largely incapable of carrying out routine law enforcement work, and that managers of the $1.1 billion training program [could not] say how many officers [were] actually on duty or where thousands of trucks and other equipment issued to police units [had] gone." James Glanz and David Rohde, "U.S. Report Finds Dismal Training of Afghan Police," *New York Times* (December 4, 2006). The report blamed U.S. contractors and "dysfunctional" efforts by the Afghan ministry of the interior for policing inadequacies. Corruption was another factor. Lt. Gen. Karl Eikenberry, commander of the U.S. forces in Afghanistan, said that "corrupt police . . . do more damage to our success than one Taliban extremist." Quoted in Lyse Doucet, "Afghanistan: A Job Half Done," BBC News (December 4, 2006).

25. See also Barnett R. Rubin and Abubakar Siddique, "Resolving the Pakistan-Afghanistan Stalemate," *USIP Special Report* (October 2006).

26. See chapter 5.

27. Ibid., table 5-1.

28. In chapter 7, Starr discusses the major missing physical linkages and how they could be provided, and there is a useful map in McKechnie's chapter.

29. See chapter 5.

30. See chapter 8 in this volume.

31. "Karzai Announces New Anti-Opium Effort," *Boston Globe* (August 23, 2006).

32. Coalition agents spent a total of $2 billion on eradication between 2001 and 2005, and approximately $500,000 was appropriated for this purpose by the ˙ S. Congress in 2005 alone. The U.S. proposed budget for this purpose in fiscal year 2(. ⁄ is just under $500,000. See *Guardian International* (June 14 , 2006); *Foreign Operations, Export Financing and Related Programs Appropriations Act, 2006,* H. Rept. 109-152, 109 Cong. 1 sess. (Washington, D.C., 2005); U.S. Department of State, *FY 2007 International Affairs (Function 150) Budget Request: Summary and Highlights of Accounts by Appropriations Subcommittee* (Washington, D.C., February 6, 2006).

33. United Nations Office on Drugs and Crime, *Afghanistan. Opium Survey 2005* (Vienna, 2005).

34. Ibid.

2 The Legacy of War and the Challenge of Peace Building

ALI A. JALALI

Afghanistan reappeared on the world center stage following the September 11, 2001, terrorist attacks in the United States. The suicide attackers who crashed hijacked passenger planes into the World Trade Center in New York and the Pentagon in Washington, D.C., were linked to Osama bin Laden's worldwide terrorist network, al Qaeda, centered in Taliban-controlled Afghanistan. However, none of those who committed the dreadful crime was an Afghan national nor was the violence inspired by Afghan politics. The tragic event that cost thousands of innocent lives and enormous material damage marked a new turn in the international war on terrorism and ushered in a new phase in the drawn-out civil strife in Afghanistan.

Sadly, it took such a devastating human tragedy for the United States to reengage in the region after a decade-long detachment after the pullout of the Soviet forces from Afghanistan and the end of the cold war. It was during this period that war-torn Afghanistan further slipped into the grip of violence and political chaos, leaving a dangerous power vacuum. The vacuum was eventually filled by the extremist Islamic Taliban regime that hosted the wealthy Saudi militant Osama bin Laden, who became a major source of financial support to the internationally isolated Taliban administration. The emerging partnership allowed bin Laden and his terrorist al Qaeda network to use Afghanistan as a training ground and base of operations for their worldwide terrorist ventures.[1] The situation turned Afghanistan into a major source of instability in the region and beyond.

The U.S.-led coalition war against bin Laden's terrorist network and its Taliban supporters at the end of 2001 scored quick and spectacular military achievements. With close cooperation of the anti-Taliban Afghan factions, the coalition succeeded in breaking up the al Qaeda establishment in Afghanistan and overthrowing its unpopular sponsor, the radical Taliban regime.

The prime reason for the U.S. military intervention in Afghanistan was to destroy the terrorist network responsible for the September 11 attack and topple the Taliban regime. Although international efforts to stabilize post-Taliban Afghanistan are considered a strategic objective in the global war on terror, the operational exigencies of the initial military action continue to cast a long shadow on the long-term development of Afghanistan.

The legacy of a long and devastating war, along with inadequate investment in postconflict reconstruction, continues to haunt the process of recovery. The enormous level of destruction and paucity of national capacity required a much wider state-building investment than the restrained rehabilitation opted for by the international community. Securing Afghanistan's future requires a long-term commitment by the international community, with a clear vision of making Afghanistan a self-supporting nation.

Distinctive Geography and Turbulent History

During the past quarter of a century, Afghanistan's political scene has been dominated by violence fueled by opposing ideologies and competing political interests. The country, which served as the last battlefield of the cold war at the end of the twentieth century, became the scene of the first global war on terrorism at the turn of the twenty-first century.

It has been the destiny of Afghanistan to serve as a battlefield for imperial ambitions since the dawn of history. Prominent British historian Arnold Toynbee, who classified countries between blind alleys and highways, thought that two countries held prominent place on the highway countries list: Syria, as a link between the civilizations of Europe, Africa, and Asia; and Afghanistan, as a bridge between the civilizations of India, East Asia, Central Asia, and the Middle East. "Plant yourself not in Europe but in Iraq," he wrote, and "it will become evident that half the roads of the old world lead to Aleppo and half to Bagram."[2] It is notable that over twenty-three centuries ago, Alexander the Great built his Alexandria-in-the-Caucasus at Bagram; two centuries later Bagram became the seat of the Kushan Empire that stretched from Central Asia to India. Bagram also served as the air force base for the Soviet occupation forces in the 1980s and is now the main military base of the coalition forces in Afghanistan.

Reaction to foreign security threats and a struggle for development have been the hallmarks of Afghanistan's recent history. The country that long blocked military clashes between imperial Russia and British India was forced to fight both powers as the last century wore on. Mostly untouched by the two world wars, Afghanistan faced security challenges at home during the uneasy peace between wars. Seven out of a dozen Afghan rulers during the century were murdered, and two were forced into exile.[3]

King Amanullah Khan's intensive reform program in the 1920s failed to create a major pro-reform constituency. The shock therapy for modernization cost him his throne and plunged the country into civil war. Restoration of peace in 1929 ushered in a period of tight government control and a strictly measured modernization process.

At the beginning of the second half of the century, Afghanistan became a peaceful battlefield of the cold war, with both superpowers vying for influence through economic assistance. But a political dispute with the newly created state of Pakistan, an ally of the West, forced the Afghan government to turn to the Soviet Union for military assistance—a move that had a major impact on the country's future. This focus coincided with democratic changes from 1963 to 1973, during which a new urban-based educated elite emerged as the core of political opposition to the government. The new elite included both a pro-Soviet communist bloc and a revolutionary Islamist movement.

The rise to power of the new elites brought enormous violence and destruction to the nation. The fall of the old regime to a pro-Moscow communist coup in 1978 opened a long period of violence that turned Afghanistan into a hotspot of the cold war. The Afghan violence that began as an antistate insurgency against the communist coup of April 1978 soon turned into a wider conflict. It led to the Soviet military intervention (1979–1989) and increased Western support of Islamic-led antiregime resistance forces, the mujahideen. Once the superpowers drew back, neighboring countries moved in to pursue their competing strategic interests by engaging and supporting rival Afghan factions who were locked in a violent power struggle.

From a "Great Game" to a "Lesser Game"

During the 1980s the United States and the Soviet Union were the two most influential actors on Afghanistan's bloody political scene. The Soviet military intervention in Afghanistan became Moscow's longest foreign war of the century. Assistance to the Islamic-led Afghan resistance turned into the largest U.S. covert operation since World War II. However, the two superpowers' engagement in the Afghan conflict was inspired by asymmetric strategic visions. The Soviet Union had militarily occupied neighboring Afghanistan in support of its distinct regional and ideological interests while the United States, located halfway around the globe, was waging a surrogate war—defensive in nature—with an ever-changing scope of military and political objectives. Continued intensification of the war forced Moscow into compromises and finally retreat while Washington gradually widened the scope of its strategic mission from bleeding the Soviets to forcing them out of Afghanistan and finally pushing for a military victory of the mujahideen over the Moscow-backed Communist regime in Afghanistan.[4]

During the Soviet occupation of Afghanistan, Islamic militants and transnational extremists became the most favored U.S.-backed fighters in Afghanistan. Dominated by religious orthodoxy, they received the bulk of U.S. and other foreign assistance channeled through Pakistani intelligence. The process marginalized mainstream Afghan forces that embraced moderate religious and nationalistic orientation but lacked strong leadership. U.S. intelligence believed that the Islamists were the most zealous and devoted anti-Soviet fighters and deserved to be supported. The United States even helped to create an international network of militant Islamists to fight with the mujahideen in Afghanistan.[5] However, this policy ignored the long-term impact of the militants' political influence in the postwar period. This perspective was swayed by the polarized nature of global politics, where international issues were often seen through the prism of the East-West ideological confrontation.

On the other hand, the Soviet policy of "divide and conquer" created and armed local and ethnic militias in support of Moscow's client regime in Kabul—a move that militarized Afghan society by popularizing the "defense of the revolution" and creating ethnic and tribal militias. The powerful Uzbek militia of General Abdul Rashid Dostum, which later dominated several northern Afghan provinces, was a product of this policy.

However, when the cold war was over, the Afghan conflict, in the words of one UN official, became a "forgotten war" and the Afghans became "a forgotten people."[6] U.S. diplomacy in support of UN efforts to end foreign intervention and find a peaceful solution to the Afghan civil war lacked consistency and perseverance. Washington's false hopes that the Taliban would be able to end the war militarily soon collapsed as the neofundamentalist militia proved to be the worst human rights abusers, record drug producers, and hosts to al Qaeda. Washington's 1998 pinprick cruise missile strikes against bin Laden's reputed terror training camps in Afghanistan, in the wake of the bombings of the U.S. embassies in Nairobi and Dar es Salaam, only raised bin Laden's global standing among anti-West militant groups. Further, the weak response helped to create the perception that U.S. retaliation against future terrorist attacks would inflict minimal pain.

The war left no party untouched. As a battleground for the two superpowers, Afghanistan sustained devastation caused by the military actions of the invaders and the support of the superpower that responded to the invasion. When the superpower contest was over, the belligerents walked away from the "great game" wreckage, opening the way for the competing neighbors to finish the destruction in a "lesser game." Afghans were the big losers. They suffered enormously during the war and failed to win the peace. The Soviet Union's defeat in a regional war was followed by its global retreat and eventual breakup. Meanwhile, the cost of Washington's victory in the Afghan power game was the advancement of the jihadi mentality, which motivated a worldwide terrorist network centered in Afghanistan.

The civil war in Afghanistan (1992–2001) became a multilateral competition involving internal armed factions with extensive foreign links, neighboring states pursuing competing strategic interests, and extraregional players with ideological, security, or economic stakes in the chaos. In the absence of a central authority, the neighboring countries furthered their policies by engaging and supporting rival Afghan factions while fueling internal strife and blocking the emergence of a broad-based legitimate government. The turmoil was both the cause and consequence of state failure in the war-torn country.

Pakistan wielded strong influence among the main actors on the Afghan political scene through its strong support of the Afghan jihad and its partnership with the United States in the anti-Soviet war of 1980s.[7] Drawing on its political leverage, Pakistan tried to manipulate Afghan politics to support its geopolitical and ideological aims. Islamabad's quest for strategic depth to counter India's geopolitical edge was one of the underlying principles of the strategy. Pakistan was also eager to compensate for its waning post–cold war strategic significance and failing economy by marketing itself as a stabilizing power in a potentially unstable region.[8]

Pakistan spared no effort to shape Afghan developments in accordance with its political ambitions. It helped to keep the Afghan mujahideen factions divided so that they could be easily controlled—a move that fueled intramujahideen power struggles and civil strife after the collapse of the communist regime in 1992.[9]

Pakistan excessively favored those Islamist parties that had close relationships with Pakistani intelligence. Pakistan policy tried to sideline Afghan nationalist forces that held independent views or were potential supporters of the irredentist Afghan demand for the creation of an independent Afghan-linked "Pashtunistan" in Pakistan's Pashtun areas. These areas were part of Afghanistan before they were annexed by the British in the nineteenth century. Islamabad heavily armed and supported Golbuddin Hekmatyar in his bid to seize power in Kabul during the early 1990s. Later, Pakistan stood firmly behind the Taliban movement and provided the radical militia with political, military, and financial support.[10]

Pakistani patronage of Islamist groups in unstable Afghanistan helped to spark militancy throughout the region. It also provided Pakistani jihadi organizations such as Harakat-ul-Mujahedin, Sipah-e-Sahaba, Lashkar-e-Jhangvi, and Lashkar-e-Toiba with training grounds and operational bases in Afghanistan. Fighters affiliated with these groups fought for "Islam" both with the Taliban in Afghanistan and in Kashmir. They gradually became part of the worldwide militant network of al Qaeda. The rippling shock of the September 11 attack forced Pakistan to break up with the Taliban and join the international community in fighting terrorism.

Iran's anti-American and anti-Western hostility limited its dealings with the U.S.-backed Afghan mujahideen. Tehran's Afghan policy evolved over the years, shifting from efforts to export the Islamic revolution to pragmatic attempts aimed at unifying the Afghan Shiite groups in a pro-Iranian front. That policy, narrow in scope and sectarian in nature, failed to pursue a well-defined strategy. Its attempt to promote Iranian culture in Afghanistan was confrontational and lacked focus, while its commitment to support the Shiite minority was too narrow and biased to influence non-Shiite parties. Iranian revolutionaries paid more attention to the

Palestinians than the Afghan mujahideen and favored Lebanese Shiites over their Afghan coreligionists.[11]

Initially, Iran targeted the country's Shiite minority living in the central Afghan mountainous area of Hazarajat. Iran's ideological crusade among the Hazaras fueled internal strife in the area, which was already undergoing profound social upheaval sparked by power struggles between the traditional establishment and the reformist forces. Iranian interference in the early 1980s divided the country's Shiite Hazara communities at a time when they were engaged in a struggle against the Soviet occupation. Iranian-backed extremist groups of the "Imam Khomeini line" (particularly the Nasr, Sepah-e Pasdaran, and Hezbollah) declared war on moderate Shiite groups, which pursued a nationalistic agenda. "Purge the domestic arrogance before dealing with outside invaders" was the motto of Iranian-inspired Afghan Shiite revolutionaries.[12] In the late 1980s, Iran mediated the unification of Afghan Shiite groups in the Hizb-e Wahdat party led by Abdul Ali Mazari.

The rise of the Taliban in Afghanistan in 1994 marked a sharp turn in Tehran's Afghan policy. Iran viewed the Taliban as an anti-Shiite and anti-Iranian fundamentalist Sunni movement supported by Saudi Arabia and other hostile forces. The Taliban's close ties with Pakistani anti-Shiite groups, its links with Saudi Wahhabis, and its alleged backing by U.S. anti-Iranian policy sparked Iran's distrust and fear.[13] The Taliban's sectarian and ethnic parochialism, coupled with its tendency to marginalize Iran-backed non-Pashtun factions and its ouster of the Rabbani government, added to the distrust. Iran saw the victory of the Taliban as part of a plot by Sunnis and the United States to isolate Iran.[14] Tehran improved the logistical infrastructure of anti-Taliban forces after the Taliban seized control of Kabul in September 1996, driving the Rabbani regime to the north. Iran continued to send supplies to the Rabbani-led anti-Taliban alliance through Central Asia.[15] The fall of Mazar-e Sharif to the Taliban in August 1998 and the killing of an Iranian journalist and seven Iranian diplomats by Taliban allies led to the deployment of about half of Iran's armed forces on the Afghan border.[16] The Iran-Afghan military standoff raised the specter of armed confrontation in a region already devastated by war and internal strife. UN mediation in October 1998 eased the tension along the Iran-Afghan border while Tehran stepped up military support to the anti-Taliban forces in Afghanistan, which continued until the fall of the Taliban.

The Fall of the Taliban

The fall of the Taliban at the end of 2001 marked the end of a protracted civil war in Afghanistan and the beginning of a recovery and healing process, opening the way for Afghanistan to free itself from extremism and international isolation. In less than two months, the U.S.-led coalition shattered the Taliban regime, broke up the al Qaeda establishment, and forced its leadership to run.

The dominance of military considerations within the U.S.-led coalition affected political developments after the demise of the Taliban. The military operation was primarily aimed at destroying the terrorist network based in Afghanistan and eliminating the security threats stemming from instability in that Central Asian country. This situation allowed Afghan anti-Taliban forces to become the allies of the coalition forces. Exploiting the sudden fall of the Taliban under the U.S.-led coalition's air strikes, the Northern Alliance, the only organized anti-Taliban military faction in Afghanistan, moved swiftly to fill the vacuum by seizing control of major cites, including the capital, Kabul.[17]

The coalition expected that the formation of a broad-based government would precede the fall of the Taliban in Kabul. But the militia's sudden evacuation of the capital opened the way for the Panjshiri-led Tajik faction of the Northern Alliance to seize control of the city in defiance of international demands. The victors immediately reincarnated the pre-Taliban bureaucracy dominated by the Shura-i-Nazar Tajiks.[18] This monopolization of power precluded the emergence of an ethnically balanced post-Taliban government. The Pashtun forces that took over in most of the southern provinces were too scattered to form a counterbalancing bloc vis-à-vis the Northern Alliance.

As military victories outpaced political arrangements, the international community rushed to broker the formation of a broad-based Afghan government that the country's diverse ethnic and political groups would support. However, negotiations on the structure of the new government between four Afghan political-ethnic groups at the UN-sponsored conference in Bonn were strongly influenced by the military situation on the ground. Having control of major cities in Afghanistan, the Northern Alliance showed no flexibility about sharing power equally with other groups, including the exiled Rome faction headed by Zahir Shah, the elderly former king, who had led the political opposition against the Taliban. The

Northern Alliance took the lion's share in the power-sharing arrangement stipulated by the Bonn agreement and signed by the Afghan factions on December 5, 2001.

Reconstruction under the Bonn Process

The challenge of rebuilding post-Taliban Afghanistan has been immense and multifaceted. It has required the creation of a broad-based national government, the establishment of security throughout the country, and the reconstruction of a war-devastated economy. These efforts had to be coordinated, directed by a unified strategy, and supported by the international community. Moreover, the process was influenced from the outset by the legacy of the protracted war in Afghanistan, the way the Taliban regime was overthrown, and competing internal and external interests.

The UN-sponsored political process aimed at unifying Afghanistan under a legitimate central government was marred by factional competition for power that intensified ahead of the Loya Jirga (Grand Council) in June 2002. The main reason factional rivalry did not develop into armed clashes similar to those in 1992 was the presence of coalition forces and international peacekeepers in the country. The process achieved a constitutional defragmentation of the country under a central authority while the military power continued to be fragmented. The nature of a crude ethnic-factional integration into state structures failed to reflect a real unification, hampered diversity in the national institutions, and affected every major decision on the reform process.

The Bonn accord called for the establishment of a six-month Afghan Interim Authority to govern the country, beginning on December 22, until an emergency Loya Jirga selected a broad-based Afghan Transitional Authority to lead the country pending the election of a fully representative government within two years.[19]

Although Hamid Karzai, a Pashtun leader from the Rome group, was selected to head the Afghan Interim Authority, the governing administration was dominated by the Northern Alliance, which controlled the military, foreign affairs, police, and intelligence. In the meantime, regional leaders and warlords who had seized control of the provinces maintained their own private armies, sources of income, foreign linkages, and autonomous administrations. The situation deepened factional distrust and fueled widespread public discontent, particularly among the Pashtuns—the largest single ethnic group in Afghanistan.

It was hoped that the emergency Loya Jirga would broaden the base of the government, assert civilian leadership, promote the democratic process, and take authority away from the regional leaders. The key result that the Afghans as well as the international community expected from the Loya Jirga was that it would correct the ethnic imbalance produced by the Bonn meeting.[20] As a linear expansion of tribal and local *jirgas* (councils) into a national institution by Afghan rulers since the beginning of the last century, the Loya Jirga traditionally lacked the cohesion and sophistication needed for making independent decisions on national issues in an incoherent state. Consequently, it was prone to being manipulated by the convening rulers. The Loya Jirga of June 2002 was slightly different for many reasons. It was not called by a ruling government, nor was it convened under the influence of a strong central authority. The situation facilitated a freer debate among the delegates but also allowed the regional strongmen and warlords to influence the process through political pressure, intimidation, and money. Furthermore, the involvement of the international community provided foreign actors with stage-managing opportunities.

The Loya Jirga brought mixed results. It was the first time in twenty-three years of war and instability that representatives from across the country came together to elect a head of state. Contrary to the recent past, the armed factions chose to advance their interests through the political process rather than resorting to violence. Despite some procedural irregularities in electing the head of state, the Jirga came up with a clear winner (Hamid Karzai) through secret balloting. In general, the outcome of the process did not live up to public expectations. Strongly influenced and manipulated by the warlords, the meeting hardly addressed the main concerns and failed to establish a balanced and representative transitional administration.[21]

As the central administration's authority barely extended beyond the capital, regional strongmen played their power games. Throughout the Bonn process (2001–2005), sporadic clashes between regional commanders continued. The conflicts stemmed from old rivalries or the desire to control or consolidate more territory. In 2002–2003, the troubled provinces of Paktia and Khost were often the scene of violent standoffs between the government-appointed governors and rebel forces under Bacha Khan Zadran. In the north, tension between forces loyal to Rashid Dostum, the leader of the Junbish Mili Islami (the National Islamic Movement), and militia units controlled by the Tajik commander Atta Mohammad frequently developed into bloody fighting that kept the region unstable. The government-imposed settlement of October 2003 virtually ended major clashes in the north and led to the cantonment of heavy weapons under international supervision and demobilization of formal militia units. Other major factional clashes took place in Samangan and areas south of Mazar-e Sharif and Faryab province. In the west, ethnic differences and rival claims for control of the Shindand district led to recurring skirmishes between militias loyal to Herat strongman Ismail Khan and those supporting the local Pashtun leader Amanullah. The conflict was ended in September 2004, following the removal of Ismail Khan from Herat and the demobilization of Amanullah's militia.

Meanwhile, post-Taliban reconstruction was strongly influenced by the ongoing war on terror and fighting insurgency. While most of Afghanistan is in a postconflict situation, large areas in the south and east are plagued by insurgency. Competing demands of fighting insurgency and rebuilding the postconflict communities have had a major impact on political, social, and economic reconstruction. In the absence of an effective central security establishment, the transitional administration has depended on the military muscle of factional militias, an arrangement that was institutionalized in the Bonn agreement. The accord stipulated that "upon the official transfer of power, all mujahideen, Afghan armed forces and armed groups in the country shall come under the command and control of the Interim Authority, and be reorganized according to the requirements of the new Afghan security and armed forces."[22]

Disarmament, Demobilization, and Reintegration (DDR) had to be reversed since factional militias were first integrated into the country's armed forces and then targeted for demobilization. Dismantling the factional militias was the key to stabilization. It entailed curbing the ability and desire of former combatants to renew violence and creating a national capacity to transform the war-instigated structures into peace-building institutions. This process involved replacing the war machines with a credible legal and political system, reestablishing public confidence in state institutions, and shifting from a culture of violent opposition to a peaceful competition for power and influence.

Breaking the war machines in the postconflict period is a prerequisite for sustaining peace. However, failure to build attractive alternatives to the life of a warrior can lead to renewal of fighting as well as proliferation of criminal activity and banditry. Deactivating the war machines is an immediate need; making them useless is a long-term goal.

The existence of too many guns in unauthorized hands and the prevalence of unruly elements that benefited from the war tended to undermine disarmament. In such cases the optimum method needs to be a macrodisarmament approach rather than a microdisarmament scheme. Macrodisarmament involves the creation of a political and security environment that can allay interfactional distrust and pave the way for voluntary disarmament as a broad-based commitment to peace. Such a strategy should eliminate the desire to use weapons rather than merely collect weapons.

Although the Japanese-supported DDR program succeeded in demobilizing over 62,000 factional militiamen and collecting over 36,000 small arms while storing nearly all heavy weapons between 2002 and 2005, reintegrating former combatants continues to be a major challenge. The second phase of the DDR that targets nearly 2,000 illegal armed groups began in 2006 under the Disbandment of Illegal Armed Groups program (DIAG). The program seeks voluntary, negotiated, and forced disbandment of more than 100,000 members of illegal armed groups. However, the upsurge in Taliban-led violence in 2006 not only slowed the DIAG program but also drove the government to rearm militias and assign them to serve as auxiliary police forces in vulnerable districts.

One of the major obstacles has been the lack of interest of the militia commanders, who felt that their interests and security were threatened by the reform process. The wartime development of distinctive local patronage networks under the leadership of regional commanders and the weakness of the central government contributed to the problem. During the drawn-out conflict, criminal elements that were incorporated into the war machines wielded significant political clout and controlled large businesses and an illicit economy. They were less inclined to give up power in the interest of peace. Reluctance to disarm grows when the postconflict government is politically fragile and militarily weak. Political fragility can be overcome by broadening the government base to include all parties. The government's political clout and coercive capacity has to be enhanced through integrating or rebuilding the national military establishment to ensure a balanced representation of diverse ethnic, regional, and political factions.

The internationally backed Security Sector Reform (SSR) provided for the creation of an Afghan National Army (ANA), Afghan National Police (ANP), and a reformed judiciary system. The SSR also included the DDR program and counternarcotics efforts. Security Sector Reform has been the flagship of the Bonn process for rebuilding Afghanistan's security forces and law enforcement. With each of its five pillars (army, police, counternarcotics, DDR, and justice) supported by a lead donor nation, SSR has developed unevenly.

Progress in building the U.S.-supported Afghan National Army has been remarkable. ANA's strength reached 30,000 as of March 2006, and it is expected to attain its goal of 70,000 by 2010. However, the ANA suffers from insufficient firepower, a lack of indigenous air support, and the absence of a self-sustaining operational budget. It continues to depend on military support from the Coalition forces and the U.S. underwriting its costs. Such a situation subjects the deployment and operation of the ANA to preapproval by the U.S. military, sometimes without concurrence of Afghan military leaders. The U.S. role in tasking the ANA causes friction and needs to be reconsidered.

Driven by operational demands to fight the insurgency and create an alternative to factional militias, the development of the ANA received a high priority. However, equal attention was not paid to other crucial aspects of the SSR.

Although building the police in postconflict societies is a more urgent need than building the army, little international attention has been paid to the development of the Afghan National Police. Yet the police have been at the forefront of fighting terrorism, illegal border incursions, illicit drug trade, warlords, and organized crime. Protecting reconstruction projects, including highways in the militant-plagued south, is another major challenge facing the ANP. As a result the ANP has lost far more men than the ANA, Coalition forces, and the International Security Assistance Force (ISAF) in fighting insurgency and criminal activity across the country. Had the police been better trained, equipped, and armed, they would have suffered less and made a stronger contribution to stability operations.

International interest and investment in developing the ANP picked up in 2004 with Germany and the United States in leading roles that have produced significant initial results. Over 60,000 police officers have received basic training. Because of the late start in a comprehensive police development, the ANP continues to be ill trained, poorly paid, underequipped, and inadequately armed. A new U.S.-supported ANP development program launched in 2006 aims to deploy a 62,000-strong, fully trained, better paid, and fully equipped police by December 2008.[23] Implementation of this program should be a top priority of the post-Bonn development strategy.

The Italian-supported justice sector reform suffers from a very low level of human resources and infrastructure capacity. The court structure is outdated, many judicial personnel are unqualified, and corruption is deep rooted. The period of violence in the country destroyed the institutional integrity of the justice system and left a patchwork of contradictory and overlapping laws. Although some progress has been made, particularly in law reform, no strategy has been agreed upon for rebuilding the system. After the inauguration of the Afghan parliament in early 2006, President Karzai nominated eight professional jurists to replace all supreme court judges. But he maintained Fazel Hadi Shinwari as the chief justice. This decision was apparently based more on political considerations than professional requirements. A strongly conservative cleric, Shinwari is widely reported to be corrupt and nepotistic. However, as head of the government-sponsored Council of Ulema, he is seen as an influential figure in gaining the support of the clerics for government policies. The Afghan parliament, in late 2006, voided Shinwari's appointment.

While the pillars are interconnected, the "lead nation" approach has been marked by a lack of close coordination, an imbalance in the level of committed resources, and the absence of a unified developmental concept. The Afghanistan Compact ended the "lead nation" concept and put the security sector reform under a joint board cochaired by Afghanistan and the United Nations.[24] The change should ensure more Afghan ownership, making the Afghan government the "lead nation," with the donor countries acting as "supporting nations" for the SSR.

Given that foreign aid covers most of the cost of security forces, the long-term sustainability of the army and police is a major challenge. It is assumed that even if the country's nondrug taxable economy grows by 10 percent a year above the current rate, the cost of maintaining the security forces will not be sustained by the country's own resources for many years.[25] There are already debates over the need to reduce the planned size of the ANA from 70,000 to as low as 45,000. A decline in foreign funding could lead to major political, security, and social crises. Given the prohibitive cost of maintaining professional forces, there is strong support in the country for the restoration of the national draft system that presumably also promotes national integration and civic education.

The Bonn agreement provided for the deployment of a UN-mandated force in Afghanistan to assist in the maintenance of security for Kabul and its surrounding areas. It was also recognized that such a force "could, as appropriate, be progressively expanded to other urban centers and other areas."[26] The UN Security Council authorized the deployment of a 4,500-strong International Security Assistance Force in Kabul. However, there were repeated requests by the Afghan government, the United Nations, and international human rights organizations to expand ISAF to other major Afghan cities in order to promote political stabilization and economic reconstruction. In a resolution adopted by the UN Security Council in October 2003, ISAF was authorized to expand beyond Kabul. The deployment outside Kabul came in the form of Provincial Reconstruction Teams (PRTs).

PRT as a Facilitator for Security and Reconstruction

The PRT is a unique structure tailored to the security and stabilization needs of a postconflict environment. It is a small military unit (less than 100 to 250 troops) with civilian representatives deployed in a province to extend the authority of the central government and facilitate the development of security and reconstruction. After the establishment of the first U.S. PRT in Gardez, the concept was internationalized, with Britain, New Zealand, and Germany setting up their PRTs in Mazar-e Sharif, Bamiyan, and Konduz, respectively. As U.S. forces shifted to stabilization operations in early 2004, the PRT network was expanded throughout the troubled southern provinces of Afghanistan. When NATO assumed command of ISAF in August 2003, it adopted the concept, and by the end of 2005 had deployed nine PRTs in a counterclockwise expansion from the north to the west. Further extension of ISAF to the south and east in 2006 brought all twenty-five PRTs in Afghanistan under ISAF command.[27]

The viability of PRTs depends on close links with larger military forces in the area. PRT is the "the tip of the iceberg" attached to a force support structure, including quick reaction forces, air cover, emergency medical evacuation, and logistic support system. A PRT without links to military forces is not conceivable. In practice, different PRTs operate in different ways, often out of control of the guiding bodies, and adopt differing balances between security and reconstruction activities. The imprecise pronouncement of the PRT mandate has opened the way for flexible interpretation. The PRT is basically military in structure and outlook, dependent on a larger political-military system—Coalition forces, NATO-ISAF, contributing nations—which shapes its operational approach and interpretation of its mandate.

A number of factors contribute to a diverse interpretation of the PRT mandate and the ad hoc evolution of the PRT concept: varied local security environment, available resources, and the political priorities of countries contributing troops. The presence of two separate military operations and commands in Afghanistan (U.S.-led Coalition forces and ISAF) and different approaches to civil-military activities add to differing perspectives. This disjunction has been magnified as more nations established PRTs with national "caveats."

While PRTs under ISAF have been less engaged in reconstruction activities and more engaged in Security Sector Reform and stabilization efforts, the U.S. PRTs have been significantly focused on supporting the U.S-led Coalition military campaign. As NATO takes over all of the PRTs in the country, it will more closely intertwine its PRT functions with the Coalition's military operations, which are taking place in a much less permissive environment than the north. ISAF will need to adapt its stabilization model developed in the north to the local dynamics.

Success has been more substantive when the PRT operational approaches were consistent with the strategic goal, mission requirement, and demands of the host government (for example, the PRT role in Gardez in April 2003, Mazar-e Sharif in October-November 2003, Herat in September 2004, and Shindand in November 2004). Actions taken with inadequate resources, those taken in isolation of the host government's needs, or those influenced by local interest groups have been less effective. The worst cases have been recorded when the PRT became more a means of serving the provider than the customer.

The ownership of the PRT system is a key to its strategic usefulness. The PRT location, structure, capacity, resources, and operations need to be adapted to the political and strategic demands of the host government as well as the realities on the ground. They must not be determined by domestic priorities of the troop-contributing countries. This shift requires the presence of effective central coordinating bodies (with effective secretariats) that can exercise direction and facilitate coordination and standardization.

The level of centralization of PRT activities and the need for flexibility in counterinsurgency operations must be balanced. While PRT-initiated quick impact reconstruction projects are effective in a counterinsurgency setting, they would be strategically more effective if carried out in accordance with the direction of the national government and in line with national development programs. Reconstruction in support of improving security infrastructure needs to be part of the PRT-initiated projects. The process is not required to emphasize providing assistance aimed at producing developmental impact on the lives of the host people, nor do PRTs have the resources to sustain such assistance.

The PRT should work to create the conditions to make itself redundant. The end state should be identified as a condition where the national government and its provincial institutions are firmly established and function without direct support from international military forces. Progress toward this end state and PRT transition needs to be benchmarked with effectiveness indicators for governance, security and stability, reconstruction, and development established and applied.

Expectations and Realities

Reconstruction of Afghanistan's war-ravaged and drought-stricken economy has been considered the key to peace and stability in the country. Rebuilding Afghanistan has also been intertwined with the strategy of the war on terrorism. In April 2002 President George W. Bush announced a major American role in rebuilding Afghanistan under a comprehensive reconstruction plan comparable to the "Marshall Plan."[28] Bush warned that military force alone could not bring "true peace" to Afghanistan, and that stability would return only when the country rebuilds its economic and cultural infrastructure.

However, the actual needs of reconstruction far outweighed the available resources. A preliminary needs assessment by the World Bank, the United Nations, and the Asian Development Bank in January 2002 estimated that reconstruction would cost about $5 billion in the first two-and-a-half years, the expected term of the transitional administration in Afghanistan. Reconstruction costs for five- and ten-year periods were estimated at $10 and $15 billion dollars, respectively.[29] In 2004, the Afghan government estimated that the amount of aid required for minimal stabilization would be $27.5 billion over a period of seven years.[30] Finally, at the early 2006 London Conference on Afghanistan, the Afghan government estimated that it would need $20 billion dollars over five years to fund its Interim National Development Strategy. However, in all these cases, only a fraction of the estimated costs were provided, mostly outside the government's control. According to UN and Afghan government data, out of $8.4 billion aid money spent in Afghanistan between the fall of the Taliban in late 2001 and the end of 2004, only $1.6 billion was spent by the government. The rest was spent by nongovernmental organizations, the United Nations, and donor governments.[31]

The absence of Afghan government control over programs funded by a deeply divided international community led to a disconnect between the development efforts. In many cases strategic goals were overshadowed by pet projects that were popular domestically in the donor nations. The slow pace of tangible reconstruction activity in the country caused public frustration.

Balancing opportunities with promises and managing expectations has been a major challenge. The unprecedented involvement of the international community in rebuilding the country raised the expectations of people who massively participated in a high-profile political process and voted for an elected government. However, the vote hardly brought significant changes in their lives. One reason was that the political benchmarks set by the Bonn agreement were not fully sequenced with other development programs and building capacities. The Afghan government met the deadlines set for the establishment of democratic political institutions such as adopting an enlightened constitution (January 2004), holding a successful presidential election (October 2004), and parliamentary elections (September 2005). But the central government's limited administrative capacity and insufficient investment in service delivery institutions hindered the functionality of the state. The state was expected to respond to the legitimate needs of the people, and the people were expected to contribute to stability and be responsible and not just to be free.

Prospects for the Future

The parliamentary elections of September 2005 in Afghanistan were the final event of the Bonn accord. Although Afghanistan met all the deadlines of the Bonn accord, it has not realized the treaty's ultimate goal of ending the conflict and establishing peace and stability. The Bonn process was neither a definitive transformation schedule nor did it envision the country's long-term development process. The struggle to secure the future of Afghanistan drags on, and the country will continue to be dependent on international support for many years to come.

The five-year Afghanistan Compact adopted in 2006 in London pledges continued international assistance to Afghanistan in the context of Afghanistan's Interim National Development Strategy. The Interim Strategy is the strategic framework for development over the next five years. It aims to enhance security, governance, the rule of law, human rights, and economic and social development. It also identifies efforts to eliminate the narcotics industry as a vital and cross-cutting goal.[32] The compact opens a new phase of partnership between Afghanistan and the international community, directed toward long-term capacity building.

Human Security and Ending the Insurgency

Security continues to be a prerequisite for political development and economic growth. The post-Bonn arrangements came against a backdrop of increased Taliban-led violence and terrorist activities, including more than twenty suicide attacks in 2005 and more in 2006. Incidents of violent expression of communal tension and a spread of violent protests hint at growing public frustration and intolerance that often stem from human insecurity. Unless significant improvement in the security situation is made, the country will be in no position to attain the objectives set by the Afghanistan Compact.

Security cannot be achieved only by securing the state. It also requires removing the threats faced by the vast majority of Afghan citizens. An international focus on fighting terrorism should not overshadow the threats emanating from militia commanders, drug traffickers, corrupt provincial and district administrators, and government incompetence. Such threats are often more damaging to the population than terrorist violence.

Security in a postconflict society finds its meaning in the notion of "human security," which ensures the sustainability of the peaceful environment. It requires opportunities more than policies and promises. The long period of war and violence has added a dimension of conflict memory to perceptions of security. Under such perceptions people tend to act more warily—and thus slowly—in investing their hope in long-term government projects aimed at peace and prosperity. This tendency affects many post-conflict issues, including disarmament, factionalism, warlordism, and the illicit drug trade. Freedom from fear and freedom from want entail the development of good governance, social security, economic development, and the protection of human and political rights. The Afghanistan Compact recognizes that security cannot be provided by military means alone but requires good governance, justice, and the rule of law, reinforced by reconstruction and development.

The Taliban-led insurgency, particularly in the south and east, the presence of illegal armed groups, and the illicit drug trade are the main security threats in Afghanistan. The Taliban and their extremist allies lack a unified leadership, a popular ideology for Afghanistan, and a sustainable logistics support network inside the country. A 2005 ABC News survey in Afghanistan indicated that 77 percent of Afghans believed that their country was heading in the right direction. Despite the prevalent economic difficulty and poverty that they face, 91 percent preferred the current Afghan government to the Taliban regime, and 87 percent called the overthrow of the Taliban good for their country.[33] In 2006, a popular disenchantment with the lack of government will and capacity to protect the people and deliver the needed services has significantly eroded the people's confidence.

The Taliban-led extremist violence in Afghanistan is more grounded in political roots than ideological ones. Using the "jihadi" movement as a cover, foreign and domestic spoilers pay or manipulate operatives to commit acts of violence in support of their political agenda. The Taliban have training camps, staging areas, recruiting centers (madrassas), and safe havens in Pakistan. The operations of a Pakistani military force, deployed in the border region, mostly in the Waziristan tribal area, have been effective against al Qaeda and non-Pakistani militants, but they have not done much to contain the Taliban. The 2006 peace deal between the Pakistan government and pro-Taliban militants in the North Waziristan border area has led to a major increase in militants' cross-border attacks in Afghanistan. More effort is needed to stop cross-border terrorist activity in Afghanistan. Pakistan's idea of constructing a fence along the border is neither practical nor politically desirable, however.[34] As long as the Taliban continue to use Pakistani territory for attacks on Afghanistan, the suspicion that Pakistan is playing a double game in Afghanistan will persist. Both Afghanistan and Pakistan are U.S. allies in the global war on terrorism. The United States has a policy on Afghanistan and a policy on Pakistan, but as Barnett Rubin rightly observes, there is no clear policy on Afghan-Pakistan relations.[35] This confusion causes misinterpretation and opportunistic manipulation of the alliance by Pakistan. Under these conditions the Taliban feel safe to operate from Pakistani territory. A strong commitment from the United States and NATO to address the sources of terrorism in the region, invigorating the tripartite U.S.-Afghan-Pakistani Commission on fighting terrorism, and close operational cooperation between Afghanistan and Pakistan are essential to ending the insurgency.

The escalated level of militant violence is more indicative of a change in tactics than capability. Suicide attacks, which are traditionally alien to the Afghans, and the more sophisticated improvised explosive device technology are al Qaeda tactics adapted by the Taliban and other terrorists. With more than seventy suicide attacks in 2006—along with the assassination of hundreds of government officials, moderate clerics, and civilians—the resurgent Taliban have become more radical, more brutal, and more sophisticated than when U.S.-led forces ousted them more than five years ago. The manner in which the insurgents wage their violence signifies how closely Taliban tactics mirror those of al Qaeda in Iraq.

The level of violence rose significantly in 2006 because of NATO's move into the militant-infested south, which triggered a defensive reaction from the insurgents; the militants' desire to exploit the impact of recent terror tactics, such as suicide bombing and the use of improvised explosive devices; efforts by Kabul to expand the reach of the central government to the remote areas as planned in the Interim Strategy; and as a response to increased government-initiated poppy eradication operations. The Taliban also exploited the weak presence of the government in the south and Kabul's neglect of local communities. An estimated 1,500 people were killed in militant-related violence in 2005, and about 4,000 in 2006, but the rebels constituted 60 to 70 percent of the dead.

While the insurgency and illegal armed groups may not have the capacity to pose an ultimate strategic threat to the government, they create a sense of insecurity, hinder economic reconstruction, and weaken government influence in remote areas. These trends have led to a much stronger insurgency capable of challenging the government. In many districts the resurgence of Taliban violence is caused more by the lack of government presence than the ability of the insurgents. Although poverty, government weakness, and corruption are not the root causes of insurgency, they can be exploited by terrorists and insurgents to gain support in rural areas.

Fighting insurgents by military action alone will never fully eradicate them, for even in their defeat a vacuum will remain, inexorably attracting new insurgents. Unless the context that nourishes the continuing violence—such as desperate economic conditions, the lack of governmental capacity, repression of communities by local thugs, and foreign interference—is addressed with the same singleness of purpose as is the insurgency, Afghanistan will remain a volatile and menacing place.

Coalition Forces and ISAF

Afghanistan continues to need an international military presence to fight insurgency and to protect the reconstruction effort until Afghan security institutions become effective and sustainable. The Afghanistan Compact provides for continued support by ISAF and Coalition forces in establishing and sustaining security and stability in Afghanistan. It also reaffirms that ISAF will continue to expand its presence throughout Afghanistan, including through PRTs, and will continue to promote stability and support security sector reforms in its areas of operation.

In addition to their operational power, the presence of about 20,000 U.S. forces and 20,000 ISAF troops deters security threats posed by internal and external spoiler forces. But the transition of command from the United States to ISAF througout Afghanistan is perceived by the Afghans as more than an operational adjustment; it has a significant psychological impact. It causes the Afghans to hearken back to the end of the cold war when the United States walked away from a devastated Afghanistan, leaving the country to descend into a brutal civil war. There is also concern that the change could embolden the insurgents and prompt some regional countries to interfere. The Taliban and their allies, as well as domestic spoilers, are playing a waiting game. Some Taliban commanders are widely quoted in Afghanistan as saying that "the Americans have all the clocks, we have all the time." The perception that the United States and the rest of the international forces will get tired and leave is spreading among friends and foes beyond the borders of Afghanistan.

Although former Defense Secretary Donald Rumsfeld stated that the U.S. military would "continue to do the heavy lifting" in Afghanistan, the operational impact of the shift depends on the nature of the expanded NATO mission in Afghanistan and its constraining rules of engagement, which are the result of disagreement among NATO members.[36] The revised Operational Plan adopted by NATO foreign ministers on December 8, 2005, focused mostly on peacekeeping security operations in coordination with Afghan security forces. With the assignment of 12,000 U.S. forces in Afghanistan to NATO, the number of ISAF troops should reach 32,000. The remaining 8,000 U.S. troops in the country will operate separately in counterterrorism operations. NATO-ISAF has established four regional commands and a forward support base in Kandahar. The alliance has not clearly addressed the operational constraints of the "national caveats."[37]

The absence of joint mechanisms to plan and coordinate the action of national and international forces in fighting security threats is a major hurdle in bringing synergy to stability operations. There is little connection between operations separately planned by the U.S.-led Coalition, ISAF, and Afghan security forces. The situation weakens effectiveness and efficiency and leads to confusion and unintended collateral damage. While the Coalition efforts to patrol the remote Afghan mountain hollows and valleys were appreciated by many, they provoked indignant protests when Coalition troops searched peaceful villages without consideration for local culture or detained inhabitants who had no known connection with hostile armed groups. Some local chiefs also directed U.S. military actions against their rivals, which often caused civilian casualties and hostile feelings among the population. Ad hoc arrangements by the Afghan government and the U.S. command in Afghanistan have been made to stave off the negative impact of U.S.-initiated searches of Afghan villages and detention of Afghan government officials by U.S. forces. However, in the absence of an institutionalized system of coordination, the results have been spotty. The establishment of a joint command and control center to plan, conduct, and coordinate joint counterinsurgency operations is of prime importance.

The Afghan parliament is expected to raise the need to adopt a status of forces agreement with the United States. A joint declaration on strategic partnership between the United States and Afghanistan was signed in May 2005. The accord provides U.S. forces "freedom of action" without an agreement on the status of forces that should reaffirm Afghan sovereignty and national security interests with regard to other states in the region. The strategic partnership needs to be translated into practical programs covering cooperation in state building and economic development.

Building Governance beyond Kabul

In reaction to the prolonged insecurity, warlordism, and factional infighting, there is a widespread Afghan desire for a strong central government that can provide security in the chaotic postconflict environment and offer needed services to war-devastated communities. In order for the central government to meet such public expectations, it needs to strengthen its control of rural areas and deliver required services.

While the central government has extensive constitutional authority over the provinces, Kabul's limited ability to intervene and its accommodation of local power brokers have left factional chiefs in control of local government. The situation is a reflection of the country's immediate past, where the breakdown of central government power led to the emergence of local leaders-warlords who set up patronage networks through access to foreign aid, weapons, tax revenue, natural resources, and illicit narcotics. The significant reliance of U.S.-led Coalition forces on the factional militia to defeat the Taliban in 2001 and to conduct stability operations led to the empowerment of factional commanders while contributing to the fragmentation of power and frustrating the reform process.

During the past three years, Kabul has successfully reduced the power of warlord-governors by reassigning them away from their geographic power bases, but their networks continue to influence provincial administration.[38] Meanwhile, former factional commanders who were appointed to government positions in police and civil administration have loaded their offices with their unqualified supporters and corrupt cronies.

With a major presence in Iraq and only a minor presence in Afghanistan, the United States has long hesitated to support the removal of defiant warlords. Despite wide public support for the national government, Kabul was reluctant to act decisively. Until mid-2006, the bulk of ISAF was based in Kabul. The PRTs deployed by ISAF in the northern and western provinces of Afghanistan have been hamstrung by policy constraints imposed by the troop-contributing nations, resource limitations, and "national caveats" in their attempts to act decisively against local thugs, drugs, and official mugs.

Given the limited coercive capacity of the central government, Afghan leaders and donor countries found it tactically convenient to integrate the demobilized militia leaders and former warlords into the government. However, failure to hold them accountable and to correct their inappropriate official behavior continues to undermine the establishment of the rule of law. It not only thwarts the legitimacy of the national government but also fosters corruption and a sense of impunity. Unless the government lives up to public expectations for providing security and services, local patronage networks will not only survive but will use their power to influence national programs and reform agendas. Government and foreign toleration of regional bullies in the hope of maintaining stability takes a heavy toll on local security.

The 2005 parliamentary elections, held on a nonparty basis, led to the emergence of a politically fragmented legislature. Elections provide the opportunity for members of different political, ethnic, and regional interest groups to wage their political fight peacefully in the parliament house rather than on battlefields. However, the absence of organized political blocs makes the parliament a wild card with a potential either to strengthen or weaken the political process in Afghanistan. Lawmakers' support of national programs will add legitimacy to the process while their emphasis on parochial and populist themes could impede government decisions on reform and put the president at odds with the diverging interests of Afghanistan's international partners. The absence of strong political parties and the prevalence of shifting political alliances foster the survival of patronage networks based on personal-client relationships. Government wheeling and dealing with such a system hinders the development of state institutions and impedes the emergence of a viable and service-oriented administration. The absence of a ruling party tends to make the president act as a "supreme khan." Much depends on the nature of emerging political caucuses and the effectiveness of mechanisms in place to enhance understanding and cooperation between the executive and legislative branches.

Removal of existing perceptional and managerial distance between Kabul and the regions is essential for the defragmentation of administration. The key is to bring a balance between creating a strong and effective central government and ensuring a level of decentralization to secure equal distribution and participation.

One of the challenges is the level of delegation of administrative and fiscal authorities to subnational government. The specter of "federalism" and the lack of clear understanding about healthy decentralization methods continue to hinder the developmental capacity of subnational government. The staffing authority of subnational administration is constrained, and Kabul's limited ability to delegate resources has put subnational administration on autopilot. Consequently, reform at the local level has been slow and difficult. People in the provinces and districts hardly feel Kabul's influence. Kabul needs to support the subnational government's political role as the sole representative of the central government and buttress its functional role as service provider.

Expanding the central government's legitimacy in the provinces would require a reallocation of financial resources and the creation of a coordinating body at the provincial level empowered to coordinate and organize government and external resources for highly focused planning and the implementation of development programs, projects, and activities. This body will serve as the Provincial Planning and Development Council, where top-down and bottom-up development meet. Chaired by the provincial governor, the council should bring together all city and district governors, representatives of the private sector, the chair of the appropriation committee of the provincial council, all members of the parliament from the province, heads of donor organizations and nongovernmental organizations, and all heads of line ministries in the province. A similar project is being pilot-tested in the Balkh province and is expected to be extended to other northern provinces.

Another key issue is the integration of formal, elected, and traditional governing bodies—including *maliks* (village chiefs), *khans* and *arbabs* (major landowners and tribal chiefs), *ulema* (religious figures), traditional *shuras* (councils), and tribal *jirgas*. The establishment of elected bodies, including the national assembly, provincial, district, and village councils further crowds the political landscape. The state needs to coalesce the traditional, local, provincial, and national government bodies into an integrated system of governance with clarity in the roles, links, power, and resources of each element. Participation and inclusiveness lead to stability.

The Afghanistan Compact gives priority to "the coordinated establishment in each province of functional institutions including civil administration, police, prisons and judiciary." Reforming the justice system is of prime importance. The Compact aims to ensure "equal, fair and transparent access to justice based upon written codes with fair trials and enforceable verdicts." Achievement of this goal hinges on a comprehensive "legislative reform of the public and private sector, building the capacity of judicial institutions and cadres, promoting human rights and legal awareness and rehabilitating the judicial infrastructure."[39]

The Compact also calls for the Afghan government to implement the Action Plan on Peace, Justice and Reconciliation by 2008. The plan adopted by the government in December 2005 envisions the promotion of peace, reconciliation, justice, and rule of law in Afghanistan and the establishment of a culture of accountability and respect for human rights.[40] The move is seen as a means of rebuilding trust among those whose lives were shattered by war, reinforcing a shared sense of citizenship and a culture of tolerance.

Counternarcotics

The problem of drugs in Afghanistan is considered the single most challenging obstacle to long-term security and development.[41] Afghanistan has a relatively short history of opium production. Emerging as part of the war economy in the 1980s, opium production soared in the past decade. The country now produces about 90 percent of the world's opium, and this income constitutes a significant part of Afghanistan's GDP. Most of the revenue goes not to Afghan farmers but to traders and distributors outside Afghanistan. Opium is not only an Afghan problem but also one of regional and global dimensions. Fighting narcotics requires a joint national and international effort.

The lessons learned during the past five years suggest that targeting traffickers and traders has fewer negative impacts and does not require provision of alternative livelihoods. However, Afghanistan's interdiction capacity is limited, and the criminal justice sector responsible for processing drug-related crime is not up to the challenge. While interim arrangements to expedite the judicial process are made, the involvement of international forces is needed to enhance the interdiction capacity. The ISAF has been reluctant to get involved in the drug war. However, as a security assistance force, it should play a role in counternarcotics operations that are security related. ISAF's role in targeting drug laboratories, opium stockpiles, and trafficking routes not only helps Afghan counternarcotics efforts but also curtails the flow of Afghan drugs to Europe.

Eradication without meaningful alternative livelihoods is not sustainable. Furthermore, eradication does not hold any promise for a near-term solution, and forcible eradication can be counterproductive. Poverty and eradication should be attacked simultaneously. Elimination of poppy cultivation should be attempted through developmental approaches determined by the size of opium revenue in the country's total GDP and not by the acreage of destroyed poppy fields. The development of alternative livelihoods is a key to achieving long-term counternarcotics goals. Alternative livelihood creation should be considered as the goal rather than the means.

Given the multidimensional nature of opium production in Afghanistan, counternarcotics efforts should be mainstreamed into all aspects of development: security, economic growth, and governance. There are no quick and simple solutions. Destroying one-third of Afghanistan's economy without undermining stability requires enormous resources, administrative capacity, and time. Attempts to simplify the problem in order to make it manageable and appealing to donor countries' domestic policies do not lead to sustained progress. Only a comprehensive and holistic approach will work.

Economic and Social Development

Since 2002 Afghanistan has made remarkable progress in laying the basis for the country's recovery. But in spite of significant economic growth, the country's recovery is fragile and cannot be sustained without prolonged international assistance. Available estimates suggest that by March 2006, the Afghan economy had grown by more than 80 percent since 2001.[42] Much of the progress is attributable to foreign assistance and the illegal drug economy.[43] Afghanistan's development index is among the lowest in the world. The majority of the population suffers from multidimensional poverty including inadequate access to productive assets, social and health services, and education.[44] The challenge of economic development in Afghanistan is a challenge of state building, where economic development is closely linked to security and political reform. Recovery hinges on the establishment of the rule of law and effective governance. Lack of progress in one area hinders recovery in other sectors.

The Afghan government's newly adopted Interim Afghanistan National Development Strategy (I-ANDS) is its overarching strategy for promoting growth, generating wealth, and reducing poverty and vulnerability. The I-ANDS is a comprehensive development approach to build infrastructure; develop natural resources, agriculture, rural economies, human capital, social protection, economic governance, and the private sector; and promote gender equality, international and regional cooperation, good governance, the rule of law, and security.

The Afghanistan Compact is based on the I-ANDS and seeks international support to pursue high rates of sustainable economic growth in order to reduce hunger, poverty, and unemployment. It promotes the role and potential of the private sector in tandem with the development of public and nonprofit sectors. It also curbs the narcotics industry, creates macroeconomic stability, and restores and promotes the development of the country's human, social, and physical capital, thereby establishing a sound basis for a new generation of leaders and professionals. Strengthening civil society and reintegrating returnees, displaced persons, and former combatants is another objective of the five-year plan.

The Afghan government also needs to widen its revenue base through raising taxes and collecting state revenues in order to support institution building and to meet the public demand for basic services. The Afghan government is critically dependent on international funding for recurrent costs. The country will need to secure guarantees from the donor countries for predictable funding for the next five years in exchange for taking concrete measures to meet revenue targets. The long-term receipt of such a significant level of foreign aid is highly uncertain and depends on the perceptions of the international community about the costs of Afghanistan's failure. It also hinges on Afghanistan's progress in making political, economic, security, and administrative reforms.

Although a recent UN General Assembly resolution on Afghanistan endorses the leadership of Afghanistan in the post-Bonn reconstruction process, the UN has indicated that giving the Afghan government direct control over funds provided by the international community depends on the development of Afghan government structures (which will take time).[45] However, what is important is that funds are disbursed in accordance with the priorities of the Afghan government, and that more transparency is brought to all levels of international aid. The overhead costs of foreign contractors who are awarded hefty reconstruction contracts are often higher than the funds eventually spent in Afghanistan. Contractors often make big money for low-quality work.

Fifty-seven percent of the Afghan population is under eighteen years of age, with little opportunity for employment. As construction projects boom, there is a shortage of indigenous skilled labor. Part of this labor is currently provided by tens of thousands of foreign workers (mostly Pakistanis and Iranians). No meaningful growth can be achieved without a substantial investment in human capital development. Capacity building in both the private and public sectors is essential for the emergence of an effective civil service and a thriving private sector.

The development of Afghanistan's private sector is not only a key to its economic growth but also a prerequisite for its active involvement in interregional trade. A recent survey indicates that Afghan firms perform better than comparable firms in neighboring Central Asian countries but lag in productivity behind Pakistan, India, and China.[46] Although new laws on investment, taxation of income, and customs reforms have liberalized the business environment, shortages of electricity, limited access to land, corruption, and issues concerning security, trade regulation, taxation, and other infrastructure are serious impediments. While there are no quick and simple solutions to these problems, removing the hurdles that deter domestic entrepreneurs and foreign investors should be given top priority.

Finally, fighting corruption is a major challenge facing the developmental process in Afghanistan. According to Transparency International, Afghanistan ranks 117th among 159 countries surveyed for the Corruption Perceptions Index (CPI).[47] Although Afghanistan is considered less corrupt than most of its neighbors (including Pakistan, Tajikistan, Uzbekistan, Turkmenistan, and Russia) and thirty-eight other countries, corruption is a major obstacle in the way of reform and development. Afghanistan planned to ratify the UN Convention against Corruption by the end of 2006 and adopt national legislation accordingly by the end of 2007. Setting up a monitoring mechanism to oversee the implementation is scheduled by the end of 2008. There is no simple and quick answer to the problem. But making the right decisions on fighting poverty, offering better salaries to law enforcement officers and civil servants, and adopting a zero tolerance policy for corrupt government officials can contribute to achieving long-term anticorruption goals.

Regional Dynamics

Afghanistan has long suffered from interference by neighboring and regional states. Despite the presence of international military forces in Afghanistan and the stated commitment of the United States, United Kingdom, and NATO to uphold the independence, territorial integrity, and sovereignty of Afghanistan, the country is still vulnerable to neighbors' influence, with the potential to spoil or promote Afghanistan's development. Stability hinges on Afghanistan's integration into the region. Promoting cooperation with neighbors and regional states in areas of common interest will go a long way toward establishing stability, peace, and prosperity in Afghanistan. One way to achieve this goal is to develop regional trade, cultural ties, and a regionally integrated infrastructure between neighboring Central and South Asian countries. Promoting regional cooperation to serve the common interests of the people in the region could contribute to confidence building, address long-standing political issues, and ease tensions.

Although disadvantaged by its landlocked location, Afghanistan has traditionally capitalized on its role as a trade and transit bridge between Central Asia, South Asia, and the Middle East. Extension of interregional economic ties can revive Afghanistan's historical role, contributing to its economic recovery. Afghanistan's recent inclusion in the South Asian Association for Regional Cooperation and the adoption of the "Kabul Declaration" on regional cooperation at a twelve-nation conference can facilitate the resurgence of Afghanistan as the hub of interregional economic exchange.[48]

Given the current diverging geopolitical perceptions in the region, neighboring countries are not much interested in Afghanistan's regional integration as long as they distrust regional security arrangements. Pakistan may wish to keep its options open for intervention in case the United States fails in Afghanistan. The U.S. strategic partnership with Afghanistan is also a source of concern to Iran, which fears that Afghan territory might be used against Iran's interests. Iran has shown signs of adopting a flexible posture regarding its relations with Afghanistan. In spite of its support for the peace process, Tehran tends to reach out to certain groups in Afghanistan to build client relationships inside the country. Finally, certain Central Asian governments feel threatened by the U.S.-backed development of democracy in Afghanistan, and such fears could facilitate wider Russian and Chinese influence in the region. Thus, for viable regional integration to be achieved, there must be sustained bilateral and multilateral diplomatic efforts aimed at building confidence among the regional states.

Conclusion

Afghanistan finds itself at a crossroads. Continued international security and economic assistance for at least ten to fifteen more years and sustained domestic leadership for reform will enable the country to build on achievements made since 2002 and become a success story in the region. The other option is to slide back into the difficult past of instability and tension. Given the potentially devastating impact of a failed Afghan state in a globalizing world, leaving Afghanistan to the latter fate can no longer be an option.

The road map for midterm development is Afghanistan's Interim National Development Strategy that underpins the Afghanistan Compact. The compact embodies a partnership between Afghanistan and the international community for rebuilding Afghanistan. Its success depends on both parties' fulfillment of their commitments. The goals and developmental benchmarks set by the Afghanistan Compact are ambitious and extensive. However, only a comprehensive and fast response to a multiplicity of interlinked challenges can move the country out of instability and economic desolation.

The key to the development of democracy and prosperity in Afghanistan is to build a viable and capable state with a robust economy. The Bonn process was dominated by an international agenda for security after the overthrow of the Taliban regime and its al Qaeda allies. The Afghanistan Compact is based on an Afghan agenda for long-term development leading to sustained peace and stability. It is closely linked to continuous monitoring of progress and introducing adjustments and course correction when needed. The Bonn process required Afghanistan to meet certain benchmarks toward democratic development. The succeeding process should identify how the international community can support the implementation of an Afghan development strategy over the next five years. Progress needs to be measured by the outcome and not by policies, pledges, or even the level of investment.

Notes

1. Peter Bergen, *Holy War Inc.* (New York, 2001), 89–90, 164–165.

2. Cited in Stephen Tanner, *Afghanistan: A Military History from Alexander the Great to the Fall of the Taliban* (New York, 2002), 2–3.

3. The murdered rulers included Amir Habibullah (1901–1919), Bache Saqao (1929), Nader Shah (1929–1933), Mohammad Daud (1973–1978), Nour Mohammad Taraki (1978–1979), Hafizullah Amin (1979), and Najibullah (1986–1992). King Amanullah (1919–1929) and Mohammad Zaher Shah (1933–1973) were forced into exile.

4. Diego Cordovez and Selig Harrison, *Out of Afghanistan: The Inside Story of the Soviet Withdrawal* (Oxford, 1995), 67–70, 266–270, 384–387.

5. John Cooley, *Unholy Wars, Afghanistan, America and International Terrorism* (London, 2000), 83–105.

6. Felix Ermacora, "Situation of Human Rights in Afghanistan," Report to the UN General Assembly UN A/45/664 (New York, October 31, 1990).

7. By 1987 Pakistani intelligence provided 67 to 73 percent of CIA-supplied weapons to the Afghan Islamist parties. See Mohammad Yousaf and Mark Adkin, *The Bear Trap: Afghanistan's Untold Story* (Lahore, 1992), 105.

8. See Dietrich Reetz, "Pakistan and Central Asia Hinterland Option: The Race for Regional Security and Development," *Journal of South Asian and Middle Eastern Studies*, XVII (1993), 28–56.

9. Cordovez and Harrison, *Out of Afghanistan*, 60–63.

10. Ahmed Rashid, *Taliban, Militant Islam, Oil and Fundamentalism in Central Asia* (New Haven, 2001), 157–182.

11. Tschanguiz Pahlavan, *Afghanistan: 'Asr-e Mujahedin ve Baramadan-e Taliban* (The Era of Mujahideen and the Rise of Taliban) (Tehran, 1999), 467.

12. Author's interviews with the late Akbar Maqsoudi, leader of the Islamic Alliance of Afghanistan Mujahideen (Etehadiya-e Islami Mujahedin-e Afghanistan), and another prominent Hazara political figure, Sayed Es'haq, Quetta, Pakistan, June 1984.

13. Wahhabi are members of a strict Islamic sect founded by Abdel Wahab in the eighteenth century in Arabia and revived by Abdul Aziz ibn Saud in the twentieth century. It opposes all practices not sanctioned by a strict reading of the Qur'an.

14. Ralph Magnus and Eden Naby, *Afghanistan: Mullah, Marx, and Mujahid* (Boulder, 1998), 190.

15. Agence France-Presse (April 21, 1997).

16. The total strength of Iran's active armed forces is estimated to be over a half-million troops (545,000). The country also can mobilize a 350,000-strong reserve force and 70,000 paramilitary troops. See Anthony Cordesman, *Military Trends in Iran* (Washington, D.C., 1998), 22.

17. The Northern Alliance was a grouping of predominantly Tajik, Uzbek, and Hazara factions that waged a long war against the Taliban.

18. The Shura-i-Nazar (Supervisory Council) was formed by the late Ahmad Shah Masoud in the northeastern provinces of Afghanistan within the predominately Tajik Jamaat-i-Islami (Islamic Society) party. Much of the group's strength was based in the Panjsher Valley, Masoud's home district.

19. The Loya Jirga is a traditional Afghan institution called into being by the state to make or endorse decisions of major national concern. It is an extrapolation from the model

of the tribal and local jirga that allows consensual decisionmaking on community matters. See "Agreement on Provisional Arrangements in Afghanistan Pending the Re-establishment of Permanent Government Institutions" (Bonn, December 5, 2001), article 1. (Hereafter referred to as the Bonn agreement.)

20. For details, see International Crisis Group, "The Loya Jirga: One Small Step Forward," Asia Briefing 17 (Kabul, 2002).

21. Author's interview with several Pashtun and Tajik commanders in Kabul, March and June 2002.

22. Bonn agreement, article 5.

23. But see later harsh critiques of the police effort in Robert I. Rotberg, chapter 1, in this volume, note 24.

24. Afghanistan National Development Strategy, "The Afghanistan Compact between the Islamic Republic of Afghanistan and the International Community" (London, January 31, 2006), www.ands.gov.af/ands/I-ANDS/afghanistan-compacts-p1.asp. Hereafter referred to as the Afghanistan Compact.

25. Islamic Republic of Afghanistan and United Nations Development Program, "Millennium Development Goals, Islamic Republic of Afghanistan, Country Report 2005: Vision 2020, Summary Report" (Kabul, 2005), www.ands.gov.af/src/src/MDGs_Reps/1.summary%20report%20english.pdf.

26. Bonn agreement, annex 1.

27. As of 2006, the PRTs were based in Kunar, Laghman, Nuristan, Nangrahar, Bamian, Parwan, Maidan-Wardak, Paktia, Paktika, Khost, Ghazni, Zabul, Kandahar, Urozgan, Helmand, Panjsher, Badakhshan, Kundoz, Baghlan, Mazar-e Sharif, Faryab, Badghis, Herat, Ghor, and Farah provinces.

28. James Dao, "Bush Sets Role for U.S. in Afghan Rebuilding," *New York Times* (April 18, 2002).

29. Author's conversation with several UN officials, Tokyo, January 21, 2002.

30. Transitional Islamic State of Afghanistan, *Securing Afghanistan's Future* (Kabul, 2004).

31. Reuters (January 3, 2006).

32. Afghanistan National Development Strategy, "The Afghanistan Compact."

33. "Life in Afghanistan," ABC News Poll (December 7, 2005), abcnews.go.com/images/Politics/998a1Afghanistan.pdf.

34. In September 2005 Pakistan President Pervez Musharraf proposed the construction of a fence along the 1,500 mile border with Afghanistan. The Afghan government dismissed the plan as unfeasible.

35. Barnett R. Rubin, *Afghanistan's Uncertain Transition from Turmoil to Normalcy* (New York, 2006), 8.

36. Lesley Wroughton, "Karzai Says Unworried by U.S. Afghan Troop Cuts," Reuters U.K. (December 21, 2005).

37. NATO, "Revised Operational Plan for NATO's Expanding Mission in Afghanistan" (December 8, 2005), www.nato.int/issues/afghanistan_stage3/index.html.

38. For example, the following governors were reassigned: Ismail Khan of Herat (2004), Gul Agha of Kandahar (2004), Haji Din Mohammad of Nangrahar (2005), Gul Ahmad of Badghis (2003), Mohammad Ibrahim of Ghor (2004), Sher Mohammad Akondzada of Helmand (2005), and Syed Amin of Badakhshan (2003)

39. Afghanistan National Development Strategy, "The Afghanistan Compact."

40. Afghan Government, "Action Plan of the Government of the Islamic Republic of Afghanistan on Peace, Reconciliation and Justice in Afghanistan" (Kabul, December 2005).

41. For an examination of the problem of opium in Afghanistan, see Cindy Fazey, chapter 8 in this volume.

42. The economy grew 28.6 percent in fiscal year 2002–2003, 15.7 percent in 2003–2004, and 7.5 percent in 2004–2005. Projected growth rate for the next decade is 10 to 12 percent. See World Bank, "Afghanistan: Data, Projects and Research" (Washington, D.C., August 2006), www.worldbank.org.af. For a comprehensive analysis of Afghanistan's economy, see Alastair J. McKechnie, chapter 5 in this volume.

43. United Nations Office on Drugs and Crime, *Afghanistan. Opium Survey 2005* (Vienna, 2005).

44. UN Development Program, *Afghanistan: National Human Development Report 2004* (New York, 2004), 4–5.

45. UN General Assembly, "The Situation in Afghanistan and Its Implications for International Peace and Security," Resolution A/RES/60/32A (New York, November 30, 2005); Jean-Marie Guehenno, Under-Secretary-General for United Nations Peacekeeping Operations, "UN Assistance Mission in Afghanistan," press conference, Kabul, December 20, 2005.

46. McKechnie, chapter 5.

47. Transparency International, "Corruption Perceptions Index 2005" (Berlin, August 2006), www.transparency.org/cpi/2005/cpi2005_infocus.html.

48. The South Asian Association for Regional Cooperation groups seven South Asian countries: Bangladesh, Bhutan, India, Maldives, Nepal, Pakistan, and Sri Lanka. The December 3–5, 2005, ministerial meeting in Kabul was attended by delegations from Afghanistan, China, the Islamic Republic of Iran, Tajikistan, Uzbekistan, Turkmenistan, Pakistan, India, Turkey, the United Arab Emirates, Kazakhstan, and Kyrgyzstan. Representatives from the World Bank, Asian Development Bank, the Group of Eight (G-8), and NATO also participated.

3 | Strengthening Security in Contemporary Afghanistan: Coping with the Taliban

Hekmat Karzai

Immediately after the horrific acts of September 11, the United States warned the Taliban, the ruling authority in Afghanistan, to hand over Osama bin Laden or suffer the consequences. The Taliban's response was very clear: Osama is a Muslim who has fought in the jihad against the Russians and to surrender him would violate our code of hospitality. Hence, on October 7, 2001, the United States and the Coalition forces started their offensive against the Taliban and their guests. Their aim was twofold—to destroy bin Laden's training camps and facilities and also to target the Taliban, with the presumed goal of destroying their morale and effecting their disintegration. This strategy was effective in destroying the camps where thousands of jihadists were trained; however, large numbers of al Qaeda members fled to neighboring Pakistan and Iran. The few battles that took place were between the allied forces, accompanied by various Afghan militias, and the hard-core extremists. The Taliban dispersed into villages and residential areas where they disappeared, chameleon-like, into the population. Within weeks, major Afghan cities such as Mazar-e Sharif and Herat fell, leading to the surrender of the capital, Kabul, on November 13, 2001.

The U.S. Operation Enduring Freedom toppled the Taliban regime in 2002. While much work remains, several surveys indicate that the overall conditions of the Afghan people appear to have improved and may actually exceed the conditions of the prewar period two decades ago.[1] A recent poll conducted by the U.S. television network ABC indicates that Afghans generally believe their country is moving in the right direction, demonstrated by the return of more than 3 million refugees. The country enjoys an elected government and an enlightened constitution. Educational opportunities have expanded and schooling is provided for all children regardless of gender.

Yet, the future success of Afghanistan is far from assured. Security remains a concern in the daily lives of the average Afghan as the Taliban, al Qaeda, and Hizb-e Islami continue to regroup and undertake terrorist attacks throughout the South and the Southeast of Afghanistan. They are learning and emulating tactics of other groups, especially the ones practiced in Iraq. In 2005, 85 American soldiers and over 1,500 individuals, including NGO workers, religious leaders, international officers, and government officials, were killed by means common to Iraq.

The United States has around 20,000 soldiers conducting combat operations against al Qaeda throughout the country. The NATO-led International Security Assistance Force (ISAF) of 10,000 was initially deployed to Kabul. The ISAF increased to about 20,000, and its mandate expanded to include the volatile South in 2006. Both the U.S. and NATO's efforts to bring security have not been very encouraging as the numbers of terrorist attacks have increased. Key leaders of the Taliban and al Qaeda, such as Mullah Mohammed Omar, Mullah Dadullah, and Osama bin Laden, are still at large and are routinely providing inspiration and motivation to their foot soldiers through modern means of communications.

The forces of Golbuddin Hekmatyar, head of Hizb-e Islami, and Mullah Jalaludin Haqani, former commander and a minister during the Taliban government, have joined the battle against the Coalition and Afghan security forces. They are known to have been operating within the porous border areas of Afghanistan-Pakistan in the provinces of Kunar, Paktia, Paktika, and Khost. They are also receiving crucial assistance from entities in Pakistan and parts of the Muslim world that are sympathetic to their extremist cause.

The objective of these groups is clear—to deter the deployment of international forces in the peacekeeping mission and eventually force the United States and the Coalition to withdraw from the country. The tactics to implement this strategy are deadly and include improvised explosive devices and suicide attacks on civilians. Of the suicide attacks that have taken place, two-thirds have been conducted since summer 2005.

The goal of preventing Afghanistan from becoming a terrorist haven, once again, rests on a number of elements: the Afghan security apparatus and whether it will be able to deal with the terrorist attacks and the booming drug trade that underpins its financial sources; the international community's commitment to the cause of Afghanistan; Coalition forces' ability to apply political means rather than military power vis-à-vis "heavy-handed tactics"; the role of external actors, and, in particular Pakistan, which has a history of interference in Afghan affairs. Finally, a consolidated and proactive legislation policy will act as both a preventative and prosecutorial strategy in relation to the broader struggle.

Historical Setting

The dominant factor in Afghanistan's recent history is continuous war since 1978.[2] This cycle of violence can be categorized in four unique stages: first, the Soviet invasion and the mujahideen resistance (1979–1989); second, the very destructive civil war among the mujahideen (1989–1994); third, the marriage of convenience between the Taliban and the Salafi jihadist group al Qaeda, subsequently leading to the September 11 attacks (1994–2001); and finally, the Taliban acting as a terrorist-militant group against the Afghan government and the Coalition forces (2002 onward).

In 1989, after a decade of war, the Soviet Union withdrew all of its troops, "condemning Afghanistan to a civil war that tore apart the nation's last remnants of religious, ethnic and political unity."[3] A culture of international neglect followed and contributed to the condition of postwar Afghanistan. Instead of uniting themselves and striving toward reconstruction of the country, the mujahideen—who defeated the Soviets—withdrew from this vacillating situation and engaged in armed conflict among themselves in competition for economic and social influence. The regrettable result was a period of immense social distress for the populace.

The Taliban, who drew much of their strength from the general disillusionment of the mujahideen, gained in popularity by presenting themselves as a viable and constructive political alternative since within weeks they had restored security in southern provinces.[4] They were not, however, a new phenomenon to Afghanistan. Participation of talibs and mullahs has been a constant feature of jihad in Afghanistan against any foreign invasion for a hundred years. They have been a component of the religious establishment and have always lived in the shadow of other military, political, and economic groups. Mullah Shor Bazar, an Afghan fighter known for inflicting heavy losses on the British during the third Anglo-Afghan war of 1919, was also a talib, as were Mirwais Khan Hotaki and Mullah Mushki Alam, who also fought against the British occupation of Afghanistan.[5]

During the Afghan-Soviet war and the subsequent war against the communist regime, the talibs and the mullahs fought under the banner of a variety of mujahideen groups and not as an organized movement. The majority fought under the Harakat-e-Inqilabi, led by Maulawi Mohammed Nabi Mohammedi, and the Yunus Khalis faction of Hizb-e Islami. After the fall of Kabul in 1992 and the establishment of a new government by mujahideen leaders, most of the talibs and mullahs went back to their madrassas to continue their study and teaching.

When they reappeared again as a military force, the majority of Afghans supported them since the broad Taliban objectives for Afghanistan were
—to end the conflict between rival mujahideen groups that continued to disintegrate the country and cause lawlessness;
—to unite the people under one central government;
—to restore peace and security for the population and protect their rights and liberties;
—to end the corruption by various parties and establish a credible and accountable government;
—to disarm the population from weapons that were abundant after the Afghan-Soviet war;
—to enforce sharia (Islamic law), establish the Islamic state, and preserve the Islamic character of Afghanistan; and
—to rebuild war-torn Afghanistan.[6]

Drawing from popular sentiment, the Interior Ministry of Pakistan, led by Nasrullah Babar, decided to further promote the Taliban and provide assistance. Pakistan has always supported various mujahideen groups for its own interests. During the resistance against the Soviets, the resources and funds coming from the United States and Saudi Arabia were channeled through the Pakistani intelligence establishment, Interservices Intelligence, which nurtured groups that were pro-Pakistan and extremist in their outlook. On this particular occasion, Pakistan sought political guarantees and found them in a group that appeared to seek stability and thus provide for secure conditions for trade with newly independent states in the north. Another element behind the Taliban emergence was Jamiat-e-Ulema Islam

(JUI), a Pakistani religious party led by Maulana Fazlur Rahman. The organization was responsible for running many madrassas.[7] Shortly thereafter, the Taliban forces advanced through Afghanistan, equipped with tanks, armed personnel carriers, artillery, and even aircraft. Their numbers rapidly expanded, and within a matter of six months, they had mobilized over 20,000 men. Most of them were given permission to come from Pakistan—many were from Pakistan—and their basic training took place in camps not only within Afghanistan but also on the Pakistan side of the border.

Financially, the Taliban were supported by many elements—Saudi Arabia and the wealthy Arabs throughout the Middle East were major contributors to the cause as they were keen on seeing a doctrine similar to Wahhabism spread across Central Asia. The Taliban were also able to generate funds from tolls on transport and the drug trade, which had started to generate major profits. Lastly, Pakistan provided millions in aid and at times even paid the salaries of the government officials.[8]

The role of Osama bin Laden and his group deserves recognition because they played a significant role in the maturation of the Taliban. The international community, led by the United States and Britain, forced the Sudan to expel bin Laden, as he was becoming a recognizable threat. As a result of the pressure, in mid-1996, bin Laden and his inner circle came back to Afghanistan, where they had already established an infrastructure, a legacy of the jihad against the Russians. Mullah Omar welcomed them and praised bin Laden for his contribution toward the jihad.

Analyzing the details of the relationship between the Taliban and al Qaeda is beyond the scope of this chapter, but the Taliban provided security and a sanctuary for al Qaeda where they trained thousands of recruits, established a state-of-the-art network, and planned various operations, including September 11. Al Qaeda's support came in several forms: they provided much needed financial resources, trained Taliban fighters in their conflict with the opposition in the north, and mobilized the well-trained 055 Brigade (a group of 500 to 1,000 Arab fighters) for key battles. Most importantly, al Qaeda ideologically influenced the Taliban leadership, which in many ways resulted in their extreme vision.

By late 1997 the Taliban had imposed their ultrapurist version of Islam on much of the country.[9] Couples were stoned to death if caught in adultery; thousands of widows were banned from employment; schools and colleges were closed to girls; men were not allowed to shave or trim their beards; TV, music, soccer, and women wearing white socks were all banned. The Religious Police Force enforced these edicts fervently. As the societal and cultural restrictions expanded, the support the Taliban once enjoyed evaporated, and Afghans sought to remove their children from the scene in order to evade conscription into the front-line action against the Northern Alliance. The vile treatment of the average Afghan continued until the attacks of September 11.

Structure of the Taliban

During their reign in power, only three countries, Pakistan, Saudi Arabia, and the United Arab Emirates recognized the Taliban as a sovereign government. At its strongest, the Taliban forces were never more than 25,000 to 30,000 men. At the early phases of the movement, the Taliban command structure was based on the following four components (figure 3-1):

—Amir ul-Mumineen (Commander of the Faithful) was the title given to Mullah Omar as the Head of State of Afghanistan and the Supreme Leader of the Taliban.

—The Supreme Shura was the highest decisionmaking body of the Taliban. It functioned as an interim ruling council. It had ten members and was based in Kandahar. Mullah Omar's friends and colleagues dominated the Shura. The original Shura was made up of these members, but military commanders, tribal leaders, elders, and the *ulema* (religious leaders) also took part in Supreme Shura meetings. The decisionmaking process remained loose and amorphous with as many as fifty people often taking part.

—The Military Shura was a loose body that planned strategy and implemented tactical decisions; however, it appears to have had no strategic decisionmaking or enforcement authority. Military strategy, all key appointments, and the allocation of funds were decided upon by Mullah Omar.

—The Kabul Shura dealt with the day-to-day operation of the government, the city, and the Kabul front against the Northern Alliance. Important issues were conveyed to the Supreme Shura, which then made decisions.

With time the leadership became more centralized and Mullah Omar took charge of issuing orders. He had four sets of very close advisors: the very few conservative Afghan clerics that shared his view, bin Laden and his top leadership, the Pakistani intelligence who served a military advisory role, and the religious body led by Maulana Fazlur Rahman and Niza-mudin Shamzi.

The military campaign against the Taliban, led by U.S. general Tommy Franks, was initially dubbed Operation Infinite Justice but quickly renamed Operation Enduring Freedom, due to perceived religious connotations of

Figure 3-1. *Taliban Command Structure*

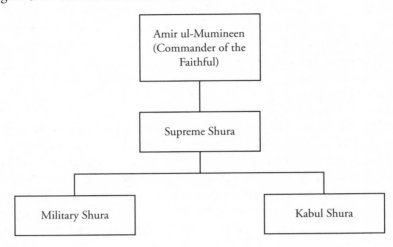

the former. The U.S. forces with their overwhelming mobile firepower achieved two very important objectives. First, they killed or captured a significant percentage of the Taliban leadership from the Supreme Shura, Military Shura, and the Kabul Shura. The detainees were secured at Bagram Air Base and the naval base at Guantanamo Bay. The Taliban began losing the ability to coordinate, and their morale began to sink. The rest of the leadership was either on the run or hiding in neighboring countries. Mullah Omar himself, after hearing the devastation brought upon the others, left his stronghold of Kandahar and still remains at large. The leadership of the Taliban was in disarray and the structure that once existed vanished.

Second, U.S. firepower destroyed the terrorist raining camps. The Taliban and al Qaeda had established many terrorist camps in Afghanistan with very specific objectives in mind. Training infrastructure has always been an essential ingredient of terrorist organizations, providing its cadre with capability for armament use and much needed indoctrination to sustain the ideology that drives the members to action.[10] One of the most important camps was the Darunta complex, which was located about eight miles from the eastern city of Jalalabad. Inside, there were four subcamps: Abu Khabab camp, where intelligence sources say chemicals and explosives were stored and terrorists were trained on how to use them to produce the most casualties; Assadalah Abdul Rahman camp, operated by the son of blind cleric

Omar Abdul Rahman—currently in jail in the U.S. for plotting to blow up the World Trade Center in 1993; Hizbi Islami camp, operated by a group of Pakistani extremists fighting in Kashmir; and lastly the Taliban camp, where religious militias were trained and indoctrinated to fight the Northern Alliance. The Tomahawk cruise missiles and the 15,000-pound daisy cutter bombs, coupled with AC-130 gunships, made the "terrorist universities" evaporate. Not only Darunta but also all the other camps and facilities that al Qaeda and the Taliban were using to recruit and train future fighters were destroyed.

Many experts allege that because of U.S. military might, the Taliban fighters and al Qaeda members established sanctuaries in major Pakistani cities and among tribal protectors in Pakistan and Afghanistan. Though the Taliban did stay quiet for some time to recover their losses, they gradually began launching cross-border attacks on nongovernmental organization (NGO) workers and civil servants. Today, they act as a terrorist group and have gained significant momentum attacking U.S. convoys and Afghan military personnel. They are clearly a much more sophisticated group than they once were.

A New Lethal Strategy

The Taliban's reemergence as a more sophisticated group rests on several factors: the reestablishment of their logistics and support from the outside, the return of foreign fighters, and financial support through the lucrative narcotics trade. The Taliban operates as a number of scattered, decentralized terrorist groups or cells that number between five and twenty-five men, each regularly crossing the border from their sanctuaries to attack their targets. The new outlook has allowed the Taliban to operate in a mobile manner and at times even capture small districts, illustrating their organizational abilities.

In view of the early setbacks in their military operations against the Coalition forces, the Taliban realized that they could not face the U.S. military with "force on force," so they shifted their strategy toward a strategic defensive posture by attacking "soft targets," such as aid workers, government employees, and civilians. They also targeted Afghans who openly criticized their actions and supported the recently installed government of President Hamid Karzai. The new strategy was effective as the UN and major international organizations, including the International Committee of the Red Cross, scaled back their operations in the south and southeast, depriving approximately one-third of the population of much-needed development assistance. Security concerns led Médecins Sans Frontières (Doctors Without Borders) to abandon their mission even though they had operated in Afghanistan for over two decades.[11] With the retreat of these vital social services, the citizens of the south and southeast grew distressed by the new administration, specifically because their basic needs, such as health care, were not being met.

In the immediate aftermath of September 11, pressure from the United States forced many of the proponents and supporters of the Taliban to abandon their ties and to support the war on terror instead. However, the Taliban has subsequently regained military training, financial support, and weapons from individuals and even entities that had supported them earlier and again wanted to exert their influence in the region by destabilizing the country. The Taliban's goal is to overthrow the perceived occupation and revert to their original ruling objectives. With time many of the restrictions that bridled foreign individuals and entities from engaging in ties with the Taliban grew soft, providing room to operate. Afghan intelligence seems to believe that since 2004, several camps were established just across the border of Afghanistan where many Taliban were trained and taught insurgency skills.[12]

Al Qaeda also became active in the region with the appointment of two of its most able commanders to Afghanistan. In particular, Khalid Habib, a Moroccan who led a group of foreign fighters and fought with the Taliban, was put in charge of the southeastern part of Afghanistan. Abd al Hadi Iraqi, a respected commander who fought against the Northern Alliance in Takhar province, was in charge of southwestern provinces. Specifically, these commanders seek to demonstrate the utter failure of the U.S. campaign in Afghanistan, beginning with the southeastern and southwestern areas and moving forward from these models of al Qaeda's success. An Afghan source close to the Taliban said, "The Taliban have divided up into groups . . . and in each unit there is a member of al Qaeda from Pakistan or an Arab, who teaches them tactics developed in Iraq."[13] Many seem to believe that members of the Taliban have gone to Iraq and trained with the insurgency, and many fighters from Iraq have come back to Afghanistan to assist the Taliban against the U.S.-led Coalition.[14] As a result of these factors, the Taliban and al Qaeda initiated an offensive posture by attacking U.S. bases and ambushing American convoys and patrols as well as Afghan national forces that were working with the Coalition. The transfer of knowledge from Iraq and resources and training from the outside provided new levels of sophistication to their operation and planning capability.

The Taliban's tactics have clearly improved. In the past the Taliban's military skills were rudimentary, but they have learned to work more closely with foreign fighters and other outside assistance; they are capable of coordinating attacks as well as executing other tactically challenging actions. This capacity is no doubt the result of the aforementioned training they have received from foreign fighters with experience in Iraq.

The increasing technical sophistication is illustrated by their use of improvised explosive devises (IEDs). The IEDs are very powerful and can destroy the most well protected tanks, Humvees, and jeeps. Taliban fighters are also able to use advanced triggering devices that allow them to set off IEDs at the time of their choosing to hit a particular target.

There have also been a number of beheadings similar to those in Iraq. While the number remains small, it is a dangerous escalation, designed to increase the terror within the local and foreign population in the country. This latter group was most recently targeted when Ramankutty Maniyappan, a driver with the Indian state-run Border Roads Organisation, was kidnapped and later beheaded. Border Roads was warned by the Taliban to leave the country and stop the road project with which they were assisting. The Indian government did not comply and afterwards called the killing "inhuman and barbaric."[15]

The Taliban have been attempting to link with the larger jihadi community. On December 25, 2005, they posted a video of the decapitation of an Afghan hostage on al Qaeda–linked websites. This video was the first ever published to show the beheading of an Afghan hostage in the hands of a terrorist cell. In what appeared to be a forced confession, Saeed Allah Khan, a resident of Khost province stated, "I worked as a spy for the Americans along with four other people. The group received $45,000 dollars and my share is $7,000 dollars." This video demonstrated how the practice of decapitation, initiated by Abu Musab al-Zarqawi, leader of Tawhid wal Jihad in Iraq, had reached Afghanistan.

More significantly, the Taliban and foreign fighters have introduced a new arsenal in their protracted war—suicide bombing (see box 3-1). Before September 11 this weapon was unknown in Afghanistan's long history of conflict, but it has gained a rapid foothold. Many Afghans allege that suicide attacks are carried out by foreign fighters because the phenomenon is alien to Afghan culture and the brand of Islam that they practice. Before his arrest by Pakistani authorities, Mullah Latifullah Hakimi,

Box 3-1. Major Suicide Attacks in Afghanistan since the Fall of the Taliban in Late 2001to Early 2006

June 7, 2003—A taxi explodes near a bus carrying German peacekeepers on their way to Kabul airport to fly home, killing four soldiers and an Afghan.

December 29, 2003—Five Afghan security officers are killed when a man they arrested blows himself up in Kabul.

January 27, 2004—A man with mortar rounds hidden under his clothes blows himself up in Kabul, killing a Canadian soldier and an Afghan.

January 28, 2004—A bomber in a taxi blows himself up near a NATO peacekeeping vehicle in Kabul, killing a British soldier.

May 8, 2005—A militant kills a UN worker from Burma and an Afghan in an attack on an Internet café in Kabul.

June 1, 2005—A suspected al Qaeda fighter detonates explosives strapped to his body in a mosque in Kandahar, killing twenty worshippers.

September 28, 2005—A militant on a motorbike kills nine Afghan soldiers when he blows himself up outside an army training center in Kabul.

October 10, 2005—Two suicide attackers explode bombs in Kandahar, killing three people.

November 14, 2005—Twin suicide car bombings target NATO peacekeepers in Kabul, killing a German soldier and eight Afghans.

December 16, 2005—A car bombing damages a Norwegian peacekeeping vehicle near the national parliament building just days before the legislature convenes.

January 5, 2006—A militant blows himself up in Tirin Kot during a supposedly secret visit by the U.S. ambassador, killing ten Afghans.

January 15, 2006—A car bomb slams into a Canadian military convoy in Kandahar, killing two passersby and a senior Canadian diplomat.

January 16, 2006—A man on a motorbike detonates explosives strapped to his body near a crowd watching a wrestling match in the border town of Spinboldak, killing twenty-one people.

February 7, 2006—A suicide bomber killed thirteen people and wounded thirteen when he set off explosives outside the police headquarters in the southern Afghan city of Kandahar.

Author's data based on field research or major news publications.

the Taliban spokesperson, warned that forty-five more suicide attackers were awaiting orders to strike. His prediction came true when, during the months of October and November 2005 alone, there were eight attacks, including one in the heart of the capital, in front of the army training center, that killed nine people and injured hundreds.

The Taliban's Media Strategy

While the Taliban were in power, they were considered to be a very conservative entity because they banned music, television, and even photography. Countless individuals were beaten and jailed for taking pictures or even for possessing a camera. Those same Taliban now utilize advanced technology in order to promote their views. The Taliban have established a media committee that is responsible for propaganda and producing their version of the news. They are constantly in touch with major radio stations like the BBC and others for news updates. One of the Taliban commanders, Mullah Osmani, even gave a television interview to the privately funded Pakistani television station GEO, where he praised his leader, Mullah Omar, and the success of the Taliban movement. Ismail, another commander of the Taliban, gave two interviews to NBC news describing the lethal attack that took the lives of several U.S. Special Forces operatives during Operation Red Wing.[16] Their most surprising evolution came when they joined the information superhighway and started to post their videos and magazines online. Today, many of their fancy videos, depicting their battles against the Coalition forces, can be seen over the thousands of jihadist websites. There are many websites, e-mail lists, and chat rooms that constantly encourage Muslims to join the Taliban in their battle against the infidel.

The Taliban's engagement with the various media channels has five main objectives: propaganda, recruitment, indoctrination, funding, and psychological warfare. The Taliban are preaching a message similar to that of Osama bin Laden: Islam is under attack and it is the duty of all Muslims to defend the lands of Islam. In a Taliban video entitled "War of the Oppressed," a Taliban member refers to the various places where Muslims are suffering and under duress by saying, "Look at our Muslim brothers that are suffering in Iraq, Palestine, Kashmir, and Chechnya from the hands of the infidels."[17]

Narcotics

In 2004 cultivation of the opium poppy had more than tripled to 510,000 acres, which meant that Afghanistan produced 90 percent of the world's opium. In a presidential report presented to Congress, Secretary of State Condoleezza Rice estimated "Afghanistan's current annual opium production at 5,445 tons, some 17 times more than second-place Myanmar."[18] While most of the drugs end up on the streets of Europe and Russia as heroin, the sale of opium also "supports terrorist groups," said a top UN official.[19]

While this fact may be alarming, the wider issue is not without precedent. For decades leftist insurgent groups in Colombia, principally the Revolutionary Armed Forces of Colombia, and right-wing paramilitaries have been financed largely by that country's cocaine trade. Some estimate the annual revenue that streams from the Afghan drug industry to be worth $2.6 billion—the Taliban clearly shares in the profits. Afghan government reports have shown that the Taliban has used the funds generated from the drugs to pay their new recruits and procure weapons.

Until very recently the United States paid scant attention to the drug issue in Afghanistan, as it was engaged in its own battle with Colombians. The United States had delegated the issue to the British, whose experience was perhaps only minimally sufficient. Only in 2005, with the backing of the Department of Defense, did the State Department develop a five-point plan designed to promote alternative crops for poppy farmers and to enhance efforts in eradication and interdiction of heroin labs and storage facilities. Both the Bush administration and the U.S. Congress supported the plan and authorized $780 million to implement and enforce it. The Afghan government has also taken major initiatives such as establishing the Counter Narcotics Ministry and Counter Narcotics Police to deal with the nexus of the Taliban and drugs.[20]

Although the governments of both the United States and Afghanistan agree on the notion that narcotics are associated with terrorist growth activity, nonetheless, the actual structure of this connection and its internal mechanisms are not yet clearly mapped. As a result, severing this relationship has proven to be an arduous task, especially as the Taliban gain deeper control of drug-infested areas in the south.

Afghan Security Institutions

Before the formation of the Afghan Interim Authority (AIA) in December 2001, most Afghan state institutions were paralyzed due to the two decades of brutal war. While state bureaucracy may have existed throughout the years, there was hardly any functionality. The problem was further exacerbated by the lack of qualified Afghans, who had migrated to the West or to neighboring countries. According to the United Nations, over one-fifth of Afghanistan's population of 25 million became refugees during the conflict.

When the AIA was given its six-month mandate to govern, it basically inherited institutions with no execution capability. The massive brain drain confronting AIA increased the grand challenge of state building. The Bonn agreement signed between the Afghans and the United Nations called upon the Security Council to deploy an international force to Kabul and eventually to other areas.[21] It was also decided that the international community would help the Afghans establish new security forces, which would consist of an army under the Ministry of Defense, a police force under the Ministry of Interior, and an intelligence service, the National Directorate of Security, an independent body that would report directly to the president. Most of the mentioned institutions were barely in existence or in the process of being established and therefore did not have the ability to execute what they were tasked to enforce. Thus, when the insurgency gained momentum, the efforts to counteract these trends were minimally effective at best.

Afghan National Army

Throughout modern Afghan history, the Afghan National Army (ANA) has been the backbone of Afghan security. Although it was mostly devoted to the government, it dealt mainly with revolts and major crises. Since its inception in the early 1900s, the ANA was considered a national institution. When the mujahideen took over Kabul in 1992, their first move was to dismantle the ANA for their own private militias. The mujahideen were under the impression that their forces would fill the vacuum of state power, but that was not the case. Instead of providing security to the Afghans, various militias started to fight with one another, and many cities were turned into ruins.

The new ANA is being trained by the United States with help from Britain and France. It started slowly due to recruitment challenges but had reached over 35,000 soldiers as of 2006 and is continuously growing. During its early training, the ANA was deployed full time only to the central garrison in Kabul, with mobile units occasionally going to the provinces. But, in response to recruitment problems and the serious Taliban attacks, the strategy changed. The ANA has been permanently deployed to four major regional military garrisons where they work to recruit new soldiers and gain a stronghold against the Taliban. On a routine basis, the ANA is embedded within the Coalition forces that engage the enemy. The ANA is gaining a great deal of experience that will contribute to its ability to deal effectively with counterinsurgency in the future.

Afghan National Police

The concept of policing is still new in most parts of Afghanistan as villages, where most of Afghanistan's population traditionally lived, provided their own security. If and when there was a conflict, the village leadership resolved it through the local mechanism of a *shura* (council). In some cases the tribal elders established a system where the Pashtunwali code of honor was used; consequently, there was no such thing as local or community policing.

Currently, Germany has taken over the job of training the Afghan National Police with the support of many Coalition partners, including the United States. They have established eight different regional centers where future officers from specific provinces and districts can be recruited. The efforts of Germany, the United States, and others have trained over 50,000 police officers who are engaged in efforts to further stabilize the country. The training provided to the police officers spans several weeks in duration and does not offer the wide-ranging skills needed to defuse effectively the threat posed by insurgent and criminal groups. Thus far, the Afghan National Police have been deployed to address a variety of operations including landmark occasions such as presidential and parliamentary elections to ensure against attacks and disruption, in provinces where warlords are in conflict with each other, and in battles with the Taliban, who at times attack and hold government checkpoints.

National Directorate of Security

Afghanistan's intelligence service—Khotwali—was given a new name and a new outlook by the KGB in the 1970s. During the communist era, most of the ruthless comrades were appointed to the State Information Service, and they were responsible for killing over 200,000 Afghans during the Russian invasion. In the late 1990s, mujahideen took over but were not able to establish any significant reform. After the fall of the Taliban, the United States, with the support of its Central Intelligence Agency, embarked on establishing a professional intelligence service. Most of the top leadership was removed and replaced with new cadres who were politically neutral. President Karzai appointed a new director of the National Directorate of Security who has also introduced new personnel and reforms.

The most needed change that has yet to occur in the Afghan intelligence community is the shift in thinking from internal to external. The KGB had trained Afghan intelligence to spy on their politicians, activists, and opposition. But at present, the immediate threat Afghanistan faces is from terrorist groups like the Taliban and al Qaeda, who are constantly planning and carrying out new attacks. Another eminent threat is the drug lords, who are generating financial support for the terrorists to conduct their activities.

The terrorist networks that were established throughout the years in the cities and rural areas by members of the various groups have not been infiltrated by the NDS. On June 1, 2005, a suicide attack on a mosque killed over nineteen people and injured more than fifty. Prior to this attack, there was intelligence that foreign fighters had entered the southern city of Kandahar; unfortunately, the human intelligence was not sufficiently developed to identify the attackers and their affiliates or to detect specific targets. The terrorist was reported to be of Arab origin, but the local support and assistance to this attacker in terms of target identification and location had been provided by the Taliban network. The "handler" of the terrorist was never brought to justice.

Foreign Troops and Cultural Blunders: A Major Liability

On October 1, 2005, Stephen Dupont, a cameraman and freelance journalist, shot the following footage while he was embedded with the U.S. Army's 173rd Airborne Brigade: five U.S. soldiers in light-colored military fatigues standing near a bonfire in which two Taliban bodies lay side by side. This incident, which took place in the southern part of the country, raised countless complaints about the soldiers' behavior, especially since Islamic belief prohibits cremation. Many wanted to punish the soldiers for their carelessness, but after an investigation, the soldiers involved were given reprimands and did not face prosecution. The report said that the incident was not criminal but illustrated poor judgment and a lack of knowledge of Afghan culture. The Afghan government stated that the U.S. military has been "very lenient" in punishing American soldiers for burning the bodies. "The burning of the bodies is against our Islamic and Afghan traditions. It is totally unacceptable, and it should not be repeated by any means under any circumstances again."[22] Afghan religious leaders also criticized the findings. "These soldiers should be severely punished," said Khair Mohammed, a senior cleric in Kandahar. "Foreign soldiers in

Afghanistan must respect our religion. If they continue to do things like this, every Muslim will be against them." In fact, local popular opinion has swayed as a result of such instances. "Continued violation of human rights by U.S. military in Afghanistan would change the minds of Afghans in favor of Taliban as they did not expect rights violation from the U.S. military when they respect them as their liberators," an Afghan tribal leader stated. "It took the Russians ten years, 120,000 soldiers, and they still were not able to dominate us, but we are working with the Americans who are still not respecting our culture," another Afghan villager noted.

Many experts agree on the notion that what injects political oxygen into the terrorist campaigns is the security force that reacts with extreme measures. In the case of Afghanistan, the notion stands correct. A recent survey conducted by an American academic states that the number of Afghan civilians killed by U.S. bombs has surpassed the death toll of the September 11 attacks.[23] Nearly 3,800 Afghan civilians have died since the conflict started. Targets have been clinics, wedding parties, and groups of tribal elders traveling to attend official business.[24] In addition, "U.S. soldiers routinely conduct search operations without the permission of the village elders, and they further lose our goodwill."[25] There have also been countless cases where male soldiers have entered houses and frisked women when relatives were not present.

There are reports indicating that at least two Afghans have died at the U.S. military detention center in Bagram Air Base, and several others have been beaten and tortured. Many Afghans do not expect such behavior from the U.S. military in Afghanistan because they were responsible for putting an end to the brutal regime of the Taliban and their harsh restrictions. "The reason why [the] U.S. military was so successful during its battles with the Taliban and al Qaeda [Operation Enduring Freedom] was due in great part to the fact that Afghans wanted them to succeed, and we supported them in every way possible."[26]

The Taliban and their radical elements have constantly capitalized on incidents such as burning bodies, torturing prisoners, and cultural ineptitude to exploit the situation for their own propaganda in order to mobilize local support. The Taliban have stated on numerous occasions that the "U.S. military powers do not value Afghan life." The central government of Afghanistan has responded by stating that U.S. troops present in Afghanistan should respect Afghan culture, and those who violate the culture should be punished. Dealing with the Taliban will require more than just military effort on the part of the soldiers—social, economic, and political measures have to be part of the broader approach. The best course of action for the U.S. coalition and Afghan forces is to apply minimum force and to "avoid a firepower-heavy operational strategy that is likely to cause significant civilian casualties, despite the 'smartness' of one's high technology."[27]

The Role of Pakistan

President George W. Bush has constantly reiterated one of the major success stories in the war on terror, that the United States has captured and killed over seventy percent of al Qaeda's leadership. It is actually with the support of General Pervez Musharraf, president of Pakistan, and his Interservices Intelligence Agency that individuals like Khalid Sheikh Mohammed, Abu Faraj al Libbi, and Abu Zubaydah were apprehended inside major cities in Pakistan. Many would argue that Pakistan is an invaluable ally in the war on terror, yet others contend that "aid has been frustratingly selective" because the Pakistani authorities have not captured many high-ranking officials even though there are many reports that they live in the major cities of Pakistan.[28]

Since March 2005 the Taliban have gathered momentum, and they are attacking with sophisticated weapons in several regions of Afghanistan that border Pakistan. As a result, many American soldiers and hundreds of Afghans have been killed. Most Afghan and even Pakistani politicians are convinced that the infiltrators are "coming from Pakistani training camps."[29] One of the most respected Pakistani journalists recently reported that "at least some training camps that were closed on Musharraf's orders have been reopened."[30]

The Slow Pace of Development

After September 11 Afghanistan became the main focus of the international community once again. Almost everyone felt sympathetic to the Afghan nation that had suffered three decades of war and destruction, and the Afghans themselves had very high expectations for help from the international community. The UN estimated that a minimum of $10 billion was needed over five years, with $15 billion needed over a decade, while Afghan officials put the figure between $25 and $35 billion over a decade. The International Conference on Reconstruction Aid for Afghanistan, held in Tokyo in early 2002, ended with just $4.5 billion in grants and loans pledged toward rebuilding the war-ravaged country.[31] The money that was paid toward rebuilding Afghanistan was mostly dispersed through international organizations and the NGO community, which comprises over 3,000 entities. The express decision not to allocate funds to the central government but rather to invigorate a parallel institution that provides social services "undermines the goal of state building and erecting institutions of governance," according to Ashraf Ghani Ahmadzai, former Afghan minister of finance. Many Afghans became disappointed with the reconstruction efforts, and they believed "the money goes to Westerners [working for nongovernmental organizations and aid groups] and is taken out of this country . . . the Afghans are still poor and jobless."[32] Furthermore, the NGO efforts are mostly focused in and around Kabul, the capital of Afghanistan. Coordination of services provided by the NGO community has also posed a challenge in that the goals of the NGOs are not defined, nor are they required to work in consultation with the strategic national vision of the central government. The lack of progress for certain segments of the population coupled with the constant propaganda that "the new government is a slave to America" has fueled resentment and led a segment of the population to sympathize with the Taliban.

Recommendations

According to a well-known proverb, success has many fathers whereas failure is an orphan. While this proverb may be true in other elements of life, it does not apply to terrorism or insurgency because volumes and volumes have been written on failed counterterrorism and insurgencies—from France's efforts in Algeria to the United States in Vietnam. Conventional wisdom would argue that experts would have learned from the errors of the past, especially in realizing that there has never been a purely military solution to terrorism, but this does not appear to be the case. One might almost apply Hegel's words: the only thing one can learn from history is that people do not learn from it.[33]

General Frank Kitson, author of the classic text *Low Intensity Operations*, articulates that in dealing with low-intensity operations, political, social, economic, and military measures are all necessary.[34] Similarly, the situation in Afghanistan requires military measures at the combat level, but there is a grave need for an indirect strategy. According to the great French strategic theorist André Beaufre, a direct strategy involves the application of military force as the primary means of imposing one's will on an enemy, whereas with indirect strategy diplomatic, economic, and propaganda instruments are orchestrated in support of the main military thrust, and military force is carefully calibrated to support—not undermine—the primarily nonmilitary means to impose one's will on the enemy.[35]

Political Strategy

In April of 2003, in a speech to religious scholars, President Karzai stated that "a 'clear line' has to be drawn between 'the ordinary Taliban who are real and honest sons of this country' and those 'who still use the Taliban cover to disturb peace and security in the country.' No one has 'the right to harass/persecute any one under the name of Talib/Taliban anymore.'"[36] The president launched his reconciliation policy, the Strengthening Peace Program (Takhim-e-Solh), which was "designed to weaken the resolve of the Taliban by breaking their ranks into good and bad Talibs."[37] Soon thereafter, an independent commission—Afghanistan's peace and reconciliation commission—was established and chaired by Sebaghatullah Mojadeddi, a former Afghan president (1992) and a respected religious scholar. The commission offered amnesty to all who would "lay down their weapons, accept Afghanistan's new constitution, and obey the decrees of Karzai's government."[38] High-level Taliban and individuals accused of war crimes were deliberately excluded from the program. The commission did prove to have a positive effect as many Taliban commanders accepted the amnesty and joined the government. It also created a rift between the conservatives and the moderates, permitting the moderates to take more of a political stand than a violent one. In the parliamentary elections held on September 18, 2005, there were many moderate Taliban candidates who ran for political seats and thus engaged in legitimate political exploits. Two former Taliban actually won seats in the lower house.

This program was the first indirect measure against the Taliban, and it yielded significant returns. Those Taliban anxious to return to Afghanistan were given an opportunity to reclaim their lives. Many government reports indicate that hard-core Taliban always preached to their lower ranks that if "you go back to our lands and villages, you will be sent to Guantanamo and Bagram prisons." The results of the Strengthening Peace Program serve as a positive illustration of how to engage terrorists and militants through political means rather than just militarily.

The international community must also remain engaged in Afghanistan until it has developed its own institutions that can deal with matters of state security and governance. Without this assistance Afghanistan's fragile institutions will crumble, repeating the history of the early 1990s, when the country was a hub of international terrorism and drug production. Most crucially, it is vital that a genuinely organic capacity of the state is developed, so that it does not appear to its citizens as the mouthpiece of the West.

The absence of a consolidated legislative structure will continue to inhibit counterterrorism and counterinsurgency processes in a number of ways in Afghanistan. The legislative vacuum is disposed to exploitation, and the command structures of all networks consistently demonstrate their knowledge of such weaknesses and where they may be manipulated. An effective prosecutorial policy will perhaps articulate an Achilles' heel or lack of political will on the issue and may encourage increased reorganization of the very entities the government is seeking to address. Without legal remedies, the government is limited in its ability to counter the opposition and the insurgents, but as Sir Robert Thompson articulates in his second principle on counterinsurgency, "the government must function in accordance with the law."[39] If this dictum is followed, then the security apparatus and the government will have the proper means to deal with the issues at hand.

Afghanistan's relationship with its neighbors is crucial to its long-term stability, and the country must establish strong ties with them, whether in commerce and trade or transfer of knowledge. Due to its landlocked status, Afghanistan must attempt to develop its relationships beyond basic diplomacy. The two most important neighbors are clearly Pakistan and Iran, and their support and assistance are crucial in the war against the Taliban and al Qaeda—who cross either of the two countries to come to Afghanistan and conduct attacks. Accordingly, it should be emphasized to these neighbors, especially Pakistan, that terrorism, if not dealt with, will have a significant impact on the state as a whole.

Social Strategy

It is imperative that strong but informal links be forged with village communities along the Afghan-Pakistani border, as some have been known to be a safe haven for the Taliban and al Qaeda operatives. The government must develop an overall plan to deal with these communities and provide them necessary services such as education and health care. The plan should include goals dedicated to improving the lives of the average villagers. Concepts such as "winning hearts and minds" must be employed. The majority of the population resents the Taliban and does not wish to go back to the draconian rule that was enforced when the Taliban were in power.

The cultural mechanisms within the Afghan communal environment are very strong and influential. Thus cultural ties should be exploited to deal with terrorism so that tribal leaders are organized into a structure that will work to further the long-term national interests of Afghanistan and desist from harboring, providing sanctuary for, or supporting terrorists.

Direct civil affairs action must take place in rural areas where poverty is rife so as to alleviate the suffering of the population. The hearts and minds of these Afghans must be won by freeing them from the perpetual poverty trap and enabling them to attain more than a subsistence living. Only then will there be success in creating a buffer between the population and terrorist groups.

Educational Strategy

There are certain cultural norms and generalizations that apply to Afghanistan that outsiders may not be familiar with, and therefore foreign soldiers should be culturally educated on the norms, customs, and traditions of the environment—particularly regarding such concepts as pawns of fate, collective identity, importance of relationships, good impressions, good intentions, associative thinking, and emotional intelligence. "Even though it can be argued that there is no recipe for dealing with terrorism or insurgency, there are, however, basic principles one can apply to deal with the situation at hand."[40] Understanding the part of the world one is in is essential.

The moderate religious leadership throughout Afghanistan should be empowered and given opportunities to spread their message at center stage. It is important to use counter-ideological measures: religious leaders should be engaged to initiate dialogue, first with the population and second with militants and their sympathizers, in order to ideologically dispel notions that terrorism is compatible with Islamic thought.

Military Measures and Strategy

Obviously, the first line of defense against the Taliban, al Qaeda, and their networks is the security services, both the Coalition forces and the Afghan police, army, and intelligence services. So far, they have found limited success, but as they develop further knowledge and understanding of the threat, they will certainly be better prepared. The following steps will further increase their success.

The military, both the Coalition forces and the Afghans, have to stop using a heavy-handed approach. Instead, they must work with the communities and develop trust between one another. On countless occasions the Taliban and al Qaeda have exploited the behavior of the Coalition forces to further strengthen their recruitment. As Mao Tse-Tung said, the insurgent's main objective should be attracting the confidence of the people because without their support there can be no battle.[41] Similarly, operations where force is used should be controlled because if one innocent civilian is killed, it diminishes the goodwill of a whole family, a community, and a tribe.

Police training in particular should be enhanced to better deal with terrorist tactics and strategies. They should receive advanced training in counterinsurgency techniques to better deal with violent groups.

The military has to familiarize itself with the Taliban's modus operandi and analyze their pattern of attacks. There are very few "hot spots" where attacks are constantly carried out; knowing that environment and protecting it will allow the military to anticipate future attacks.

The military must improve intelligence activities in areas, whether in Afghanistan or Pakistan, where the majority of the Taliban leadership resides and plans their operations. Most of the intelligence will come from within the population if there is goodwill and if they see the government as a protector.

The local police must refrain from engaging in corrupt activities; winning social trust is crucial. Also, the police must improve their image by maintaining effective neutrality. The population must not feel that the police are biased toward a particular clan or tribe because it will create a further distance between the state and the locals.

The institutions involved in military measures and security must share whatever intelligence and ideas they have with partners for regional cooperation. The more allies, the better the response. Coalition forces must continue to work with the Afghan security forces and share operational knowledge, which will further enhance the local capacity.

Conclusion

If Afghanistan is going to succeed in dealing with its security problems, it must overcome three vital challenges. First, it has to defeat the Taliban and their supporters, who are conducting terrorist attacks and hurting the population's morale. Second, it must curb the narcotics problem—which is a major source of revenue for the terrorists—by securing a sustainable decrease in cultivation, production, trafficking, and consumption of illicit drugs with a view to complete and sustainable elimination. And finally, it must train its security apparatus of police, army, and intelligence better to deal with the long-term threat. Each of these challenges requires strategy and long-term commitment.

Clearly, establishing security throughout Afghanistan is the job of the Afghans, but they will need the financial assistance and political support of the international community. Led by the United States, the international community has to be committed and much more generous to the cause of Afghanistan.

President John F. Kennedy once said, "Today's problems are the result of yesterday's solutions."[42] We learned the significance of this statement when the international community abandoned Afghanistan in 1989 after the withdrawal of the Soviet Union. Afghanistan subsequently became a hub of terrorism and a sanctuary for the masterminds of the September 11 attack. The question is really whether we are willing to make the same mistake all over again.

Notes

1. "Life in Afghanistan," ABC News Poll (New York, December 7, 2005), abcnews. go.com/images/Politics/998a1Afghanistan.pdf.; Asia Foundation, "Voter Education Planning Survey: Afghanistan 2004 National Elections" (San Francisco, 2004); International Republican Institute, "Afghanistan: Election Day Survey" (Washington, D.C., October 9, 2004), www.iri.org/10-21-04-AfghanistanSurvey.asp.

2. Larry Goodson, *Afghanistan's Endless War: State Failure, Regional Politics, and the Rise of the Taliban* (Seattle, 2001), 54.

3. Martin Evans, *Afghanistan: A Short History of Its People and Politics* (Surrey, Britain, 2002), 238–260.

4. The name "Taliban" is derived from the Arabic word *talib*, which means a student or one who seeks. In Arabic, *taliban* means two students. The word *talib* in Arabic is not used strictly for religious students. In fact, it is used for students at all levels, including those who study in university. In Pashto and Dari (Farsi), the two official languages of Afghanistan, *taliban* is a plural form of *talib*. It strictly refers to those who seek religious (Islamic) scholarship in traditional circles of learning in *deeni madaris* (Islamic schools or *madrassas*), part time or full time. The students in theological and Islamic studies in modern universities are not called *talib*.

5. Kawun Kakar, "An Introduction of the Taliban" (Fall 2000), www.institute-for-afghan-studies.org/AFGHAN%20CONFLICT/TALIBAN/intro_kakar.htm.

6. See Sayyid Rahmatullah Hashemi, "The Truth about the Taliban" (March 10, 2001), sydney.indymedia.org/front.php3?article_id=8468; "Facts and Realities under Taleban Administration" (date unknown), web.archive.org/web/20010216174708/www.taleban.com/taleb.htm; Ahmad Rashid, *Taliban: The Story of the Afghan Warlords* (London, 2001); University of Nebraska, *Afghan Atlas Project* (Omaha), 22; Michael Rubin, "Who Is Responsible for the Taliban?" *Middle East Review of International Affairs*, VI (2002),

meria.idc.ac.il/journal/2002/issue1/jv6n1a1.html; Kakar, "An Introduction of the Taliban"; "Interview with Abu Abdul Aziz Al-Afghani," *Nidau`ul Islam*, XVIII (1997); Tony Karon, "The Taliban and Afghanistan," *Time* (September 18, 2001); U.S. Embassy (Islamabad), "Meeting with the Taliban in Kandahar: More Questions than Answers," cable, document no. (declassified) 1995ISLAMA01686 (February 15, 1995), www.gwu.edu/~nsarchiv/NSAEBB/NSAEBB97/tal7.pdf.

7. Evans, *Afghanistan*, 255.

8. Daniel Byman, *Deadly Connections: States That Sponsor Terrorism* (New York, 2005), 194.

9. Peter L. Bergen, *Holy War, Inc.* (New York, 2002), 158.

10. In fact, religious indoctrination was considered far more important than battlefield or combat training. Rohan Gunaratna, *Inside Al Qaeda: Global Network of Terror* (Melbourne, 2002), 73.

11. Cheryl Benard, "Afghanistan without Doctors," *Wall Street Journal* (August 12, 2004), www.rand.org/commentary/081204WSJ.html.

12. Author's interviews with several Afghan intelligence personnel, September 2005.

13. Mitchell Prothero, "Taliban Regroups to Fight U.S. Troops," *Washington Times* (September 3, 2005).

14. Author's interview with Afghan intelligence officers, September 2005.

15. "Body of a Kidnapped Indian Man Has Been Found in Southern Afghanistan," BBC News Service (November 23, 2005).

16. Lisa Myers and the NBC Investigative Unit, "Interview with a Taliban Commander," NBC News (December 27, 2005), www.msnbc.msn.com/id/10619502.

17. "War of the Oppressed," translation from Pashto to English by the author. See www.intelcenter.com.

18. Robert Longley, "Afghanistan on Verge of Becoming a 'Narcotics State'" (March 2005), usgovinfo.about.com/od/defenseandsecurity/a/afghandrugstate.htm.

19. Paul Watson, "Afghanistan: A Harvest of Despair," *Los Angeles Times* (May 29, 2005).

20. For more information on the Afghan government's policy and actions, see Hekmat Karzai, "Afghanistan's War on Narcotics,"*e-Ariana.com* (June 1, 2005), e-ariana.com/ariana/eariana.nsf/allArticles/51A627F618D0DBF7872570130071B63D?OpenDocument.

21. For complete analysis of the Bonn agreement, see "Agreement on Provisional Arrangements in Afghanistan Pending the Re-Establishment of Permanent Government Institutions" (August 2006), www.afghangovernment.com/AfghanAgreementBonn.htm.

22. Daniel Cooney, "Afghan Government: U.S. 'Very Lenient,'" Associated Press (November 28, 2005).

23. Marc Herold, "A Dossier on Civilian Victims of United States' Aerial Bombing of Afghanistan: A Comprehensive Accounting [revised]" (2002), www.cursor.org/stories/civilian_deaths.htm#1.

24. For further incidents and attacks see Kathy Gannon, *I is for Infidel: From Holy War to Holy Terror* (New York, 2005), 114–125.

25. Author's interview with village elder in Kandahar, September, 2005.

26. Ibid.

27. Kumar Ramakrishna, "Coping with Asymmetric Threats the 'Propaganda-Minded Way': Lessons from 1950s Malaya," speech presented at "Coping with Terrorism" conference (August 6, 2005).

28. Editorial, "Afghanistan's Forgotten War," *New York Times* (August 5, 2005).

29. Maulana Fazlur Rehman, chief of his own faction of Jamiat Ulema-e-Islam and leader of the opposition in the National Assembly, mentioned that Pakistan is sending infiltrators to Afghanistan. Ahmad Rahid, "Musharraf's Double Game Unravels," *International Herald Tribune* (August 10, 2005).

30. Paul Watson, "Pakistan Connection Seen in Taliban's New Tactics," *Los Angeles Times* (July 28, 2005).

31. For details on the Tokyo conference, see Ministry of Foreign Affairs of Japan, "International Conference on Reconstruction Assistance to Afghanistan," www.mofa.go.jp/region/middle_e/afghanistan/min0201.

32. Prothero, "Taliban Regroups to Fight U.S. Troops."

33. Martin Van Creveld, "On Counterinsurgency," in Rohan Gunaratna (ed.), *Combating Terrorism* (Singapore, 2005), 294.

34. Frank Kitson, *Low Intensity Operations: Subversion Insurgency and Peacekeeping* (1971; reprint, Dehra Dun, India, 1992).

35. André Beaufre, *Strategy of Action* (London, 1967). Also see Kumar Ramakrishna, "An 'Indirect' Strategy for Trumping Al-Qaeda in Southeast Asia" (2002), www.ndu.edu/inss/symposia/Pacific2002/ramakrishnapaper.htm.

36. As quoted in Amin Tarzi, "Afghanistan: Is Reconciliation with the Neo-Taliban Working?" Radio Free Europe/Radio Liberty (June 2, 2005).

37. Ibid.

38. Ron Synovitz, "Karzai Confirms Amnesty Offer Is for All Willing Afghans," Radio Free Europe/Radio Liberty (May 10, 2005), www.rferl.org/featuresarticleprint/2005/05/7b099d96-969a-4c2c-837e-f12bc916b9f2.html.

39. Robert Thompson, *Defeating Communist Insurgency: The Lessons of Malaya and Vietnam* (Westport, Conn., 1966), 55–58.

40. Interview with Gerard Chaliand, leading counterterrorism-counterinsurgency expert and author of *Guerrilla Anthologies: An Historical Anthology from the Long March to Afghanistan* (Berkeley, 1982), September 2005, Singapore.

41. *Selected Military Writings of Mao Tse-Tung* (Peking, 1963).

42. David Kilgour, "Canada and the Global Drug Problem," remarks at the 12th International Conference, "Drugs, Criminal Justice and Social Policy: New Alternatives for An Old Problem," International Society for the Reform of Criminal Law, St. Michael, Bridgetown, Barbados, August 9–12, 1998, www.david-kilgour.com/secstate/drugs.htm.

Neither Stable nor Stationary: The Politics of Transition and Recovery

PAULA R. NEWBERG

> Democracies preclude contending absolutisms and the dicta of fixed identity. They have to do with identity in flux, with culture, and cultures, constantly transforming, molting into something new—something surprising and different and open-ended and free.
>
> —Jane Kramer, "Images," *New Yorker*, February 27, 2006.

> We will make the land beneath their feet like a flaming oven.
>
> —Mullah Mohammed Omar, Taliban leader,
> as quoted by Drake Bennett, "The Other Insurgency,"
> *Boston Globe*, April 16, 2006.

Like many small, insecure states, Afghanistan's political development is subject to the assumed prerogatives of its neighbors, allies, patrons, and enemies. But Afghanistan occupies more than simply another unstable space among countries living in volatile neighborhoods. Its path from civil instability to regional war and back again reflects the deeply seated contradictions between the external imperatives that fuel the war against terrorism and the country's efforts to build a political system based on internationally accepted standards of rights and democracy. Afghanistan's recovery not only reflects this contradiction but also duplicates it in many ways and challenges the diagnosis on which Afghanistan's recovery has been defined and pursued. The international community's desire to use the development of democratic institutions to forestall conflict—a highly instrumental and deliberate view of political change—has been thwarted by the same community's overriding military objectives against al Qaeda and the Taliban.

The reconstruction community's interventions in Afghanistan have been premised on the hope that conflict is over, rather than the reality that conflict persists. Despite the enormous strides that have been made since the anarchy of the late 1990s, efforts firmly to establish representative government will continue to falter on the twin grounds of external aggression and internal war. Until the assumptions of reconstruction are rigorously reviewed rather than half-heartedly sustained, democratic development and longer-term recovery will remain tantalizing and elusive goals.

More than five years after an emergency Loya Jirga confirmed Hamid Karzai's presidency, the Taliban movement has regained military strength in southern Afghanistan, compromised security, and reasserted civic power through parallel (and unsanctioned) institutions of justice.[1] Its reemergence, even if not permanent, is also not surprising. Continuing conflict along the Pakistani-Afghan border—a region of the country already beset by poverty, inequity, and a sense of civic abandonment—has been an inevitable result of the Western coalition's antiterror campaign and erratic antistate activity on both sides of the border. The international community's distinction between the Taliban and al Qaeda (conceptually and militarily, locally and globally) has been unclear for years. But as NATO battles Taliban forces, the Taliban's incursion into civic culture, including the imposition of local Islamic courts, now copies its insertion into Afghan life in the 1990s. By forcing NATO, Afghans, and their government to fight a past war in the context of current conflict, the Taliban fundamentally challenges the writ of the Afghan state and its capacity to change democratically under the Karzai government.

Transition

The resumption of war in October 2001 was, for many Afghans, the first step away from decades of violence and toward something resembling peace. From 1989 to 1996, half-hearted consociation had declined into rampant warlordism and, ultimately, anarchy. When the Taliban ascended sequentially to power in Kandahar, Herat, Jalalabad, and Kabul in the period from 1994 to 1996, a limited and false security reigned. It was soon replaced by the movement's tendentious efforts to whip an otherwise independently minded society into ideological conformity. As the country's meager resources became increasingly devoted to the Taliban's efforts to gain control over the territory held by the United Front (later renamed the Northern Alliance), society and the economy came close to their breaking points. With international assistance at an all-time low and peace brokering virtually absent, Taliban rule was increasingly infected by, and premised on, its relations with foreign fighters and patronage from al Qaeda. Despite flash-in-the-pan edicts to end the opium trade—market correction disguised as public relations—the country's place in its region and the world eroded into the illegalities of poppy and terror.

Within two months—from mid-October to mid-December 2001—it appeared that the equations of power were radically reversed. As the Tajik-dominated Northern Alliance marched into Kabul, Afghans convened in Bonn to craft a postwar compact to reestablish legitimate governance across the country. The Bonn agreements provided a framework far more than a road map: they set an early agenda for renewed relief, rehabilitation, and reconstruction, and placed the idea of political revival at the center of the country's future development.

The agreements were crafted through individual participation (under the umbrella of the United Nations) rather than delegation and representation.[2] At the outset, therefore, what was to count as democracy—and specifically, the relationship of democratic means to democratic ends—was only vaguely defined. The agreements were meant to bridge the considerable physical, political, and ideological distances between warriors and the victims of war, refugees and returnees, majority and minority ethnic groups and tribes, ideologues and technocrats, entrepreneurs and laborers, and the poor and the poorest.

Perhaps most strikingly, the agreements tried abstractly, if not practically, to balance the ideas of restitution and opportunity for political groups with very different historical memories. The spare language of the agreements implicitly recognized the different interpretations that former communists and their opponents (read: prisoners, refugees, and mujahideen) brought to political history. Floating alliances of sparring freedom fighters often represented alternative interests, and the Taliban (initially a collection of disenchanted mujahideen and later a fragmented force that tried to appear united) and its opponents viewed their own conflicts and those that preceded them through distinct lenses. Given these conditions, an outline for future political and judicial bodies could only be indicative and not prescriptive.

Additionally, the trajectory for future reconciliation was set in semi-institutional contexts that were often at odds. The United States—and implicitly, the United Nations—had hoped that the international community would take charge of Kabul, not the proxy fighting force under the banner of the Northern Alliance that marched into the capital. They—like the Alliance itself—were well aware that a minority-controlled armed group could exacerbate ethnic tensions already heightened by the Pashtun-centered experience and ideology of the Taliban and the historically Tajik-centered governance of Kabul and the Afghan state. Negotiations among individuals and among Western donors brought in a provisional government that recognized ethnic identity and past loyalties as valid criteria for political appointment. At the time of their drafting, the agreements tacitly considered the Alliance's current power and set the language of politics in terms that could accommodate ethnic politics or a broader view of equal citizenship.

In 2006—after presidential and parliamentary elections, billions of dollars of international assistance, the seeming demise and subsequent rise of Taliban insurgency, and after the Bonn agreements were superseded by the Afghanistan Compact—these contextual elements for political development were worth remembering and revisiting. Assumptions are important in politics, and those that reflect negotiated settlements between domestic and foreign actors, donors and aid recipients, feuding fighters and nascent democrats are all the more important for the complexity that they represent. Paramount among these assumptions, however, was and remains a conviction that Afghanistan can become a successfully functioning, pluralistic, democratic state. (Some Afghans argue that it can be prosperous as well, but that prediction may tax the imagination of observers even more than the prospect of democracy rising from the ashes of antidemocratic war.) International assistance, whether for political, economic, or military purposes, arrived in support of this goal.

Recovery

At first blush, Afghanistan's recovery statistics are heartening. At least 60,000 militiamen have been disarmed, and at least 5 million children have returned to school.[3] Reconstruction produced a temporary economic boom, a sharp rise in GDP, and the beginnings of a domestic revenue stream to support the government. In a sense, however, these figures are a harvest of low-hanging fruit. Obstacles to fulfilling the promise of recovery and reconstruction remain significant and sobering. International assistance has not kept pace with recovery needs; the lion's share of foreign funds has been used to support military operations for the Coalition and NATO, and the latest international agreement to support future reconstruction, heralded in London at its signing as a vote of confidence in Afghanistan's future, is seen by close observers as reflecting the international community's "strategic failure" to put the country on a strong enough footing to withstand the perilous assaults of narcotics and insurgency.[4] One reflection of the problem is the weakness of the domestic police and defense apparatus, which remain tied to antistate armed groups and thus to trafficking in illegal substances and terror. Neither nongovernmental organizations nor regional donor assistance providers (including multidonor Provincial Reconstruction Teams) have been able to override the critical absence of state infrastructure and local and national political power that might otherwise break the link between arms and power.[5] The scope of reconstruction is clearly limited; international assistance cannot yet support locally grounded, politically acceptable (and indeed, politically generated) recovery.

Compromise and Political Change

The Afghan state and its citizens have attempted to stand war on its head without discarding many practices and habits that either predated its wars or laced through their aftermath. Discontent in 2006 focuses more on old frustrations than new ones. Reform preempted outright revolution, and obeisance to history persists even when history has been proven wrong. Old warlords have disarmed at least partially, but most—disarmed or not—have retained political and economic muscle. Mujahideen have turned into jihadis or politicians, the rural poor remain economic outcasts, and the urban poor are not embraced by the engines of growth envisioned in innumerable planning documents. Even though insurgency has revived, there has been little hint of insurrection or uprising. No doubt even the Taliban insurgency would have lost strength had the border with Pakistan been less porous. Popular sentiment still sides with a civilian leadership that is representative rather than dictatorial—although this opinion almost inevitably wanes in the face of rising insecurity—and poverty has not displaced a yearning for—and a semblance of—peace, even where security is notably lacking.

Rebuilding a state is always an uneven process. In Afghanistan as elsewhere, the road to peace is scarred with good intentions and bad, technical expertise and incompetence, autonomy and dependence, and promise and

fear of uncertainty. The miracle of Afghanistan's post-2001 political environment is that it has moved forward at all—because of but also despite
international political and economic experimentation. Afghanistan's politics
could be better, but they could also be much, much worse. The country now
has a national constitution that was drafted with imperfect countrywide participation, but participation nevertheless. Presidential and parliamentary
elections, feared for the fragmentation that they might have reflected or
engendered, turned out to define and satisfy important benchmarks of participatory politics—not all, but enough to restart state institutions.

Glaring restrictions on political parties—which the government seemed
to believe would empower jihadi groups rather than promote legitimate
political interests—constrained relations between the executive and the
new parliament, the parliament and the judiciary, and national and local
institutions. Indeed, these constraints on party development and activities,
spearheaded by the president over the objections of many donors who otherwise supported elections, clearly juxtaposed fears of conflict with hopes
for the future and weakened democratic development. In an ideal political
world, the influence of jihadi groups would have been limited by the very
success of the electoral process; in a world defined by ideological and military conflict, such progress has been easily compromised.

These political activities accompanied a reconstruction process that has
barely begun and may never be completed. To the degree that plans remain
unfulfilled, they have been held hostage to the perniciously cumulative
effects of jihadi politics, porous borders, and the illegal drug trade. Political progress has been thwarted by complex problems of political enfranchisement and empowerment exacerbated by the reality of a young,
refugee-returnee population whose experience with governance of any sort
ranges from limited to nonexistent.

Political failures are complicated by choices rendered all the more difficult by the diffusion of responsibility in a state still host to war. The hard-
est questions to answer in Afghanistan since 2002 have been those that
arise from the impossibly close relationships between internationally
funded reconstruction and a politics colored by tenuous foreign policy—
and thus reveal the incomplete foundation of political responsibility. Is the
government's first priority to extend the authority of the central state or to
use the prospect of universal political enfranchisement to defuse dangerous
ethnic politics? Is a weak (although seemingly stable) presidency the fault
of personalities, competing claims to command foreign armies on Afghan
soil, or a choice to maintain an uncontested center among competing

peripheries? Are unfinished plans for local level redevelopment the responsibility of local actors or of internationally funded and executed projects that miss their mark? Is insecurity a hallmark of poor governance, an outgrowth of wrong-headed policies, a failure of international actors to ensure safety, or the fault of rapacious, antistate warlords and insurgents for whom peace is an inconvenience? Who, in the end, is responsible for Afghanistan's success?

These questions reflect the fundamental uncertainties that lie at the heart of postconflict political development. Their answers are heatedly debated in Afghanistan, as in most states attempting to rise above the divisiveness of long war, and of course among donor governments. Afghanistan may not differ fundamentally from other countries seeking to restore political engagement to the center of national life. It is, however, among the latest and largest internationally assisted experiments in joining reconstruction to locally determined, democratic development at a time when peace has not, really or realistically, broken out.

Old Uncertainties and New

Until the end of 2001, conflict was perhaps the most certain element of civic life. For those who lived through civil strife, ideological contest, foreign intervention, and proxy wars, the deprivations of war were enormous. By the time war resumed in late 2001, millions of Afghans had left the country, conflict had subsumed neighboring regions, and major powers seemed paralyzed by political stalemate and ideological conflicts that no one was quite willing to confront.

The events of September 2001 catalyzed the United States and its allies into renewing war within the borders of Afghanistan. War did not, however, alter the outlines of Afghan politics. The political stasis that Afghanistan seemed to show the world through the 1990s had been but a façade; while anarchy reigned, dozens of nascent, national power holders and local power brokers continued to refine and redefine their interests and the terrain on which future politics might be built. The October 2001 war reinforced personal and political alliances; revived proxy war helped to set the stage for future political contests. Expatriate politics was overlaid onto the shifting alliances within Afghanistan, and all components joined, in one way or another, in Bonn.

Was Afghan democracy the intended outcome of this iteration of war? Not really. The Western-led coalition was far more interested in establishing stability than democracy and defined that stability in terms of al Qaeda's removal from the country and the region, and the removal of the Taliban movement from power. For stalwart democrats the distinction between stability and democracy is a false one, but in the context of recent Afghan history, it is telling. Proxy war itself limited choice: the only Afghan forces capable of using Coalition resources were old mujahideen, commanders and warlords for whom democracy was not (yet) as vital an interest as securing territory, influence, and wealth. (That some of the same actors reappeared as candidates for local and national office in 2004 and 2005 simply proved their tenacious pursuit of power.) The events of late 2001 underscored commonalities and deep differences among Afghan groups dedicated to removing foreign forces from Afghan soil and regaining control of national life—even if many of these groups agreed on little else. Perhaps more than any other single factor, this conflation of goals into a rubric of "taking back Afghanistan for ourselves" set the context for the emergency Loya Jirga that confirmed President Karzai, the subsequent constitutional jirga that set the rules of political engagement, and the presidential and parliamentary elections that followed.

Many Afghans may have thought that war should bring democracy; few thought that it would. Interviews undertaken by the U.S.-based National Democratic Institute for International Affairs in 2002 and 2003 reflected the perceived chasm between stability and democracy: stability sounded like an achievable goal; democracy did not and could even be thought of as a deterrent to stability.[6] When U.S. Ambassador James Dobbins noted shortly after the Bonn meeting that most Afghans were anxious not to go back to war, he was reflecting popular sentiment as well as U.S. support for President Karzai—and, indirectly, the fact that fear of renewed violence constrains the kinds of political choices that citizens feel they can take.[7] This "fear of the future, lived through the past," as Vesna Pesic described the former Yugoslavia, has retained political and military meaning in the post-Bonn years.[8]

Among the most difficult challenges for those engaged in recovery and reconstruction—whether domestic or foreign actors—is determining where and when to set boundaries between past, present, and future. It can easily be argued that by empowering old mujahideen, the Western-led coalition reasserted the primacy of groups whose strength and legitimacy might otherwise have continued to wane. By seeking to balance political representation in the early cabinet, major political actors reified an ethnic dimension of political participation that might otherwise have been best left to the past.

By seeking to create a postwar government before war had ended—in effect, to act as if the Bonn agreements were a peace treaty rather than a prelude to peace or, more perniciously, a prelude to a new kind of war— the Coalition, the United Nations, and donor governments became party to some of the very struggles that they were trying to defuse. Little wonder, then, that each stage of political recovery has been matched or thwarted by the intrusions of fighting on battlefields, in political institutions, and within the processes of reconstruction.

It can also be argued that by recognizing some of the basic assumptions of Afghan political life—including those that predate the beginnings of war in the 1970s—the Bonn framework offered a handy realism in contrast to high-handed and impractical idealism. In some ways institutional developments prove this point. Elections in 2005 were relatively peaceful, with 12.5 million registered voters, 6.8 million of whom voted in parliamentary elections for the national legislature and thirty-four provincial councils. There were no formal, schismatic postelection problems, and a working parliament emerged that was able to approve a presidential cabinet.[9] In the months since it convened, parliament (with male and female members working together) has been able to create an environment for discussion and debate—not always friendly and perhaps not always fair but potentially resilient.

The political fulcrum in Afghanistan is thus neither stable nor stationary. It tries to balance continuing and profound instabilities fostered separately by the uncertainties of the foreign-led antiterrorism (and increasingly, anti-Taliban) campaign and by the incomplete institutions established to govern the state. Thus far, equilibrium has been difficult to maintain. Whether democratically leaning state institutions will be a sufficient placeholder for a full democracy to come depends in part on three related questions: What counts as a just state and an appropriate environment for political justice? How much space for democratic and institutional development can be carved out of ongoing hostilities, and will it be expansive enough to sustain the momentum for peace rather than future war? Can democratic development link local and national initiatives to establish a reasonable political foundation for the state?

Justice and Recovery

The corrosive certainties of war are perpetually dangerous. Afghanistan remains among the world's poorest countries, dependencies have flourished under foreign aid, and the uneven distribution of resources—and the chances to receive, create, or acquire them—is a threat to stability, political participation, and democratic development. The essential elements of a humanitarian crisis, ranging from poverty to powerlessness, remain in many parts of the country. Tribal safety nets—the backbone, in many instances, of refugee communities—have eroded, and particularly in the southern Pashtun belt, the intersection of poverty and resentment has helped the Taliban to flourish.[10] These phenomena underscore not only the fragility of national unity where it is most effectively challenged by insurgency but also the clear link between economic degradation, local concepts of political opportunity, and the capacity of reconstruction to reverse the fragility that emerges from so many years of state failure.[11] They undercut the state capacity that Afghans need in order to believe that their futures might be more stable and prosperous than they are today.

If lessons from other transitions apply to Afghanistan, then stability will depend on the way that citizens (and their representatives) are able to imagine legitimate alternatives to current uncertainties. If those alternatives are available only through violence, then democracy is inaccessible. If they are available only through the illegitimate seizure of power—a reasonable fear in an unstable state—then democratic development is at best stunted.

Afghanistan's new parliament represents the country's cautious, troubled, and incomplete recovery from decades of war. The relative success of elections suggests that many Afghans believe a better future is indeed possible. Afghans have thus vested their hopes in a parliamentary system that will require considerable support and increasing peace in order to succeed. (Indeed, one important role of electoral rules will be to erase future divisiveness that might otherwise arise from the perception of unfair resource competition.) On the one hand, parliament shows Afghans what political contest might look like in postwar Afghanistan armed with words rather than guns. But the political future offers far greater challenges than the seating of one elected institution can provide, and embedded in parliamentary elections and electoral politics are many of the broader problems that Afghanistan continues to face. Host to an international campaign against terrorism and to all the insecurities of postwar poverty and displacement, Afghanistan demonstrates how tenaciously difficult postconflict recovery and reconstruction can be and how easily retrogression can triumph.

To keep open the possibility of success within the domestic political orbit, however, the state's paramount needs are an assured means to guarantee rights for its citizens and a structured rule of law that is transparent, accountable, and accessible. Rights and rule of law require many forms of protection, including a fully fledged articulation of legal rights that has yet to be made concrete in either law or practice, and palpable mechanisms for the state to deliver on the promise of those rights: independent and accountable judiciaries, functioning legislatures, and transparent electoral administrations that can anchor the role of participation in a nascent democratic process.[12] Thus far, in the absence of adequate, formal, judicial protections, the Electoral Complaints Commission has offered the only secure way for citizens to file complaints against either individuals or the state—a popular vehicle during the parliamentary election period that nonetheless could not, for the most part, address such grievances.[13] The success of electoral politics and the stability of the state are premised, necessarily if not sufficiently, on a cogent system of rights promotion and protection.

The Bonn agreements provided for the development of a human rights commission, a quasi-governmental organization that has straddled the line between state critic and defender with considerable finesse. Foreign-based rights organizations have been allowed relative freedom to work in Afghanistan and have been able to promote rights protections (most notably for women) and publicize criticisms fairly openly; the United Nations has also been able to conduct its human rights work without major difficulties. The imbalance between central authority and peripheral challenges to it, the porous nature of Afghan society, and the presence of a huge reconstruction community and foreign military forces have all conspired to weaken the government and, perhaps counterintuitively, to allow unexpected space for rights promotion. This experience differs markedly from Afghanistan's neighbors, where critique is prohibited and rights promotion is often impossible. Maintaining democracy in a sea of regional authoritarianism will remain a special challenge.

Nothing can substitute for an independent judiciary, however, and this critical institution is still missing across the country.[14] The parliament's vote against ideologues on the supreme court may seem heartening to rights advocates—even though their appointments no doubt seemed like tactical protection for a president whose own political sentiments are sandwiched between extremes he cannot control—but its own prospective work crafting protective laws to depoliticize the judiciary is likely to be far more important.

Laced through discussions about justice in Afghanistan, however, are two paramount concerns: the question of impunity for crimes committed during decades of war and the problems of crimes committed in the course of the ongoing antiterror campaign.[15] In both arenas domestic and international responsibilities are intertwined in ways that seem to surpass the writ or will of the Afghan government—illuminating, once again, its tenuous hold on rights and related concepts of due process. When, for example, a national security tribunal sentenced to death a communist-era intelligence chief in March 2006—the first effort to hold a former government official accountable for past crimes—the proceedings were reportedly so compromised by basic rights violations that justice could not even remotely be seen to be done.[16] Similarly, another case concerning the rights of a Christian convert exposed the chasm between civil and Islamic law as well as the incomplete rendering of citizenship rights. With some domestic groups clamoring for the prosecution of war crimes—whether among communist-era authorities, Taliban officials, or other leaders of armed struggle during the past three decades—the cabinet's late 2005 plan to establish a system of transitional justice has become among the most critical pieces of policy passed since the interim government took office. At this stage in Afghanistan's transition toward recovery, overlapping, intersecting, and conflicting loyalties remain potent and divisive forces within the polity, and state instrumentalities are not comfortable mediating the conflicts that such tensions so often produce.

Establishing a system of justice—more than the simple articulation of a rule of law—is inevitably complex in a country where retrospective and prospective justice are so closely related and where neither the state nor its citizens have yet come to a shared reading of the country's history. The process of rereading and rethinking this history has been additionally complicated by the gross violations of rights committed by foreign forces within Afghanistan and in prisons overseas as part of the continuing antiterror campaign. These actions have, in a particularly poignant way, robbed the country of some of the legitimacy of its own recovery.

Setting a course to correct human rights abuses, while difficult, is an essential prerequisite for political progress. If it is not crafted well and quickly, with the cooperation of the international community in ways that allow the Afghan state to lead rather than follow, then the state is likely to be seen as complicit in the kinds of rights violations that fully fledged political recovery would otherwise prevent. Here again, Afghanistan faces two related problems. First, nascent democracies require time and space to establish institutional balance: stability on behalf of the state and its citizens requires stability within the state. Stable states can craft and recraft relationships within, between, and among the branches of government, and competition between instruments of the state can often produce stronger rights protections for citizens. Unstable states live differently. Few Afghans are likely to believe that their elections produced a confident and capable government, but fewer still can survive the insecurity that weak government fosters.

Second, strains on representative government come from within but also from outside the electoral system and the state itself. Every decision that the Afghan state must make in the near term must balance competing power centers—center and periphery, military and civilian, foreign and domestic—against the imperatives of maintaining the state's literal existence. Warlords, insurgents, dissatisfied constituents, and recalcitrant ideologues—vestiges of the past that define individual culpability and collective justice in the present—all represent governance challenges beyond the capacities of a young administration to confront directly.

Reconstruction, recovery, rights, and democracy meet on this shaky ground. Although the Bonn agreements, their iterative processes, and subsequent policies empowered politicians and political processes, the responsibility implicit in them was not matched by the authority accessible to government or fully embraced in reconstruction operations. This lack has been most evident in the unfinished reintegration of combatants as well as in incomplete security sector and judicial reform, which strikes at the heart of both democratic development and material reconstruction.[17] The factors that drive the course of domestic politics exist in a delicate, difficult relationship to the state's technical abilities and political adaptability. Instrumental reconstruction can fix structures and systems, but it can at best repair history only obliquely. At the same time, rights regimes can address retrospective abuses and establish the grounds for future protections but cannot guarantee political toleration. Democracy—as a principle, a means, and a political end—can set a context for recovery but cannot guarantee political revival.

In the longer term, the stirrings of democratic participation and the rights protections they can set in place can become the real arenas for democratic transition. If, and only if, reconstruction can be moved toward this goal—with leadership from within Afghanistan—will a condition approximating peace seem even marginally within the country's reach. Even then, preparing for democratic governance can provide only false hope until the state and its nascent representative institutions control territory, men, materiel, and decisions about the prosecution of war. These crucial relationships between peace and political security will ultimately require a recasting of the reconstruction agenda.

Just short of the critical five-year success point for postconflict governments, Afghanistan has reached a decisive crossing. Its short course in electoral politics may offer hope—albeit fragile and occasionally faint—that fair and equitable political participation can set the context for reconstruction, development, and justice. But an overarching environment of insecurity, instability created by the antiterrorism campaign, the desperation of local populations squeezed between foreign military forces, a weak government, and the increasing presence of armed, nonstate actors may well compromise the best hopes for participatory governance. If reconstruction becomes immutably separated from democratic development, the state's political trajectory will be seriously compromised, and political choice may well be limited to the discomfiting, dangerous, and paradoxical choices between further conflict, the erosion of state power, and authoritarianism.[18]

Notes

1. Carlotta Gall, "Taliban Surging in Afghan Shift from U.S. to NATO," *New York Times* (June 11, 2006).

2. The Bonn agreements, signed in December 2001, established a transitional structure under the auspices of the Afghan Interim Authority, set the stage for an international security force, and established a timetable for a Loya Jirga (which met in June 2002) and for elections in October 2004 and September 2005.

3. See Simonetta Rossi and Antonio Giustozzi, "Disarmament, Demobilisation and Reintegration of Ex-Combatants (DDR) in Afghanistan: Constraints and Limited Capabilities," London School of Economics, Crisis States Working Papers II (2006).

4. Ahmed Rashid, "Afghanistan: On the Brink," *New York Review of Books*, LII (June 22, 2006).

5. See Robert M. Perito, *The U.S. Experience with Provincial Reconstruction Teams in Afghanistan: Lessons Identified* (Washington, D.C., 2005), www.usip.org/pubs/specialreports/sr152.html.

6. National Democratic Institute (NDI) for International Affairs, Focus Group Report, "Afghan Perspectives on Democracy" (Washington, D.C., 2002); NDI Focus Group Report, "A Society in Transition" (Washington, D.C., 2003).

7. Drake Bennett, "The Other Insurgency," *Boston Globe* (April 16, 2006).

8. Vesna Pesic, remarks to the Institute on Global Conflict and Cooperation Working Group on the International Spread and Management of Ethnic Conflict, University of

California at San Diego, October 1, 1994. Cited in David A. Lake and Donald Rothchild (eds.), *The International Spread of Ethnic Conflict: Fear, Diffusion and Escalation* (Princeton, 1998), 7.

9. See European Union Electoral Observation Mission, "Democracy-Building in Afghanistan: An Integrated Dimension for the Way Forward" (Kabul, 2005).

10. Cross-border assistance to the Taliban in conservative regions of Pakistan's tribal agencies has helped the Taliban to survive on both sides of an increasingly porous border. The social and economic environments in Pakistan and Afghanistan are not the same, but together their presence is changing political society in both countries. See Declan Walsh, "Pakistani Taliban Take Control of Unruly Tribal Belt," *Guardian* (March 21, 2006). See Bennett, "The Other Insurgency," on the complex causes for insurgency. See also Sebastien Trives, "Afghanistan: Tackling the Insurgency: The Case of the Southeast," *Politique Étrangère*, I (2006), 105–118. This article argues for stronger counterinsurgency operations rather than solutions to the political and economic problems of the region.

11. Paula R. Newberg, "Surviving State Failure: Internal War and Regional Conflict in Afghanistan's Neighborhood," in Cynthia J. Arnson and I. William Zartman (eds.), *Rethinking the Economics of War: The Intersection of Need, Creed, and Greed* (Baltimore, 2005), 206–233. See also Ashraf Ghani and Clare Lockhart, "Rethinking Nation Building," *Washington Post* (January 21, 2006).

12. Antonella Deledda, "Afghanistan: The End of the Bonn Process," *Transition Studies Review*, XIII (2006), 155–171; U.S. Agency for International Development, "Afghanistan Strategic Plan, 2005–2010" (Washington, D.C., 2005).

13. Joshua Wright, "Warlords in Parliament: How It Happened" (February 17, 2006), www.tcf.org/list.asp?type=NC&pubid=1371.

14. In early 2005, Minister of Justice Ghulam Sarwar Danish complained to the UN news service that as many as 50 percent of Afghans had no access to judicial and legal services, despite huge sums of foreign aid designated for this sector. Later that year domestic and international critics took on the Afghan judiciary for imprisoning an editor who questioned Islamic punishments meted out by the courts; the editor was later released.

15. "A pervasive culture of impunity exists, unchecked by an effective legal system or transitional justice efforts that would address past human rights abuses. Forces opposed to democratization are well entrenched at all levels of society. The institutions designed to represent citizens' interests and protect human rights are weak." NDI, "Statement of the NDI Pre-Election Delegation to Afghanistan" (Washington, D.C., July 8, 2006).

16. Human Rights Watch, "Afghanistan: Conviction and Death Sentence of Former Intelligence Chief Flawed" (March 2, 2006), hrw.org/english/docs/2006/03/02/afghan 12744.htm.

17. See Rossi and Giustozzi, "Disarmament, Demobilisation and Reintegration."

18. Suhrke describes reconstruction as an essentially goal-determined activity and development as open ended. In these terms democratic development would require a commitment to a process whose ends are essentially uncertain; the process itself would be the guar-

antor of success. The language of donor assistance often glosses over these differences. See Astri Suhrke, "The Limits of Statebuilding: The Role of International Assistance in Afghanistan," paper presented at the International Studies Association annual meeting (San Diego, March 21–24, 2006), www.cmi.no/pdf/?file=/publications/2006/isapapermarch2006.pdf; Adam Przeworski, "Problems in the Study of Transition to Democracy," in Guillermo O'Donnell, Philippe C. Schmitter, and Laurence Whitehead (eds.), *Transitions from Authoritarian Rule: Prospects for Democracy* (Baltimore, 1986), 47–63.

5 Rebuilding a Robust Afghan Economy

ALASTAIR J. MCKECHNIE

The recovery of the Afghan economy has made remarkable progress since the collapse of the Taliban government in November 2001. From 2001–2002 until the end of the Afghan fiscal year 2004–2005, legal real GDP is estimated to have grown by 60 percent and has now recovered to at least the highest level reached before the wars (see figure 5-1).[1] However, figure 5-1 also shows the huge loss in potential income from the wars if the Afghan economy had grown at the same rate as other low-income countries. For example, in the period from 2004 to 2005, the loss of GDP amounts to around $3.8 billion, equivalent to about $180 per capita in current prices. Continued strong growth of 14 percent in the 2005–2006 period seems likely, which would bring the increase in GDP since 2001–2002 to about 80 percent. This picture of rapid recovery

This paper has not undergone the review accorded to official World Bank publications. The findings, interpretations, and conclusions expressed herein are those of the author and do not necessarily reflect the views of the International Bank for Reconstruction and Development, the World Bank and its affiliated organizations, or those of the executive directors of the World Bank or the governments they represent. The World Bank does not guarantee the accuracy of the data included in this work.

Figure 5-1. *Afghanistan GDP, Constant 2000 Prices*[a]

Billions of U.S. dollars

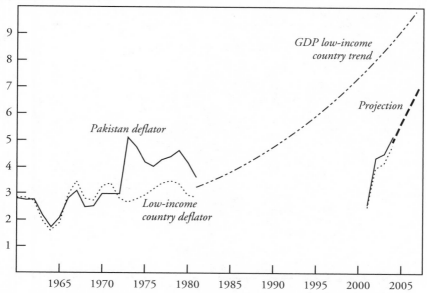

Source: World Bank databases, staff estimates.
a. Current price Afghan GDP data were deflated by the implicit GDP deflators for Pakistan and all low-income countries. The GDP trend growth rate for low-income countries is 4.43 percent per year. The GDP growth rate for low-income countries was estimated by regression analysis for the years 1981–2004.

from war and the associated jump in per capita incomes is reinforced by the obvious changes since 2001 that have taken place not only in cities such as Kabul and Herat but less obviously in the repairs to infrastructure, farms, and housing that are taking place in the countryside.

The government's National Solidarity Program in 2006 reached half of Afghanistan's 20,000 villages, and democratically elected Community Development Councils received around $10 million a month in block grants. The critical north-south road from Central Asia to Kandahar through the Salang Tunnel and Kabul has been rehabilitated, and the road from Iran to Herat has been rebuilt.

A healthy, educated population is not only a desirable social goal but also the basis for economic development. A vaccination campaign has virtually eliminated polio. Nongovernmental organizations (NGOs) contracted to

Figure 5-2. *Outpatient Visits per Capita per Year since 1-1383 (March 2004) in Selected Provinces Where NGOs Are Working*[a]

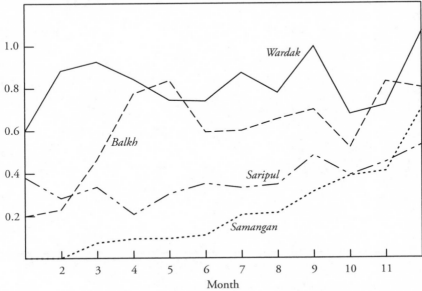

Per capita consultations

Source: Islamic Republic of Afghanistan, Ministry of Public Health, information system, unpublished data; World Bank, "Afghanistan: Managing Public Finances for Development," Report 345822-AF (Washington, D.C., 2005).

a. Values corrected for underreporting.

the government are providing basic health services in eight provinces, and the initial results suggest that publicly funded, NGO-delivered, basic health services could have significant health benefits. For example, in these provinces during the first year, the number of pregnant women receiving prenatal care went from 3.3 percent to 62 percent, contraceptive use went up by a factor of fifteen, and clinic consultations tripled overall (see figure 5-2). The aggregate demand for education is the strongest in the history of Afghanistan, as shown in the actual enrollment. Less than 1 million students, almost all boys (93 percent), were enrolled in 1999. In 2004 almost 4.5 million children were in schools, of which 34 percent were girls, although enrollment, particularly of girls, shows wide regional variations.[2]

Economic progress occurs in an environment where there are successes in related areas. The Bonn political process is almost complete. Presidential and parliamentary elections were carried out more or less on schedule and with little violence. There have been two smooth changes of government since 2001. The Afghan National Army is now a force of 28,000 to 30,000, and most militias have been disbanded so that 63,000 combatants have been demobilized. More than 4.2 million refugees have returned to Afghanistan since the beginning of 2002.

Despite this progress, recovery is inherently fragile and may not be sustainable without prolonged international assistance. High rates of growth in the legal economy are due to special factors like the end of a three-year drought, overflow from the illegal drug economy to the legal economy, and high rates of foreign assistance. Opium poppy and heroin production have been estimated to amount to 35 percent of total GDP, legal and illegal, and expenditures and payments by those benefiting from the drug industry feed into the legal economy. Foreign aid disbursements amounted to $2,817 million in 2004–2005, or 47 percent of GDP, yet 89 percent of foreign assistance disbursed was off budget and only loosely under the control of the Afghan authorities. The long-term sustainability of this extraordinary level of foreign assistance is highly uncertain and depends upon the international community recognizing the regional and global implications of failure in Afghanistan. This recognition in turn depends upon Afghanistan maintaining the pace of political, administrative, and economic reforms that deliver results and ensure security. Security not only depends on these reforms but also on increasing the rule of law, extending the effectiveness of Afghan security forces that are trusted by the population, and providing clean and efficient public administration.

While there are islands of comparative excellence, institution building in Afghanistan has made slow progress. Institutional capacity was never high before the war. A World Bank report from that era states,

> When all is said and done, it is the capacity of the administration to carry out these programs which will determine the pace of Afghanistan's development. So much has been written about the weakness of the administration with so little effect that the reader must judge whether we are brave or foolish to raise the subject yet again. . . . But if there is to be a breakthrough, if the rate of growth is to reach five or six percent in real terms, if basic needs are to be met, then the administration will need to make a far more positive contribution to development than in the past.[3]

Added to this low base is a tradition of modern government that is essentially Soviet. Government regulations, procedures, and institutional culture are a legacy of the socialist government and the technical assistance that preceded it. Afghanistan has an economic transition to complete that parallels Eastern Europe and Central Asia after the dissolution of the Soviet Union.

State Building in Afghanistan

Rebuilding Afghanistan is more than the reconstruction of infrastructure or reviving the legal economy; it is nothing less than the rebuilding of the state itself. Economic development is only one of several interconnected pillars on which the state is built. Security, political reform, and economic development are interrelated; failure in any one of these areas could lead to the failure of the new Afghan state. Without government that is representative, efficient, effective, accountable, respects minorities, and has domestic and international legitimacy, it is difficult to create a climate of security, establish the rule of law, or create an environment for the economy to flourish. Without economic development, the legitimacy of government is undermined; incentives increase for young men to associate with predatory militias that provide them and their families with income and security.

Economic development is dependent upon establishment of the rule of law, which in turn depends on effective government. Government cannot be effective without establishing the monopoly use of force so that it can convince citizens that their lives and property are protected. This credibility is necessary for development to take place. The challenge for Afghanistan is to neutralize the power of militias and criminal elements that had locked Afghanistan into an informal, low-level equilibrium at the end of the wars (see figure 5-3).

Building the Formal Economy

Rebuilding the Afghan economy involves a shift from activities that are illegal to those that are legal and from a low-productivity informal economy to a high-productivity formal economy.[4] A striking feature of the Afghan economy is the prevalence of informal activities, not just in agriculture (32 percent of GDP in 2003) or through opium cultivation (35 percent of

Figure 5-3. *The Informal Equilibrium*

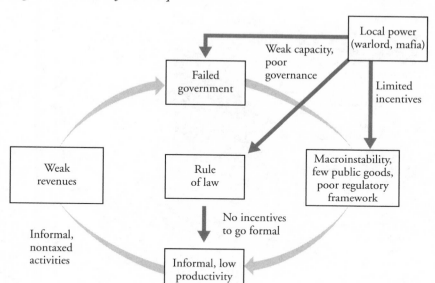

Source: World Bank, "Afghanistan: Managing Public Finances for Development."

GDP) but also in most other sectors, including unlikely areas such as electric power, where small-scale generators provide much of the output of that sector (see figure 5-4).

Economic activity in Afghanistan can be classified into five types:

—*formal,* those activities that are registered with the government or pay tax;

—*in-kind,* where there is no market transaction, for instance, subsistence agriculture, or sharecropping or other arrangement that offers agricultural crops as payment for services or goods;

—*extralegal,* which involves a market transaction and where the activity would be legal if it were registered, for example, small shops, construction, small manufacturing;

—*irregular,* where production and transactions for output would be legal if laws were followed, for example, trade in illegally exploited natural resources such as gemstones, timber, and construction materials, as well as smuggling, that may account for as much as $1 billion a year; and

Figure 5-4. *The Informal Economy in Different Sectors*[a]

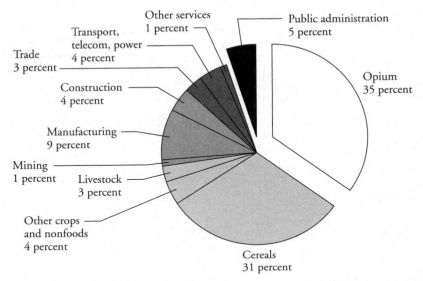

Source: William Byrd, *Afghanistan—State Building, Sustaining Growth, and Reducing Poverty* (Washington. D.C.).

a. Note: percent values refer to share of sector in total GDP; the shadings are very rough estimates of the percentage of the informal economy in the sector.

—*illegal,* where opium production is the most well known and employs as many as 2 million people, but also including other criminality such as the appropriation of customs revenues and illegal taxation, trafficking in people and body organs, forced labor, practices similar to slavery, export of archaeological artifacts, arms trading, land seizures, and real estate speculation based on armed force or corruptly obtained contracts.

Although the state failed, Afghan society survived. While building a robust economy involves a shift from an informal economy to one where activities are more formal (see figure 5-5), informal institutions may provide a solid base on which to build. One feature of Afghanistan has been the resilience of traditional institutions such as the *jirga* or *shura,* where communities make decisions through consultation and consensus. The elected Community Development Councils formed at the village level under the National Solidarity Program are consistent with this tradition. Analysis of land markets in Kabul has shown that while 80 percent of housing is informal, there is a well-functioning informal system of property rights and adjudication of property disputes.[5] Informal systems of dispute

Figure 5-5. *The Formal Equilibrium*

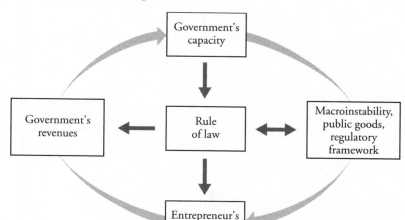

Source: World Bank, "Afghanistan: Managing Public Finances for Development."

resolution may have to be the norm for resolving differences over property rights and small contracts until the formal judicial system can be made functional over several years. Even once a formal, trained judiciary is in place, capacity constraints may make it more an appeals system for the informal dispute resolution process.

In 2004 the Transitional Government of Afghanistan presented "Securing Afghanistan's Future," which outlined a strategy for national development to Afghanistan's development partners at the Berlin Conference.[6] This paper recognized the challenge that the wartime, illegal economy posed for state building in Afghanistan and set out two scenarios for the future. One scenario proposed a program of action that would create a self-sustaining country that can fund its operations from its own resources. The other scenario, "Putting Afghanistan's Future at Risk," presented a descent into lawlessness and increasing drug production, or at best muddling through at low levels of growth and poverty reduction, unlikely to lead to a sustainable modern state.[7] To secure Afghanistan's future, the paper set forth a broadranging program of reforms and investment, supported by official development assistance and private investment. Such a program would generate high rates of economic growth to overtake the illegal economy and create expanding opportunities for legitimate activities. Under this scenario GDP

Figure 5-6. *Required, Feasible, and Projected Rates of Economic Growth*

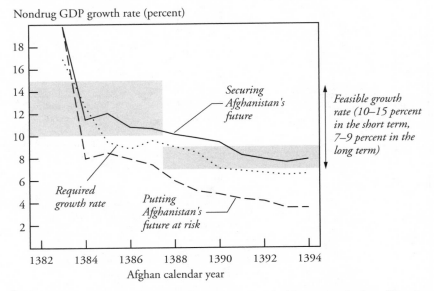

Source: Taken from Transitional Islamic Government of Afghanistan and others, "Securing Afghanistan's Future," p. 10, figure 1-1.

would need to grow at rates approaching a feasible—but high—10 to 15 percent a year in the short term and 7 to 9 percent a year in the longer term (see figure 5-6). The "at risk" scenario had a disengaging international community, whereas the scenario for "securing" Afghanistan's future required substantial donor support: around $28 billion over seven years. Pledges made at the 2004 Berlin Conference substantially met the needs of the first two years of the program. The outcome of the London Conference on Afghanistan in February 2006 indicated that this level of support would continue.

In addition to political reform and security, the transition from illegality and informality requires development in five economic areas:

—creating an environment that enables the private sector to flourish;
—boosting the rural economy and assisting the poor and vulnerable;
—defining the role of the state and establishing government capacity;
—increasing the effectiveness of foreign aid; and
—developing Afghanistan as part of a wider Central Asia region.

Developing the Private Sector

A decade of socialism followed by a decade of civil war devastated the Afghan private sector, and Afghanistan was unable to benefit from the capital flows arising from globalization. Consequently, the private sector is largely informal and undocumented. Despite some notable exceptions such as the mobile phone companies, new entrants, in general, and foreign investors, in particular, have been slow to establish themselves. The sector covers the spectrum from a very few large enterprises that employ more than 250 workers and are mainly foreign financed, to medium-size enterprises—employing 50 to 250 workers—that are found mainly in construction and a few services and are largely financed locally, to small and microenterprises, and finally to businesses that have been registered as NGOs.

A recent survey has shown that existing firms perform comparatively well when compared with firms in neighboring countries in Central Asia. Afghan firms tend to have higher output per worker than in Tajikistan and Uzbekistan but only a third of the output of small firms in India and Pakistan.[8] Regarding investment during 2004, 71 percent of Afghan firms invested, only marginally less than the rate for small firms in China (see table 5-1). While the relatively good performance of Afghan firms may be unexpected, table 5-1 also shows how far Afghanistan has to go to catch up with the performance of small firms in China, India, and Pakistan.

What are the constraints that firms face in Afghanistan? Investment climate surveys have been carried out recently for firms in five cities in Afghanistan.[9] The results are summarized in figure 5-7. Electricity shortages, access to land, corruption, and financing were rated as the largest problems by 50 percent or more of managers responding. There was some regional variation in the ranking; for example, electricity as a constraint was ranked higher in Kabul, where there is a major shortage, and lower in Herat, where supply is more adequate. Second-rank constraints were anticompetitive behavior, customs and trade regulations, regulatory policy uncertainty, taxation, telecommunications, and transport, again with differences among cities depending on local issues, for instance, quality of telecommunications services.

What is perhaps surprising is the low rank of security as an issue (crime, theft, and disorder), which was ranked highest in Jalalabad (41 percent of respondents) and Kabul and Herat (16 percent of respondents), whereas only 4 to 5 percent of respondents in 2005 in Mazar-e Sharif and Kandahar

Table 5-1. *Comparative Performance of Afghan Firms
versus Others in the Greater Region*[a]
Units as indicated

Country	Median output per worker (U.S. dollars)	Average capacity utilization (percent)	Median capital-labor ratio (dollars per worker)	Firms investing in 2004 (percent)
Afghanistan	3,330	62	1,500	71
China	20,374	71	3,170	74
Pakistan	10,043	...	2,063	5
India	9,146	78	2,307	38
Syria	4,333	60	570	42
Tajikistan	1,859	91	721	36
Uzbekistan	567	73	229	26

Source: World Bank, "Investment Climate Surveys"; World Bank, "The Investment Climate in Afghanistan."
a. Data are for firms employing fewer than 100 workers.

thought security was a major or severe issue. This finding conflicts with the widespread perception that security is the greatest barrier to investment in Afghanistan. For example, the *Euromoney* country risk indicators rank Afghanistan 183 out of 185 countries, below Zimbabwe, Burundi, Liberia, Somalia, the Democratic Republic of the Congo, and Cuba but above North Korea and Iraq.[10] The survey indicates that established firms make arrangements to cope with insecurity, such as hiring private security services or negotiating agreements with local power brokers. The downside of these arrangements is their cost; the survey showed that security accounted for 15 percent of the cost of sales of Afghan firms, ten times more than in China (see figure 5-8). New entrants are discouraged by the uncertainty and cost, and there is the risk of anticompetitive arrangements by incumbent firms supported by local power brokers who provide their security.

Afghanistan ranks well in some comparative regulatory measures, particularly in starting a business, hiring and firing workers, and paying taxes. New laws on investment, taxation of income, and customs reforms have substantially liberalized the business environment. Nevertheless, a large number of "nuisance" taxes or fees and bureaucratic procedures remain that provide opportunities for poorly paid officials to extract rents.

Figure 5-7. *Percentage of Firms Citing Constraint as Major or Severe*

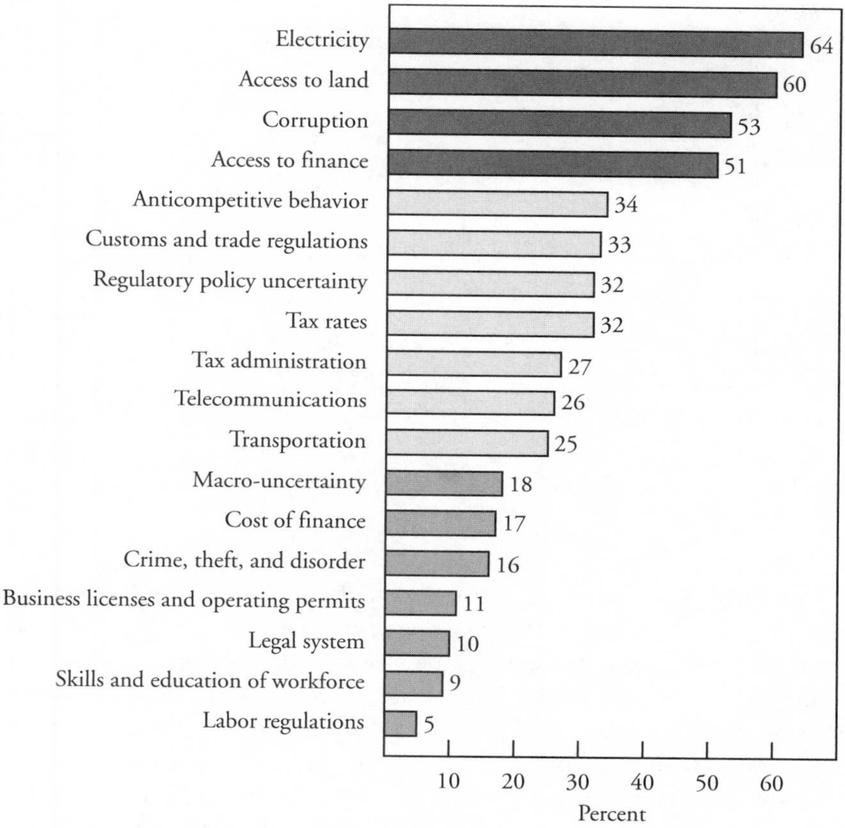

Source: World Bank, "The Investment Climate in Afghanistan."

Corruption is endemic to Afghanistan and adds to uncertainty facing businessmen. It is especially threatening to foreign investors or Afghans returning from overseas who do not have powerful patrons or understand the system.[11] Surveys have shown that bribes to get things done account for 8 percent of the cost of sales in Afghanistan, compared to around 2 percent in other countries in the region (see figure 5-9).

Access to land is another major constraint, almost unique to Afghanistan, that arises from weak governance at the municipal or provincial levels of government and policies that constrain the supply of land.[12] A World

Figure 5-8. *Security Costs as a Percent of Sales*

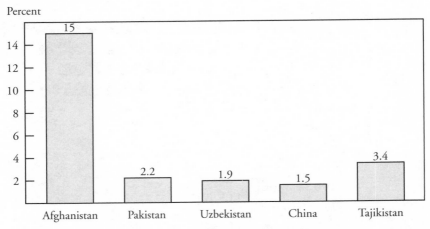

Source: World Bank, "The Investment Climate in Afghanistan" and "Investment Climate Survey"; also World Bank–European Bank for Reconstruction and Development, Business Environment and Enterprise Performance Surveys.

Bank report on urban land in Kabul describes how the formal system for recording land ownership and resolving disputes has become dysfunctional, with extralegal seizures of land taking place through corruption and use of force.[13] This problem is symptomatic of a postwar environment where land has changed hands during conflict, the supply of serviced land has not expanded, and population has grown rapidly through migration—the population of Kabul grew by 13 percent per year between 1999 and 2002.[14]

Infrastructural deficiencies also add significantly to the costs of doing business in Afghanistan. Investment climate surveys show that 76 percent of Afghan firms own a generator, compared to 42 percent in Pakistan and 2 percent or less in Central Asia. Cargo loss from international shipping amounts to 4.6 percent in Afghanistan, compared to 1.2 percent in China and less than 1 percent in Central Asia.[15]

The extreme underdevelopment of the financial sector has constrained private investment and initially allowed only cash payments for international and domestic transactions. After the fall of the Taliban administration, there were no functioning banks, and the central bank was a shell that could only communicate with the outside world through a single satellite phone. Three variants of the Afghani were circulating, and the currency had lost value due to inflation. Foreign currencies such as the U.S. dollar, Pak-

Figure 5-9. *Average Unofficial Payments to Get Things Done as a Percent of Sales*

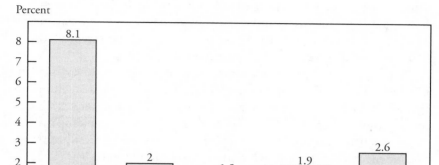

Source: World Bank, "The Investment Climate in Afghanistan."

istani rupee, and Iranian rial were used in domestic transactions, all of which were in cash. To meet the growing demand for money, central bank employees had to travel abroad and bring foreign banknotes back in suitcases.

Early financial sector reforms built capacity into the central bank, both human and infrastructure, to allow electronic funds transfer. A successful currency reform introduced a new national currency that has maintained its value against foreign currencies, in part due to foreign reserves arising from aid flows and the opium economy. New banking and central banking laws were introduced, and several foreign banks have been licensed and established in Kabul. Two state-owned domestic banks have also been licensed.

Many of the constraints to private sector development have no simple solutions or will take many years to resolve. Investment in trunk road infrastructure is inherently slow even with accelerated design, bidding, and construction. While much of the national ring road system has been rehabilitated, some major sections such as Kandahar-Herat and roads linking Afghanistan to Pakistan remain to be completed during the next few years. It will take three years to complete the power line across the Hindu Kush mountains to bring cheap power from Central Asia to Kabul. Even with supply assured, performance of the power utility, Da Afghanistan Breshna Moassese, will need to be drastically reformed if rehabilitation of the distribution system is to be completed and revenues are to be collected.

Similarly, fixing the land market and addressing corruption requires lengthy reforms of institutions, laws, regulations, organization, and human skills as well as behavioral changes. Reforming the financial system requires fundamental restructuring of the state-owned banks and implementation of legal and credit information systems that allow the recently arrived banks to provide finance for investment.

All of these reforms need to be implemented quickly, but there is a danger that it will take too long to institutionalize the business environment that will facilitate investment to meet the ambitious growth targets laid out in "Securing Afghanistan's Future." Reforms and capacity building need to be well sequenced so that the constraints that have the greatest impact on investment and can be removed relatively easily are addressed first. The performance of the Afghanistan Investment Support Agency will be critical in using the power of the state to overcome the informal arrangements and corruption that deter overseas investors. Fortunately, ways exist to create enclaves where there is land, security, infrastructure, and transparency, such as industrial parks and free trade zones, where the state can extend its authority.

Looking to the medium term, development of Afghanistan's considerable mineral deposits, such as copper, iron, and gemstones, offers considerable potential for increasing both national income and government revenues. However, experience in other countries that have suffered the "resource curse" clearly indicates the need for a solid regulatory regime and government capacity to implement it, as well as transparent budget processes to ensure that natural resource rents are invested to provide a stream of income as the resources become depleted. There are plenty of foreign firms that will develop and export mineral resources. However, it is the value added that accrues to Afghanistan, not gross production, that should be the objective, and the best way to maximize the value added is through a transparent bidding process for the rights to the minerals within a transparent system of rights, royalties, and taxes.[16] Afghanistan is in the process of establishing a new minerals law, but the regulations to operate the law still need to be developed.

Agriculture and Rural Development: Productivity, Livelihoods, and Reducing Poppy Cultivation

Afghanistan is essentially a rural society—over 85 percent of the population lives in rural areas—and agriculture, which accounts for 53 percent of legal GDP, is the largest economic sector, employing 67 percent of the labor force. The opium poppy industry accounts for 35 percent of legal and nonlegal GDP. Overall, the licit and illicit rural economy accounts for at least 68 percent of total GDP.[17]

Although the Afghan economy is primarily agricultural, only 12 percent, or 7.9 million hectares, of its total land area is arable. Wheat, the primary cereal crop, covers about two-thirds of the cultivated area, with most production (75 to 80 percent) on irrigated land. Wheat yields are low, 1.5 to 2.0 tons per hectare on irrigated land and less than 1 ton per hectare on rain-fed land, substantially less than in neighboring countries. Yields in Iran, Pakistan, and Uzbekistan of 2.6 to 2.8 tons per hectare are about 50 percent higher than in Afghanistan, indicating substantial potential for increasing productivity and production.[18] Indeed, "Securing Afghanistan's Future" projects that cereal production will grow by 10 to 20 percent per year during the next few years.[19]

The horticultural sector was hit badly by scorched earth policies during Afghanistan's wars and drought. Fruit and nuts were a major cash crop and accounted for over 40 percent of export earnings in the 1970s. Grapes, almonds, apples, apricots, and pomegranates account for roughly 2 to 3 percent of the cultivated area. However, the sector is slowly recovering, and exports, particularly of grapes, are starting to recover.

Livestock is a major source of food and income, and range pasture has accounted for about 45 percent of the land area. Drought and animal disease have led to a serious decline in the livestock population. Livestock is critical to incomes, food security, and reducing vulnerability, particularly for women.[20]

In 2004, opium poppy was farmed in all provinces of Afghanistan but accounted for only 2.9 percent of the cultivated area. About 2.3 million people, or 8 percent of the total population, were engaged in poppy cultivation. Figures from the UN Office on Drugs and Crime put the value of poppy production in 2005 at $4,600 per hectare, compared to $390 per hectare for wheat.[21] Although the value of opium production is higher than all alternative crops, the distribution of this value is uneven and skewed toward large landowning farmers and traders.[22]

Addressing the issues of rural poverty, vulnerability, and the opium drug economy, as well as realizing the growth potential from the rural economy, requires a strategy that not only increases agricultural productivity but also goes beyond agriculture. Creating off-farm employment through activities that add value to agricultural output—for example, fruit processing, production of agricultural inputs, and handicrafts—would constitute part of a livelihoods strategy, but it would also face the same constraints as any other private sector activity in Afghanistan, such as inadequate infrastructure and credit. Once security has been established fully, reviving tourism has long-term potential for the rural (and urban) economy. Human development is another way to enhance rural development. Healthy people are more productive farmers, and education can improve productivity and promote the spread of new ideas and technologies.

The government's agricultural strategy has three priorities: increasing wheat productivity, rebuilding perennial horticulture, and livestock development. Wheat productivity can be enhanced through increased application of fertilizer, use of improved seeds, rehabilitation of irrigation, greater mechanization, and improved weed, disease, and pest management. Key issues in horticulture are establishing orchards and vineyards, and investing in processing and market development. There are plans to set up a public-private horticultural council that would provide grants to establish orchards and vineyards, acquire planting material, develop extension services, and provide venture capital for processing and storage and for market development. A livestock improvement program will be created to improve animal health through vaccinations, and there will be community programs aimed at nomadic Kuchis, who are dependent on livestock grazing on rangeland for their livelihoods.

There are other key measures needed for development of the rural economy.

Irrigation

The priority is to rehabilitate existing systems that have fallen into disrepair during the wars and droughts. Rehabilitation is cost effective, quickly increases water supply, and does not raise riparian issues with neighboring countries. Institutional capacity to manage rehabilitation is the greatest challenge, and past efforts to buy in implementation capacity are starting to bring results. Work also needs to start on identifying and assessing new irrigation projects and managing any riparian issues. Cost recovery to ensure good maintenance and to contribute toward financing new investment is an issue in many countries, and Afghanistan also needs to start preparing for a sustainable irrigation sector. Community-based approaches to managing water rights and irrigation systems show promise, especially for smaller schemes.

Access to Finance

Progress in reforming the formal financial sector has been slow, and regular banking institutions do not offer a short-term solution to the lack of credit. However, microfinance has taken off quickly in Afghanistan. By the end of September 2005, the number of loans made by microfinance institutions operating under the umbrella of the Microfinance Investment Support Facility for Afghanistan numbered more than 200,000 and amounted to $35.7 million. Loans were mostly under $200, and 82 percent of borrowers were women. Most loans have been for trade and services (58 percent), some of which supported provision of agricultural inputs, although 15 percent was directly for agriculture and 8 percent for handicrafts. While microfinance has an important part to play in the rural economy, such as for financing small livestock holdings and artisanal handicrafts, it is not sufficient to guarantee an adequate supply of rural finance. Other short-term solutions include extending credit through agricultural input dealers, such as scaling up the Rebuilding Agricultural Markets Program financed by the U.S. Agency for International Development and scaling up some of the microfinance institutions. The existing private banks have made only hesitant moves to open branches outside of Kabul, and their lending has not yet taken off. A promising approach to creating a branch banking system that farmers could access lies in restructuring Bank-e Milli Afghan (National Bank) and Pashtany Tejaraty Bank (Pashtany Commercial Bank), the existing state banks that have provincial branches and that could be rehabilitated into a modern bank operated by a private management company. In the longer term, this modern bank should be privatized. The existing agricultural bank has not obtained a license and has little capacity. Specialized agricultural banks in other countries generally have been unsuccessful.

Access to Roads

Roads are necessary to get crops to market in good condition. Secondary roads in Afghanistan were never well developed. The primary ring road system is partially rehabilitated and there should be a reasonable primary road network by 2008. Well-maintained gravel roads can provide adequate access to the ring road system. The successful emergency public works program, designed to provide cash-based employment at the end of the war and the last years of drought, mainly through road repairs, is being reformulated into a rural access program. Administrative and implementation capacity to scale up rural access exists, and the constraint is funding.

Other Infrastructure Improvements

Improvements to other rural infrastructure are being implemented through the highly successful National Solidarity Program. This program

Table 5-2. *National Solidarity Project Program Implementation Status,*
November 2005
Units as indicated

Activity	Current status
Villages where community mobilization is completed	10,361
Villages having elected Community Development Councils (CDCs)	9,785
Villages having final community development plans prepared by CDCs	9,230
CDCs that have received block grants	7,140
Subproject proposals submitted	13,437
Subprojects financed	12,687
Villages with completed subprojects	2,617
Total block grant disbursements (U.S. dollars)	142.5 million
Total block grant commitments (U.S. dollars)	185 million

Source: Ministry of Reconstruction and Rural Development.

has built upon existing NGO capacity and was modeled on an equally successful community-driven development program in Indonesia. Half of
Afghanistan's 20,000 villages have democratically elected village development
councils, and nearly all of them have prepared community development
plans with the assistance of NGO facilitating partners. By November 2005
this program had disbursed $142 million in block grants to villages under the
guidance of the facilitating partners (see table 5-2). Most grants have been for
irrigation, water supply, access roads, electricity supply, schools, and income-
generating activities. This program has scaled up rapidly and is currently dis-
bursing around $10–12 million a month in block grants.

Electricity is a necessary input for value-enhancing activities and can
also allow irrigation from groundwater if water is managed sustainably and
if electricity is priced to recover costs. Since electricity supply is inadequate
in all of Afghanistan's cities, extension of the grid system will take time and
may not be economical in many parts of the country. However, there is
considerable scope for renewable micropower or small hydropower in areas
where grid connection is uneconomical or too distant. Implementation
could be through already established village development councils with
central technical support.

Knowledge Services

Applied research, improved agricultural statistics, and the extension of
agricultural technology underpin productivity improvements in the agri-

cultural sector. While the Ministry of Agriculture is strengthening its extension system, existing NGO capacity could be contracted to scale up provision of knowledge services with public financing under government supervision.

Government Involvement

Government capacity in the agricultural sector is only starting to be strengthened. While the Ministry of Agriculture has carried out some reforms and attracted some leaders, further work is needed to clarify its role and organization and to ensure adequate managerial and staff skills. This effort is needed to balance development in the rural sector since the rural development ministry tasked with the nonagricultural aspects of the rural economy is one of the strongest ministries in the government.

Counternarcotics Efforts

Finally, rural development and development of agriculture is the essential pillar of a counternarcotics strategy. Since opium poppy is already growing in every province in Afghanistan and can quickly spread from one area to another in response to eradication campaigns, eliminating opium poppy cultivation requires nothing less than the acceleration of economic and social development in rural spaces. This chapter does not attempt to cover the complex issue of counternarcotics strategy except to note that elimination of the poppy will succeed or fail along with broader rural development.[23]

Government Capacity

Strengthening government capacity is critical to Afghanistan's success in order to formulate sector strategies, carry out reforms, implement investment programs, and provide a regulatory environment that encourages modern, formal business. The government has set clear policies in favor of a market economy with a regulatory role for the state. It has put forward the principle of a merit-based civil service and restraining civil service employment.[24] Both these principles mark a break with the recent past where clientelism was a feature of the mujahideen governments, leading to increased public employment of supporters who often lacked the skills needed for the job, as well as a reversal of the shift toward production by state-owned enterprises in the socialist period.

Nevertheless, much remains to be done to put these principles into practice at the sectoral level. Few ministries have clearly set out their objectives and realigned their organization to meet the new mandates. There is frequently lack of clarity about the role of the government or public sector in service delivery or production, and public utilities have yet to be moved out of their parent ministries. Some progress has been made in some sectors, such as telecommunications and contracting out publicly financed delivery of basic health services to NGOs. Although the government is preparing plans to close, privatize, or restructure state-owned enterprises, many are close to the bosom of parent ministries, and there is no plan to deal with employees left without a job.

Across-the-board civil service reform has been difficult to achieve in countries with stable administrations, let alone in a postconflict situation. Accordingly, the Interim and Transitional Administrations decided to pursue reforms in ministries, or even departments within a ministry, where there was clear ownership of reform and where reform could have a significant impact on development outcomes. This was the Priority Reform and Restructuring program, which allowed reforming institutions to pay higher salaries to staff selected competitively for positions in the new organization. Employees without a position in the reorganized institution were kept on the books of the ministry or, in some cases, transferred to the Ministry of Labor and Social Affairs. This approach was pragmatic but piecemeal. Some ministries, such as finance, carried out wide-ranging restructuring; some others, such as commerce, carried out partial reforms; and the reform process hardly started in key spending ministries such as those of education and of energy and water.[25] More recently, the government has indicated that it will carry out a pay and grading review in order to select qualified staff for defined positions with competitive salaries. Establishing a merit-based civil service will require protecting the independence and strengthening the capacity of the Independent Administrative Reform and Civil Service Commission.

Given the shortage of capacity when the first Karzai government was established, it was not surprising that nongovernmental actors provided services that would normally be supplied by government. During the Taliban administration, NGOs and UN agencies provided services funded by donors outside the government budget. This well-developed capacity was harnessed after the Taliban administration collapsed. However, services provided by nongovernmental actors and funded by donors outside the government budget undermined indigenous capacity building and created a populist backlash.[26] Some government programs, funded externally, appointed NGOs and UN agencies as service providers through competitive procurement that provided transparency, efficiency, and accountability.

But too often NGOs, consultants, and contractors were funded directly by donors, off budget and through opaque processes.[27]

Coordinating Role of Government Budget

Good development practice is to use a multiyear government budget as the central coordinating and organizing mechanism for development. However, in Afghanistan, government revenues are insufficient to pay salaries, let alone other operating and development costs. Government revenues in Afghanistan amount to 4.5 percent of GDP, compared to 10 to 20 percent for other low-income countries and 45 to 55 percent for countries in the Organization for Economic Cooperation and Development. Consequently, Afghanistan is dependent on the international community for funding the budget. Even worse, in 2004–2005, 75 percent of expenditure was completely off budget and funded directly by donors, with sometimes limited interaction with the government. Government revenues amounted to only $269 million and financed 8 percent of the total government budget, or 48 percent of the recurrent budget (see table 5-3).[28] Such a high level of aid dependency makes Afghanistan vulnerable to shifting donor priorities.

Whether the volume of aid received by Afghanistan is adequate in relation to other postconflict countries has been controversial.[29] Official Development Assistance (ODA) per capita has clearly been lower than for postconflict countries in the Balkans, for small countries such as East Timor, and outliers such as the Democratic Republic of the Congo (see appendix 5A, which shows data for a sample of conflict-affected and drug-influenced economies). However, when ODA is plotted against population, there is a clear inverse correlation between aid and population, and Afghanistan appears to receive more aid per capita than comparator countries of its size. One might expect that higher-income countries would receive more aid per capita than lower-income countries on the grounds that their absorptive capacity is greater, and in the case of postconflict countries, the costs of repairing damaged assets are greater, since the stock of assets is higher in middle-income countries. Figure 5-10 indicates that there is indeed a positive correlation between ODA per capita and income per capita. Again, Afghanistan appears to be receiving a level of aid above the trend.

Raising government revenues is one of the key challenges faced by Afghanistan. Even in the 1970s, Afghanistan never managed to generate revenues much greater than 7 percent of GDP. Rubin has described prewar Afghanistan as a "rentier state" and explained how declining foreign aid was

Table 5-3. *Three Illustrative Fiscal Scenarios*
Millions of U.S. dollars unless otherwise indicated

Scenario	Actuals			Projections							
	2002–03	2003–04	2004–05	2005–06	2006–07	2007–08	2008–09	2009–10	2010–11	2011–12	2012–13
Base case											
Domestic revenues	129	208	269	379	532	677	853	1,033	1,220	1,393	1,593
Core expenditures	342	558	874	1,226	2,116	2,360	2,434	2,614	2,376	2,588	2,597
Operating expenditures	342	449	558	678	892	1,094	1,251	1,431	1,535	1,576	1,585
Wages	...	282	374	460	562	649	749	845	900	940	948
Fiscal deficit before grants	213	350	606	847	1,584	1,684	1,581	1,581	1,156	1,195	1,005
Operating deficit	213	241	289	299	361	417	398	398	315	183	(8)
High case											
Domestic revenues	129	208	269	393	569	770	1,046	1,315	1,618	1,954	2,225
Core expenditures	342	558	874	1,226	2,116	2,398	2,471	2,651	2,407	2,588	2,597
Operating expenditures	342	449	558	678	892	1,131	1,288	1,468	1,566	1,576	1,585
Wages	...	282	374	460	562	685	785	882	930	940	948

Fiscal deficit before											
grants	213	350	606	833	1,546	1,628	1,425	1,336	789	634	373
Operating deficit	213	241	289	285	323	361	242	154	(52)	(378)	(640)
Low case											
Domestic revenues	129	208	269	353	443	527	651	804	970	1,125	1,303
Core expenditures	342	558	874	1,226	2,046	2,254	2,285	2,406	2,117	2,350	2,431
Operating											
expenditures	342	449	558	678	823	988	1,102	1,224	1,276	1,338	1,418
Wages	...	282	374	460	545	631	694	754	794	854	931
Fiscal deficit before											
grants	213	350	606	874	1,603	1,727	1,634	1,602	1,146	1,225	1,128
Operating deficit	213	241	289	325	380	460	451	420	306	213	116
Memo											
GDP growth											
(real terms)	28.6	15.7	8.0	13.6	11.2	10.8	9.7	7.5	7.5	7.5	7.5
GDP deflator											
(percent)	(22.2)	6.4	17.0	10.0	8.0	5.0	5.0	5.0	5.0	5.0	5.0
Exchange rate											
(AFA to $U.S.)	45.3	49.0	47.7	48.5	48.5	48.5	48.5	48.5	48.5	48.5	48.5

Source: World Bank, "Afghanistan: Managing Public Finances for Development."

Figure 5-10. *2003 Official Development Assistance (ODA) versus 2004 Population and versus 2004 Gross National Income per Capita, Cross-Country Comparisons*

ODA per capita (U.S. dollars)

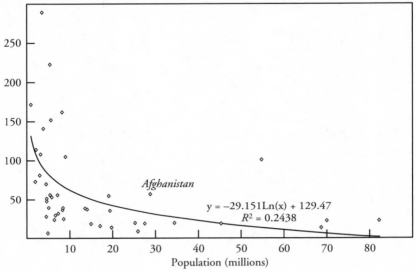

Population (millions)

ODA per capita (U.S. dollars)

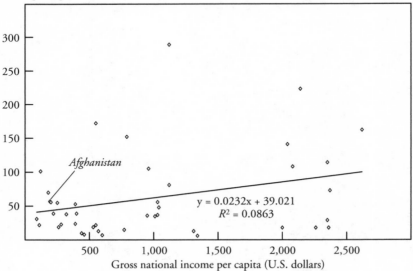

Gross national income per capita (U.S. dollars)

Source: See data from appendix 5A.

one of the factors that diminished local support for the Daoud Khan government in the late 1970s.[30]

Recent studies by the World Bank have set out three scenarios for domestic revenue mobilization (see table 5-3).[31] These show that in the base case scenario, revenues are not sufficient to cover the operating costs of government until 2012, whereas in an optimistic but achievable high case scenario, revenues cover operating costs in 2010 and by 2012 are financing nearly two-thirds of public investment. It seems clear that the international community will need to continue substantial funding of wages and operating costs of government for at least the next five years and possibly longer. These are the costs with highest fiduciary risks that donors are most reluctant to fund. At the same time, there is a risk that after nearly a decade of having such costs funded from outside, government and parliament may find it difficult to make the hard choices needed to mobilize revenues. What is needed is a compact between the government and the international community to guarantee funding for a period of at least five years, based on the government taking concrete measures to meet revenue targets. Such an agreement will not be easy, since donor government budgetary processes often do not allow such long-term commitments, and multiyear programs of revenue reform can run aground as constituencies opposed to them build strength.

Aid Effectiveness

In addition to the long-term demands for donor funding, there is an issue of the form in which foreign assistance is provided. Currently, about 75 percent of foreign aid bypasses the government budget and is provided in-kind by the donor. Almost all of this aid is for projects or technical assistance provided through consulting firms. Of the $3.058 billion of external finance during the fiscal year 2004–2005, $2.503 billion was in the "external" budget, over which the Afghan authorities had little influence. Large bilateral donors such as the United States, Japan, and the European Commission account for the largest share of the external budget, which excludes some categories of Afghan security expenditures. The cost of foreign and international military expenditures, such as for the Coalition and the International Security Assistance Force, are not included in the external budget and may be in the order of $15 billion.

As others have noted, providing assistance off budget can actually undermine state building.[32] Governments become passive recipients of aid, and their legitimacy can be reduced as citizens see services being provided by foreign governments, not their own.[33] Furthermore, the little government capacity that exists is weakened as the best staff leave for higher paid jobs with contractors or NGOs. And most important, the capacity of the state is not built through "learning by doing."

The Afghanistan Reconstruction Trust Fund (ARTF) was set up to finance government programs and the recurrent budget, minimize the administrative burden on the government from having to deal with a large number of donors, and coordinate donor assistance and align it with government programs and procedures.[34] The ARTF is managed by a committee consisting of representatives of the Asian Development Bank, Islamic Development Bank, UN Assistance Mission to Afghanistan, UN Development Program, and the World Bank. The World Bank also provides day-to-day administration and takes fiduciary responsibility. Contributions from twenty-four donors have exceeded U.S. $1 billion and disbursements have almost reached the U.S. $800 million mark. The majority of resources channeled through the ARTF are used to support the recurrent costs of government—primarily civil servant salaries (payroll) and operations and maintenance expenditures—and the ARTF has financed only a little more than $200 million in commitments to investment programs due to lack of funds. In 2004–2005 the ARTF funded 52 percent of the government budget and constituted only 9.4 percent of external funding to Afghanistan that year (the sum of budget financing plus the external budget; see table 5-4).

There are also questions about the effectiveness of bilateral aid, which is often highly fragmented into projects that are designed and executed by consultants and contractors from the donor country and may not effectively utilize local knowledge or resources. Most of this information is anecdotal, but research on comparative efficiency of aid delivery systems is overdue.[35] In the case of the World Bank, its disbursement ratio on Afghanistan projects in 2004–2005 was 44 percent, and the ARTF disbursement ratio on projects was 118 percent, compared to a World Bank–wide average of 23 percent, which indicates that government execution is not necessarily less efficient than direct execution by donors.[36]

Development in a Regional Context

Afghanistan lies at the intersection of Central Asia, South Asia, and the Middle East. Before the entry of European powers into this area in the eighteenth century, Afghanistan was a natural land bridge between these regions.

Afghanistan has historically been a trading nation with strong private sector traditions. Disruption of historical trade and transit corridors has been a consequence of the entry of powers from abroad or interference from neighbors. The dissolution of the Soviet Union, the end of widespread internal conflict, and cooperation from border counties, as expressed in accords such as the Good Neighborliness Agreements, offer the possibility of regional integration that would expand economic opportunities for Afghanistan and the countries with which it shares common borders, as well as the outer tier countries such as Turkey, United Arab Emirates, India, and Russia.

Infrastructure in Afghanistan can be part of regional networks—for example, the ring highway in Afghanistan connects Iran to South Asia and connects Central Asia to Iran, Pakistan, and the ports in the Persian Gulf and Indian Ocean. Afghanistan already imports power from three of its neighbors and, in the longer term, it can benefit from the transit of energy from energy-rich Central Asia to relatively energy-poor South Asia. Water storage in Afghanistan can produce benefits for downstream riparian countries, as well as irrigation and power benefits for Afghanistan. Infrastructure planning in Afghanistan needs to be carried out with regional linkages in mind and with incremental financing for additional investments that produce regional benefits but are not justified by benefits solely within Afghanistan.

The most promising areas for furthering regional integration include

—*Transport.* The southern section of the ring road and its connections to neighboring countries is planned for completion by the end of 2007. However, the north-south transport corridors through Afghanistan face competition from alternative routes from Russia via the Caspian and Iran and from China from the Karakoram highway to Pakistan. The use of Afghanistan as a transit route also depends critically on adequate security being maintained along the highways. Moreover, the constraint to goods passing across Afghanistan is increasingly due to bottlenecks in trade and transit facilitation at borders. Finally, opening the Pakistan-India border to land trade will increase transit and trade opportunities substantially but depends on continued progress in bilateral relations between these two countries.

—*Trade and transit.* There are wide differences in tariff rates and non-tariff barriers among the countries in the region. Border policies such as customs procedures and transshipment requirements as well as corruption impede movement of goods across borders. Within the transport sector, visa restrictions, cartels, fees, and capacity constraints lower the transit of goods within countries and encumber trade generally. Reforms to trade

Table 5-4. *Medium-Term Fiscal Financing Requirements,*
Fiscal Years 2002–2003 to 2007–2008

Millions of U.S. dollars

	Estimates			Revised budget	Projections		
	2002–03	2003–04	2004–05	2005–06	2005–06	2006–07	2007–08
A. Domestic revenues	131	208	269	468[a]	410	500	600
B. Expenditures (B1 + B2)	346	617	829	1,900	1,300	1,500	1,775
B1. Ordinary expenditures	346	452	560	693	640	750	875
Wages	...	299	396	425	425	500	600
Goods and services	...	95	88	129	125	150	175
Capital expenditures	...	41	41	38	40	50	50
Others	...	17	35	101	50	50	50
B2. Development expenditures	...	165	269	1,207	660	750	900
C. Budget deficit (A – B)[b]	(215)	(409)	(561)	(1,432)	(890)	(1,000)	(1,175)

D. Float and adjustments	(15)	35	5	...	...	...	...
E. Financing	230	375	555	1,432	890	1,000	1,175
Afghanistan Reconstruction Trust Fund	79	217	288	398	398	400	400
Law and Order Trust Fund for Afghanistan and Army Trust Fund	17	36	54	67	67	65	60
Programmatic Support for Institution Building	...	...	80	80	80	80	80
Other external financing	114	118	374	887	375	425	585
Domestic financing[c]	20	4	(241)	0	(30)	30	50
Memo							
External budget	503	2,182	2,503	2,169	2,000	1,800	1,600

Source: World Bank budget documents and staff estimates from William Byrd, *Afghanistan—State Building, Sustaining Growth, and Reducing Poverty*.

a. Includes an expected payment for telecom licenses.

b. Excluding grants.

c. Change in currency deposits. Note: the exchange rate for 2005–2006 and beyond is based on 48.5 Afghanis per U.S. dollar.

and transit regimes probably offer the best hopes for growth in trade and transit. Such reforms are best carried out through coordinated regional agreement, or as a second best, among contiguous, like-minded countries.

—*Energy.* Trade opportunities exist in the short term through Afghanistan buying power from its neighbors, which in most cases would cost no more than domestic power production and would allow supply shortages to be relieved. In the longer term, Afghanistan can participate in transit of power and gas from Central Asia to South Asia.

—*Water resources management.* Regional integration would allow for flood control and dry-season supply to downstream countries and provide the confidence needed for Afghanistan to finance large irrigation and power projects.

—*Labor.* The migration of labor to Iran, Pakistan, and abroad and the flow of remittances back has provided Afghanistan with a social safety net during times of war and drought. Almost no migration has taken place between Afghanistan and Central Asia. More than 2 million refugees have been repatriated since 2001, and those remaining in host countries are increasingly seen as economic migrants, although these refugees are not necessarily integrated into the social and economic fabric of the host countries and may not be covered effectively by national worker protection laws.

—*Security and border management.* Secure borders are a concern of all countries in the region and a constraint to greater integration.[37]

Moving forward with regional integration will require a combination of approaches involving regional trade organizations such as the Central Asia Regional Economic Cooperation program, Economic Cooperation Organization, and South Asian Association for Regional Cooperation; focused discussions on the issues mentioned above; and much closer cooperation among coalitions of countries willing to cooperate on particular reforms or transactions. In the short term, power trade and cooperation on trade and transit with the eastern Central Asian countries, Pakistan, and Iran seem to offer the best opportunities.

Conclusion

After several years of successful state building and economic recovery, Afghanistan is at a crossroads. Two paths lie ahead. One is a continuation of the recent past that enables Afghanistan to wake from the nightmare of the last twenty years and become one of the economic success stories of Central and South Asia. The other is a resurgence of past tensions, increasing insecurity, slow development, and little alleviation of poverty. Strong leadership, continued reforms, and sustained support from the international opportunity can allow Afghanistan to permanently break out of the low-level informal equilibrium characterized by violence, poverty, and political instability. Modernizing governments have been overthrown twice in Afghanistan's modern history and replaced by conservative elements who have appealed to traditional values in the name of Islam. The pace of change that can be tolerated by a broad range of Afghan society is a political decision that only Afghans can make. Afghanistan will require high levels of international financial, security, and political support for the foreseeable future, yet how this support is delivered, as well as its level, will determine how rapidly Afghanistan can transform itself. After bloody encounters with the outside world, Afghanistan was left in isolation and poverty as a theater for regional actors to play the Great Game. The blowback from this neglect has shown that in a globalized world, leaving Afghanistan to its own devices is no longer an option. Contagion from drugs alone would affect both its neighbors and countries far abroad. Afghanistan has opted for the path of moderation, poverty reduction, and membership in the community of nations. A robust economy is one of the keys to this future.

Notes

1. Afghanistan uses a Persian solar calendar where the new year begins on March 21. Fiscal, or solar, year 1383, presented in the report as 2004–2005, corresponds to the period from March 21, 2004, to March 20, 2005.

2. World Bank, "Afghanistan: Managing Public Finances for Development," Report 345822-AF (Washington, D.C., 2005).

3. World Bank, "Afghanistan: The Journey to Economic Development," Report 1777a-AF (Washington, D.C., 1978).

4. The discussion in this section is based on William Byrd, *Afghanistan—State Building, Sustaining Growth, and Reducing Poverty* (Washington, D.C, 2005).

5. World Bank, "Kabul: Urban Land in Crisis" (Washington, D.C., 2005).

6. Transitional Islamic Government of Afghanistan and others, "Securing Afghanistan's Future: Accomplishments and the Strategic Path Forward" (Kabul, 2004).

7. Ibid., 12.

8. See World Bank, "The Investment Climate in Afghanistan" (Washington, D.C., 2005).

9. Ibid.

10. Euromoney, "Country Risk" (September, 2005), www.euromoney.com/article.asp?PositionID=1896&ArticleID=1000448.

11. World Bank, "Investment Climate in Afghanistan."

12. World Bank investment climate surveys have not found access to land to be such a significant problem, even in postconflict countries such as Mozambique. See World Bank, "Investment Climate in Afghanistan."

13. See World Bank, "Kabul: Urban Land in Crisis."

14. Ibid.

15. World Bank, "Investment Climate in Afghanistan."

16. See Byrd, *Afghanistan—State Building, Sustaining Growth, and Reducing Poverty.*

17. World Bank, "Afghanistan: Managing Public Finances for Development."

18. See World Bank, "Afghanistan: Agricultural Development Proposal (1384–1386)," unpublished (Washington, D.C., 2005).

19. Transitional Islamic Government of Afghanistan and others, "Securing Afghanistan's Future," 8, table 1.4.

20. Ibid.

21. United Nations Office on Drugs and Crime, "Afghanistan Opium Survey 2004" (Vienna, 2004).

22. Christopher Ward and William Byrd, "Afghanistan's Opium Drug Economy," World Bank Report SASPR-5 (Washington, D.C., 2004).

23. Ministry of Reconstruction and Rural Development. See Ward and Byrd, ibid. See also Cindy Fazey, chapter 8 in this volume.

24. See, for example, Transitional Islamic Government of Afghanistan and others, "Securing Afghanistan's Future."

25. See Michael Carnahan and others (eds.), *Reforming Fiscal and Economic Management in Afghanistan* (Washington, D.C., 2004).

26. Francis Fukuyama, *State-Building: Governance and World Order in the 21st Century* (Ithaca, 2004). Former Planning Minister Ramazan Bashardost campaigned for parliament on a platform that criticized the role of NGOs, some of which were contractors taking advantage of tax exemptions and the "misuse" of foreign aid; he was elected in Kabul with the third-highest vote count.

27. A minister told the author of the difference in performance of the same consulting firm working on a contract with the ministry and a separate contract with a bilateral donor. Confidential communication, Kabul, 2004.

28. World Bank, "Afghanistan: Managing Public Finances for Development."

29. See Barnett R. Rubin and others, "Building a New Afghanistan: The Value of Success, the Cost of Failure" (New York, 2004), www.cic.nyu.edu/archive/pdf/Building.pdf.

30. See Barnett R. Rubin, *The Fragmentation of Afghanistan* (New Haven, 2002, 2nd ed.).

31. See World Bank, "Afghanistan: Managing Public Finances for Development."

32. See for example, Fukayama, *State-Building.*

33. Visiting parliamentarians from donor nations expect to see their national flag flying over projects as a sign of recognition by the recipient country.

34. For more information on this fund, see World Bank, "Afghanistan Reconstruction Trust Fund," www.worldbank.org/artf.

35. See David Rohde and Carlotta Gall, "Delays Hurting U.S. Rebuilding in Afghanistan," *New York Times* (November 7, 2005).

36. Disbursement ratio is defined as funds disbursed during the year, divided by the stock of commitments (project approvals) net of the cumulative disbursements at the beginning of the year. The disbursement ratio can exceed 100 percent due to disbursements on projects approved during the year. The typical implementation period of a standard World Bank project is around five years, which is consistent with a disbursement ratio of around 20 percent. Afghanistan projects are processed under emergency procedures that require an implementation period of three years.

37. For further discussion of regional integration, see World Bank, "Prospects for Regional Development and Economic Cooperation in the Wider Central Asia Region," paper presented at the Kabul Conference on Regional Economic Cooperation (Kabul, December 3–4, 2005).

Appendix 5A. *Aid Flows for a Sample of Conflict-Affected and Drug-Influenced Countries, and by Income and Region*
Units as indicated

Country	Population, 2004 (millions)	Gross national income per capita, 2004 (dollars)	ODA per capita, 2003 (dollars)
Afghanistan	28.8	192	57
Albania	3.2	2,080	108
Angola	14.0	1,030	37
Armenia	3.0	1,120	81
Azerbaijan	8.3	950	36
Bangladesh	140.5	440	10
Bolivia	9.0	960	105
Bosnia and Herzegovina	3.8	2,040	141
Burundi	7.3	90	31
Cambodia	13.6	320	38
Colombia	45.3	2,000	18
Congo, Democratic Republic of	54.8	120	101
Côte d'Ivoire	17.1	770	15
Croatia	4.5	6,590	27
Egypt	68.7	1,310	13

(continued)

Appendix 5A. *Aid Flows for a Sample of Conflict-Affected and Drug-Influenced Countries, and by Income and Region (Continued)*
Units as indicated

Country	Population, 2004 (millions)	Gross national income per capita, 2004 (dollars)	ODA per capita, 2003 (dollars)
El Salvador	6.7	2,350	29
Eritrea	4.5	180	70
Ethiopia	70.0	110	22
Georgia	4.5	1,040	48
Haiti	8.6	390	24
Honduras	7.1	1,030	56
Jordan	5.4	2,140	223
Kazakhstan	15.0	2,260	18
Kyrgyz Republic	5.1	400	39
Lao People's Democratic Republic	5.8	390	53
Lebanon	4.6	4,980	51
Macedonia	2.1	2,350	114
Mozambique	19.1	250	55
Namibia	2.0	2,370	73
Nepal	25.2	260	19
Nicaragua	5.6	790	152
Pakistan	152.1	600	7
Peru	27.5	2,360	18
Rwanda	8.4	220	39
Serbia and Montenegro	8.2	2,620	162
Sierra Leone	5.4	200	56
Sri Lanka	19.4	1,010	35
Sudan	34.4	530	19
Tajikistan	6.4	280	23
Timor-Leste	0.9	550	172
Turkmenistan	4.9	1,340	6
Uzbekistan	25.9	460	8
Vietnam	82.2	550	22
West Bank and Gaza	3.5	1,120	289
Yemen	19.8	570	13
Income			
Low income	2,388.1	510	14
Middle income	3,006.2	2,190	9

(continued)

Appendix 5A. *Aid Flows for a Sample of Conflict-Affected and Drug-Influenced Countries, and by Income and Region (Continued)*
Units as indicated

Country	Population, 2004 (millions)	Gross national income per capita, 2004 (dollars)	ODA per capita, 2003 (dollars)
Region			
East Asia and Pacific	1,870.2	1,280	4
Europe and Central Asia	472.1	3,290	22
Latin America and Caribbean	541.3	3,600	12
Middle East and North Africa	294.0	2,000	26
South Asia	1,447.7	590	4
Sub-Saharan Africa	719.0	600	34
Nepal	25.2	260	19
Nicaragua	5.6	790	152
Pakistan	152.1	600	7
Peru	27.5	2,360	18
Rwanda	8.4	220	39
Serbia and Montenegro	8.2	2,620	162

Source: World Bank, "World Development Indicators" (2005); staff estimates.

6

Revitalizing Afghanistan's Economy: The Government's Plan

Hedayat Amin Arsala

S ome scholars argue that "geography is destiny." Afghanistan's history has been a witness to the importance of geography, with a location that has for centuries been a strategically
vital crossroads for trade and politics, part of the land bridge
connecting Asia and Europe known as the Silk Road. While
geography may be less important in today's world than it once
was, there is little doubt that Afghanistan's location will continue to have a significant influence on the country's future political and economic prospects. Afghanistan still occupies a
vitally important location with links to Central and South Asia
as well as to Turkey and Iran. Future economic prosperity and
political stability throughout this entire region will inevitably
be strongly affected by the successful revitalization of Afghanistan's economy and political institutions.

The author was appointed as the senior minister of the Islamic Republic of
Afghanistan after serving as senior advisor to the president and the minister of
commerce. Prior to these appointments, he held a number of senior positions in
the government, including vice president, minister of finance, minister of foreign
affairs, and head of the Independent Administrative and Civil Service Commission and of the National Economic Coordination Council. The views expressed
in this paper are presented in his personal capacity and should not be attributed
to the government of the Islamic Republic of Afghanistan.

Beginning with the Soviet invasion in 1979 and throughout much of the ensuing conflict, Afghanistan's economy was largely cut off from the rest of the world. As with all entities controlled from Moscow at that time, the state quickly assumed the dominant role in the economy. As a result, private sector businesses were generally limited only to trading for basic needs. Almost one-third of the country's population had little choice but to flee as refugees, going mostly to Pakistan or Iran. Consequently, the country lost many of its most highly qualified people. What national assets the Soviet occupation failed to destroy were eliminated during the internal conflict and political turmoil that followed. It took a particularly heavy toll on the infrastructure of the country.

Today, Afghanistan faces an enormous fourfold challenge that requires the country simultaneously to provide internal security, build a capable representative democratic government, establish a strong private sector–led economy able to provide productive employment, and bring an end to the opium economy. Few countries have ever had to face one or two challenges of this magnitude, let alone four at once. Even Japan and the countries of Europe that were decimated during World War II had stronger foundations on which to build their postwar successes than does Afghanistan.

But as great as are the challenges that the country must meet, the assets that are available for what will be a major national transformation are greater still. The world recognizes the vital importance of succeeding in these tasks, and it stands with Afghanistan as a fully committed partner. More important, the Afghan people—who have suffered so much for so long—recognize that they must rebuild their country to take their rightful place as responsible, productive members of the international community. The inherent strength and determination of the Afghan people to succeed in this endeavor is undoubtedly the country's greatest asset, despite the incredible difficulties that people face in their daily lives. After all, the Afghan people demonstrated their strength and determination in the long and difficult struggle against Soviet occupation and during the subsequent conflict, which left more than 1 million dead and many more injured and at the same time left almost everyone without access to education or the means to earn even a minimum income.

It is already apparent to many of those who have been actively engaged in this initial transition period that the situation Afghanistan faces is unique. The traditional approaches to promoting economic development and public sector reform are not going to be adequate to the task. To succeed, the country cannot simply resume the process of economic development from the point where it was disrupted in 1979. The goal is rapidly to approach economic parity with the other countries in Central and South Asia in order to provide a foundation for full integration into the world economy and to ensure high rates of economic growth. The government of Afghanistan and its partners in the international community need to recognize that new models must be developed and applied if growth is going to occur.

One of the principal sources of difficulty is that many of the changes to be implemented will have significant impacts on the way people work; in some cases there may be a loss of jobs. It has to be recognized that a large proportion of the country has little or no direct experience or understanding of how a free market economy functions. Many continue to look to the government to control the economy, set prices, and provide employment for large numbers of people. There is much that needs to be done to educate the public on the way a market economy works and what it requires of them. It will take time for people to adjust to their changing world. In the government one of the most important tasks underway is an intensive effort to build public employees' skills so that they can assume the new responsibilities necessary to carry this process forward. The foundation of any successful market economy is based on efficient markets for the factors of production: land, labor, and capital, alongside an open trading environment. The successful revitalization of the economy will depend on ensuring that these key factor markets develop and function efficiently.

Afghanistan cannot afford to repeat the mistakes that were made elsewhere in the past, but it has the advantage of recognizing many of these mistakes. For example, at the time of the Soviet invasion in 1979, most developing countries were attempting to industrialize using strategies based on import substitution and maintaining relatively high trade barriers. In retrospect, this approach largely failed to deliver the anticipated economic benefits. Instead, Afghanistan should look to those countries that have been more successful economically by adopting export-led strategies.

It is clear that one of the greatest challenges is finding ways to ensure that reforms are effectively implemented. For the most part, the policies and institutional reforms needed to make progress in social and economic development are reasonably well understood. But for a variety of reasons, they often prove to be very difficult to implement successfully. The government of Afghanistan fully recognizes the extent of this challenge and is focusing a great deal of attention and resources on building the necessary capacity in the public and private sectors.

The Afghanistan National Development Strategy

In order to manage the extensive program of economic and institutional changes needed to transform Afghanistan and make the best use of the available resources, in early 2005 the government established the Presidential Oversight Committee to develop a national strategy.[1] The Afghanistan National Development Strategy (ANDS) that was produced was the result of twelve months of intensive consultations among the government, a wide array of stakeholders from the private sector, civil society, nongovernmental organizations, the United Nations, donors, and other members of the international community. According to ANDS, "Our vision for the Islamic Republic of Afghanistan is to consolidate peace and stability through just, democratic processes and institutions, and to reduce poverty and achieve prosperity through broad based and equitable economic growth."[2]

The development strategy provides a five-year framework that is built on three pillars: security; governance, rule of law, and human rights; and economic and social development.[3] There are, in addition, five important "crosscutting" themes that form an integral part of objectives established with each of the three pillars: gender equity, countering narcotics, regional cooperation, anticorruption, and environment.

The government is using the ANDS framework as the basis for developing the detailed tasks to be undertaken as part of the implementation and monitoring of the strategy. This process is taking place in all of the government's ministries and agencies and also includes the participation of the private sector, civil society, and the international community.

It was apparent early in the transition process that in order to implement and manage economic reform, fundamental changes in the structure and organization of the government would be required. To begin to address this urgent issue prior to the development of the ANDS, the Priority Reform and Restructuring program was introduced as a key element in broader public sector reform. This program is leading to a smaller, more qualified, and better paid public sector workforce, with hiring based on merit and carried out in a more transparent and competitive manner.

Key Economic Issues

National Economic Integration

One of the most pressing priorities of the government's economic strategy is to integrate a highly fragmented national economy. Much of the commercial activity focuses on local markets. (Investment in the telecommunication industry is an important exception.) The commercial connections linking these local centers remain largely undeveloped. This fragmentation in part reflects the years of conflict that damaged much of the social and economic infrastructure, physical as well as institutional, that normally bind together the disparate elements of a national economy. Furthermore, the extensive socioeconomic disruption and lack of consistent and coherent economic policies led to a severe restriction on the development of private sector business activity, with the exception of relatively small-scale trading activities. In addition, a great many businesses choose to operate in the informal economy, outside of the reach of legal and regulatory requirements and the taxation system.

One of the major challenges facing the government is to create a sound economic environment that will foster the reestablishment of a viable, confident private sector. Good progress is being made in this area, reflecting the prominent role that commerce has always played in traditional Afghan culture. Admittedly, much more remains to be done.

At the same time, an environment that encourages businesses to choose willingly to operate in the formal economy is equally important. Virtually all of private business, in all sectors and in all provinces, operates informally to some extent, with the possible exception of the few larger firms—including foreign ones—that have been established. There are, however, increasingly significant additional costs for firms that continue to operate in the informal sector.[4] For example, they typically have very limited access to bank credit, which causes them to remain smaller and less competitive than would otherwise be the case. It is also very difficult for firms operating informally to take part in international trade, severely reducing their available market opportunities and their prospects for expansion.

Experience in other countries has shown that the size of the informal sector is an important indicator of the quality of the economic policies and institutions—including the effectiveness of the legal system—that define the environment in which business operates. If the environment is supportive of business activities, the size of the informal sector will tend to be small. What we see today in Afghanistan is a very large informal sector that reflects the strong antibusiness environment that prevailed for much of the last three decades. But as far-reaching institutional, legal, and regulatory reforms take effect, it is hoped that there will be a substantial shift of business activity into the formal sector.

Employment Creation and Poverty Reduction

The eventual attainment of the country's political, security, and economic objectives will depend crucially upon whether the economy will be able to produce the large numbers of productive jobs that are needed to begin to fulfill the aspirations of Afghan men and women. Although the magnitude of unemployment and underemployment is difficult to estimate, it is clear that a very large proportion of the potential workforce is in desperate need of adequate employment.

The urgently needed expansion of employment opportunities will come about only through sustained high rates of private sector–led economic growth. Increased growth is also critical if people's expectations concerning the pace of economic progress are sufficient for them to have confidence that they will be able to share equitably in the country's future success. But there is an added challenge that can also only be met through sustained high growth—that is, shifting the significant amount of economic activity devoted to the production of illegal narcotics to legal alternatives. The ANDS estimates that this goal will require a sustained real economic growth rate of at least 9 percent for more than a decade.

Only one country, China, has been able to achieve an average growth rate of 9 percent or more for over a decade. It averaged 10.1 percent growth between 1985 and 1997.[5] Matching this performance will be a daunting task. However, during the last several years, official statistics indicate that Afghanistan's GDP growth has been in the range of 13 to 16 percent, reflecting the large initial gains resulting from the early stages of economic recovery and the large expenditures of the international community in support of Afghanistan's efforts.

There are two principal sources of economic growth: increased investment and increased productivity arising from the reallocation of resources to more productive uses. These fundamental economic facts make clear that the government must maintain an economic environment that will be attractive to investors as well as ensuring that legal and regulatory reforms are implemented that will encourage the most productive employment of *all* of the country's resources. Some important steps in this direction have already been taken and more are under way. These include, for example, the establishment of a well-supported investment promotion agency; the passage of the new laws covering banking, private investment, the tax system, and customs; and a commitment to privatize many state-owned enterprises.

Achieving and maintaining a 9-plus percent growth rate over time cannot be deemed a success, however, if it does not also lead to significant re-
ductions in poverty. Afghanistan is one of the poorest countries in the
world, where a substantial proportion of the population struggles to survive on less than $1 per day. The average per capita GDP is estimated to be
about $300 for 2005–2006.[6] This extreme poverty is also reflected in the
country's low rank in the 2004 UN Human Development Index (173 out
of 178 countries).[7]

A pro-poor growth strategy requires that barriers that unduly restrict
the opportunities of the poor to participate fully in the country's economic
recovery be removed. One of the most significant steps that can be taken
in this regard is to make it possible for the poor to utilize better the assets
that are already in their possession, particularly land. The government,
with the help of the donor community, is introducing programs to help
secure people's property rights, including strengthening land registration
systems. These measures are aimed not only at preventing illegal land grabs
but also at providing the means for the poor to gain greater access to credit,
which can be used for investment. In addition, provisions that more clearly
establish land ownership will help to ensure more equitable access to social
services such as water and power.

Eliminating the Opium Economy

Afghanistan faces yet another major hurdle that must be overcome if the
economy is to be successfully revitalized: eliminating the prominent economic role being played by the cultivation of poppies and production of
narcotics.[8] According to the UN Office of Drugs and Crime, in 2005 Afghanistan produced 87 percent of the world's illicit opium, valued at
$2.7 billion or approximately one-third of GDP.[9] While poppy growing
directly employed only 8.7 percent of the population, it indirectly provided economic support for many more. However, it is important to emphasize that this is an activity that is still inconsistent with prevailing social
mores and the religious beliefs of almost all Afghans. For the most part,
people find themselves compelled to engage in growing poppies because
they have no alternative means of earning an income to provide for their
families.

The government fully recognizes that eliminating the opium economy
is an essential element in any strategy aimed at increasing internal security
and political stability as well as promoting economic development and

reducing poverty. As a result, counternarcotics activities play a major cross-cutting role in Afghanistan's development strategy. While these activities are generally aimed at developing alternative livelihoods, substantially extending eradication efforts, and improving law enforcement, there is nevertheless a direct and vital linkage between the elimination of the opium economy and the more general revitalization of the economy.

A New Vision for Afghanistan's Private Sector

To create a robust and dynamic private sector, the government and the private sector must establish a working relationship that allows private businesses to succeed and to move beyond basic survival. The most pressing issues on which this working relationship should focus are strengthening the financial sector, investment in basic infrastructure, investment in human resources and skills development, securing property rights, a stable environment for private investment, and strengthening institutions for good governance.

Strengthening the Financial Sector

In a 2004 survey of business people, access to finance was identified as the third most serious problem faced by business, with finance-related issues accounting for three out of the top ten problems that businesses must confront.[10] The financial sector faces a number of significant constraints, but these do *not* include the amount of funds that are available for lending in the banking system; rather, it is the limited capacity of many banks to analyze business plans and make sound commercial decisions on loan proposals. Studies have shown that banks, especially state-owned banks, are only lending approximately 20 percent of their available capital.[11] Bank lending is also severely constrained by the lack of reliable legal protection for the recovery of collateral when borrowers default.

The private sector must also strengthen its business capabilities so that it can more effectively communicate its financial requirements to banks. In particular, improvements in two broad areas are needed: internal accounting and documentation systems, and business plan development. Local business people typically have strong entrepreneurial skills, but they often lack the background and experience necessary to introduce accounting systems or to prepare effective business plans. In the short run, the emergence of the business development services industry will help firms that do not have the required accounting and financial skills internally to improve their business practices.

Investment in Basic Infrastructure

Private sector competitiveness depends on access to productive infrastructure, particularly roads and power generation. A modern road system is important for both the Afghan and regional business communities. As a landlocked country, roads are the main transport link to the rest of the world—over 95 percent of all goods that cross the border travel by road.[12] In addition, an improved national road network would bring major social and economic benefits to the rural population and would contribute substantially to the increased integration of the national economy.

In the same 2004 survey of business people referred to above, power generation and road and transport problems were identified as the first and fourth most serious problems facing businesses. Shortcomings in these areas result in higher costs for businesses and put them at a competitive disadvantage.[13] The UN Development Program estimated that simply rehabilitating transport and energy infrastructure alone will cost $3.7 billion over the next ten years.[14] (The total cost of rehabilitating, upgrading, and undertaking the additional infrastructure investments needed for full economic recovery will cost substantially more.) Improving infrastructure presents an opportunity to attract private investors with financial resources using one of the many successful public-private partnership models that have worked in other countries, such as Malaysia.[15] Without this investment it will continue to be difficult for business to become competitive.

A well-developed road network would also considerably increase the opportunities for intraregional trade, taking advantage of Afghanistan's strategically important location linking Central and South Asia as well as Iran and Turkey. Much of the intraregional trade bypasses Afghanistan because of security concerns, poor infrastructure (roads and handling facilities), and lack of compliance with international transit agreements.

Power generation also represents a major infrastructure problem for the private sector. Seventy-six percent of firms must operate generators to ensure a regular and high-quality power supply—the highest share in the region.[16] Use of generators is expensive, unsustainable, and degrades the environment. Effort is being devoted to rehabilitating much of the former power generation capacity that deteriorated during the years of war. Another way to ameliorate this problem in the short term is to rely more on industrial parks, which can provide an integrated solution for some of the private sector's biggest problems: security, electricity, and land titles. The government, with the assistance of international donors, is rehabilitating neglected facilities as well as developing a number of new industrial parks.

There is also enormous untapped potential for increased trade in energy within the region. One indication is the construction of a major power transmission line from Uzbekistan to Kabul. There continues to be considerable interest in pipeline investments that would bring gas from Central Asia and Iran to markets in Pakistan and India. In addition to these traditional energy sources, there are increasing numbers of innovative and sustainable solutions that could be developed to help meet energy requirements. For example, miniature hydropower units have considerable potential, particularly in remote areas with ample river flow.

Investment in Human Resources and Skills Development

Over two decades of conflict and political turmoil have left a crippled educational system and led to the emigration of large numbers of the country's most educated and skilled people. The adult literacy rate is about 35 percent. Because of the lack of a skilled workforce and the limited capital with which they have to work, the productivity of Afghan workers is low compared to other countries in the region. On average, Afghan workers produce only $333 in output compared to $10,043 for workers in Pakistan and $20,374 for workers in China.[17] Overcoming this challenge will require major investments in all levels of education over an extended period.

Of particular importance for accelerating private sector development is providing ample facilities for vocational and technical training. It is going to be extremely difficult for local producers to take advantage of the export opportunities that are increasingly available without the training necessary to permit them to meet the requirements of the international trading system. For example, those wishing to export horticultural produce, including dried fruits and nuts, must be able to improve quality and be able to obtain the international certifications necessary to earn higher profits. Workers and managers at the farm and factory level need to be instructed on how to maintain quality to conform to international standards. The establishment of the Afghanistan National Standards Authority is an important step in supporting this process. In addition, business people and entrepreneurs must also reeducate themselves in order to acquire the skills required to compete in international markets, particularly using advanced marketing and production methods. These types of total quality management are little known in Afghanistan.

Securing Property Rights and Land Tenure

Land tenure is a particularly severe problem in Afghanistan. In a World Bank survey, 60 percent of firms surveyed identified access to land as a major or severe constraint to expansion, the second highest ranking problem after electricity.[18] In the same study, the World Bank noted that although access to land is almost always a significant constraint to private sector development, the problems in Afghanistan are substantially greater than elsewhere, even when compared to other postconflict countries such as Mozambique.

The principal problem is access to secure land titles. Years of conflict, politically driven land reform, and nationalization have left the country with a confused system of property rights characterized by multiple claims and unclear procedures for establishing ownership. In the absence of transparent procedures, obtaining clear land titles becomes time-consuming and expensive.[19] Until the question of property rights is adequately resolved, private investment will be significantly constrained because of the inability of businesses to use land as collateral or to acquire suitable land to construct factories and other facilities.

A Stable Environment for Private Investment

Substantially increased levels of private investment will be necessary if higher economic growth rates are to be achieved. Much of this additional investment will have to come from foreign investors willing to commit their resources in an untested market. In order to attract the needed foreign direct investment, the government must reduce the risk of doing business in Afghanistan by maintaining stable and predictable economic policies. Numerous surveys of actual and potential investors have consistently reported on the critical importance of offering a transparent and unchanging set of rules for both foreign and domestic investors.

Tax rates, business registration procedures, land regulations, and requirements for the repatriation of capital must be clearly spelled out and consistently implemented. Progress in addressing these issues has been made with the introduction of a new tax code as well as new banking, private investment, and customs laws. Additional steps aimed at streamlining business procedures are being taken by the Ministry of Commerce and the Afghanistan Investment Support Agency, a semiautonomous agency under the Ministry of Commerce and Industry with a mandate to promote both foreign and domestic investment.

Strengthening Institutions for Good Governance

There are a number of governmental and civic institutions that must be modernized and strengthened if the private sector is to realize its potential and lead the economic revitalization of the country. These bodies have three essential institutional functions that must be fulfilled: maintaining internal security, eliminating corruption and improving transparency, and creating a stable and competitive environment for business.

Considerable progress has been achieved in each of these areas, although much more still needs to be done. A survey of Afghan business leaders gives an indication of the extent of the work that still remains. For example, there are still concerns about improving security, despite the considerable progress that has been made in the training of domestic police and army units and the continued support of foreign forces.[20] Security problems result in higher costs for businesses that must provide their own security. The survey also pointed to corruption as an important concern of the private sector—as it is for the government, which recognizes that corruption is a problem that must be addressed forcefully. Finally, many in the private sector indicated that they believe that the government does not respond effectively to private sector needs, for example, by providing efficient business support services, a modern infrastructure, and a business-friendly legal environment. There is no doubt that there needs to be more and better communication and a deeper understanding on both sides in the private sector–public sector relationship. Like the government, the private sector is adapting to a more open and competitive economic environment.

In recognition of the critical role that good governance and strong public institutions will play in achieving the social and economic development goals of the country, the government has placed these issues at the center of the ANDS. Far-reaching institutional, legal, and procedural reforms are under way throughout the public sector that will result in new organizational structures that correspond more closely to the requirements of the market-oriented economy being adopted by the country, including the Priority Reform and Restructuring program, which is leading to major restructuring efforts that will substantially strengthen the public sector. Virtually all commercial laws and regulations will be significantly reformed within the next several years. One indication of the procedural reforms that are under way is the changes that have been introduced by the Ministry of

Commerce and Afghanistan Investment Support Agency in business registration requirements. According to a World Bank study, Afghanistan has
one of the most efficient registration systems in the world.[21] However, it
should also be remembered that institutional reform is among the most
difficult and time-consuming changes to implement effectively because it
involves people's livelihoods and the way that they function in the work-
place—which is as true for the private sector as it is for the public sector.

A Supportive Legal Environment

A modern, reliable commercial legal system is critical to attract the investment needed to revitalize the economy. Like many of the other aspects of
the institutional and infrastructural foundations that support the economy, decades of conflict have left the legal system in need of substantial
reform and strengthening. In the words of the ANDS: "As much of the
[country's] current commercial legal framework is governed by outdated
legislation, the development of the legal and regulatory framework, based
on international standards and best practices, will be critical to the ability
of Afghanistan to attract investment, to promote exports, ensure the safety
of goods in the domestic market, and to ensure adequate levels of competition necessary for the equitable operation of the marketplace."[22]

The legal system is composed of three occasionally overlapping systems:
sharia (Islamic law), *jirga* (traditional systems of informal justice), and the
formal system based on the 2004 constitution. The Afghanistan Commercial Code of 1955 remains the law for business dispute resolution. Beginning in 2003, the government, with the help of international legal experts,
began the process of drafting updated laws to bring this code up to international standards.

The legal system also suffers from a number of deep-seated institutional
weaknesses that must be addressed. Underlying these weaknesses has been
the long disruption of legal education and training, which has seriously
depleted the human resources required for any legal system to function
properly. One result is that the formal legal system is used infrequently by
the private sector to resolve commercial disputes. As an alternative, private
firms have often turned to the informal jirga system to settle their problems
despite a lack of consistency across jurisdictions.[23]

The government, with the assistance of the international community, is
engaged in a comprehensive program of reviewing and updating virtually all
commercial laws. The first important steps were the passage of banking, tax,

private investment, and customs laws. But this process is exceedingly complicated, not least because all new laws must be accurately translated and fully consistent in three languages: Pashto, Dari, and English. These legal reforms are also taking place in the context of Afghanistan's more active engagement with a number of international bodies and agreements, including the World Trade Organization (WTO) and the International Monetary Fund. These organizations impose important legal requirements of their own. Nonetheless, the government is fully aware of the key contribution that reforming its commercial laws and legal procedures will make in fostering prosperity and economic growth and is giving this effort its highest priority.

The Commitment to Eliminate Corruption

The reform of the legal system and a strengthened commitment to maintaining the rule of law are essential preconditions in the fight against corruption. Shortcomings in public sector management and continuing corruption impose additional costs and put the country at a substantial competitive disadvantage. The government recognizes that corruption is a serious problem and for that reason anticorruption efforts are one of the most important crosscutting themes in the ANDS: "Government's long-term aim is to eliminate corruption in the public and private sectors in order to improve the effectiveness, transparency, and accountability of government and to create an environment conducive to investment."[24]

There are four key elements to the anticorruption strategy included in the development strategy: strengthening public sector management, strengthening public accountability systems, strengthening the legal framework and judicial system, and controlling corruption within counternarcotics institutions.

It will not be possible to make significant progress in revitalizing the economy without also making substantial progress toward eliminating corruption. Corruption introduces a major disincentive for investment, increasing transaction costs throughout the economy. It also plays a major role in discouraging commercial activity from taking place in the formal economy, which cripples the government's attempts to enforce customs and tax regulations used to raise revenues.

International Trade and Regional Economic Cooperation

As a relatively small, landlocked country with a limited domestic market, Afghanistan must rely to a great extent on increasing international trade to propel the higher rates of economic growth necessary to revitalize the economy and achieve the country's core economic objectives. There are three key elements in the government's strategy aimed at promoting trade based on rapid reintegration into the global economy, expanding access for Afghan goods in foreign markets, and maximizing the economic benefits of increased trade:

—a broad program of trade liberalization that will establish an open and transparent trading environment, made more stable through accession to the WTO;

—more active regional economic cooperation, based on extending regional and bilateral trade agreements in order to maximize market access for domestic producers; and

—an ongoing program to improve trade facilitation and reduce transportation costs.

Trade Liberalization

The ANDS establishes a commitment to implement a general policy of trade liberalization that encompasses wide-ranging initiatives, including policy and regulatory reforms and steps to reduce nontariff barriers to trade and investment. These goals are essential to establish the open and transparent economic environment needed to foster competitive commercial activities. It is well understood that the free movement of goods throughout the region is central to the country's prosperity and a critical condition for better integrating the national economy.

A more liberal trade environment will also greatly benefit agriculture and the rural economy, which has largely been left behind in the economic recovery that has taken place since the end of the Taliban regime. During the last two decades, exports declined to a fraction of the levels that existed before the Soviet invasion in 1979. Exports consist almost entirely of agricultural goods: fresh and dried fruits, seeds, hides and skins, wool, and cotton. Handwoven carpets, which were largely made with domestic wool, have been the other notable export. Increased international trade will almost certainly begin with expanding markets for what have been Afghanistan's traditional exports. Greater access to markets for its products will directly lead to more rapidly increasing incomes and employment opportunities in rural areas, where the incidence of poverty is especially high.

Considerable effort is also being devoted to the country's process of acceding to the WTO. Having been granted observer status in 2004, the government is giving high priority to completing the requirements for full membership as quickly as possible. The benefits of WTO membership go beyond allowing the country's exporters to compete on a more level playing field in foreign markets. The process of preparing for accession is itself providing a highly useful framework within which the process of reviewing and reforming commercial institutions, laws, and regulations can proceed more systematically and in line with international standards. When the process is completed, it will not only lead to Afghanistan becoming a full member of the global economic community, but it will also send a strong signal to international investors and traders with regard to stability.

Regional Economic Cooperation

Regional integration is among the highest priorities for Afghanistan's trade policy. Afghanistan has actively pursued trade agreements with countries throughout the region.[25] Integration is also a crucial part of the broader ANDS theme of pursuing greater regional cooperation. The ANDS states that "Government's goal is to contribute to regional stability and prosperity, and to facilitate the enabling conditions for Afghanistan to resume its role as a land bridge between Central and South Asia in order to benefit from increased trade and export opportunities."[26]

Afghanistan is an active member of the Economic Coop   ion Organization (ECO), which promotes trade liberalization and integration within the region. Member countries include Azerbaijan, Iran, Kazakhstan, the Kyrgyz Republic, Pakistan, Turkey, Turkmenistan, and Uzbekistan. In early 2005 a preferential trade agreement, the ECO Trade Agreement, was signed. It reduces intra-ECO tariffs to a maximum of 15 percent over the course of the next fifteen years and also provides for cooperation in the reduction of nontariff barriers and other trade-related charges.

With the agreement of the South Asia Association for Regional Cooperation (SAARC) in November 2005, Afghanistan became a full member of that organization.[27] The South Asia Free Trade Agreement entails the phased reduction and eventual elimination of intra-SAARC tariff rates for a substantial number of goods (that is, goods not included on each country's sensitive lists). It also provides a formal regional institutional mechanism with which to address other trade- and transit-related issues. This free trade agreement offers Afghanistan preferential access to one of the world's largest and fastest growing markets.

Afghanistan's preferential trade agreement with India grants 50 to 100 percent tariff concessions for a number of the country's most important exports, including fresh and dried fruits, seeds, medicinal herbs, and precious stones. The market shares of products in the Indian market have substantially increased.

The government is also exploring the potential for participating in a number of additional regional and bilateral trade arrangements. These arrangements include, for example, participation in the Central Asian Regional Economic Cooperation (CAREC) program, which seeks to promote increased coordination in customs, energy, trade facilitation, and trade policy. CAREC in 2006 included Azerbaijan, China, Kazakhstan, the Kyrgyz Republic, Mongolia, Tajikistan, and Uzbekistan.

Trade and Transit Facilitation

Particular attention is being given to addressing transit and customs procedures that add unnecessary costs to trading activities. As a landlocked country, it is especially important to strengthen transit agreements with neighbors to permit improved access to lower the costs of transportation for goods to and from regional countries as well as the seaports through which Afghanistan exports to other important international markets. In addition, with assistance from the international community, there is a great deal of activity under way to construct new, more efficient, fully integrated border posts that will incorporate new systems to facilitate trade, including the computerization of customs. Investments aimed at securing the borders will contribute significantly to improving security and aid in the fight against the narcotics trade. Improved systems at the borders, along with the trade policy reforms being enacted, will also do much to eliminate official corruption by reducing the incentives for traders to smuggle.

Like many other countries, Afghanistan is increasingly looking at more general ways to facilitate trade, especially reforms that need to take place "behind the border." These include the simplification and harmonization of trade-related procedures, such as product standards, customs clearance, and activities involved in the collection and processing of data required for goods being traded internationally. This list includes a wide range of activities including procedures relating to licensing, sanitary, and phytosanitary requirements; transport formalities; and cross-border payments, insurance, and other financial requirements. But improving trade facilitation also entails reducing barriers to international investment, improving international telecommunications facilities and transportation infrastructure, as well as providing better access to business visas and the movement of people between countries for business purposes. The liberalization of trade in services throughout the region is an explicit goal in the development strategy.

The government recognizes that trade facilitation should be seen as an ongoing process, not a checklist of specific steps that can ever be achieved with finality. All of the areas mentioned above are constantly altering as economic conditions change. Ensuring the maximum possible contribution toward effective trade facilitation is very much a moving target. What is needed is a comprehensive and effective framework with which to guide and manage the ongoing process of trade facilitation. Establishing an environment where the entire array of these issues can be addressed effectively will depend upon the government and the private sector working together to create a mind-set where initiatives aimed at streamlining and reducing trade-related transaction costs can be continually identified and implemented.

The Way Forward

This chapter has sought to convey some sense of the scope and complexity of the tasks facing Afghanistan in rebuilding the nation after years of occupation, conflict, and political turmoil. When one first looks at the immensity of the challenges, addressing them may seem too ambitious, almost beyond reach. However, when the strategies for meeting these challenges are carefully considered and broken down into well-defined tasks, the way forward begins to look more manageable. It must be recognized that no government could carry out such a comprehensive program on its own. Afghanistan has been fortunate to have much of the rest of the world engaged as an active working partner in these endeavors, providing financial assistance and technical expertise. More important, the country has been able to draw on the strength and resilience of the Afghan people, including the growing number of Afghan refugees, in 2006 estimated to be as many as 4 million, who are returning to participate in the rebuilding of their country.

The revitalization of the economy will depend on a number of factors, each of them critical. The first task has been to establish a comprehensive, consistent economic framework that sets out the structure of the economy that will emerge from the process. From the outset there has been fundamental agreement that Afghanistan would have a free market economy, with the private sector responsible for making the key commercial decisions regarding production and investment. Most of the rest of the world has seen that this model is essentially the only workable solution. Afghanistan has had the opportunity to learn this lesson itself. Based on widespread consultation with all local and international stakeholders, this framework has been translated into an Afghan development strategy for the way forward.

Investment in both physical and economic infrastructure will also play a major role in the revitalization of the economy. Improved physical infrastructure, especially the rehabilitation and new construction of roads, as well as increased capacity for power generation, will not only provide essential services for expanding production but will also provide much needed employment opportunities in the short term. (Increased infrastructure investment will also provide a basis for greater regional cooperation because the amount of work that will be required is well beyond the capacity of domestic firms.) Equally critical is additional investment in economic infrastructure—especially legal reform and institutional strengthening; deepening of democratic political processes, inextricably linked with improved public education on economic issues; and establishing and maintaining pubic security.

Notes

1. The Presidential Oversight Committee was chaired by the senior economic advisor to the president. The members included the minister of commerce as well as the ministers of finance, foreign affairs, economy, and rural rehabilitation and development.

2. The preparation of the Afghanistan National Development Strategy (ANDS) is an ongoing process. The documents were originally published in 2005 as the *Interim Afghanistan National Development Strategy* and include the summary report and volume I, which lay out overall policy objectives, strategies, and programs; volume II, which contains a summary of sectoral programs; and volume III, which is a collation of strategic plans developed by line ministries. Quote is from Islamic Republic of Afghanistan, *Interim Afghanistan National Development Strategy. Summary Report: An Interim Strategy for Security, Governance, Economic Growth, and Poverty Reduction* (Kabul, 2005), 3.

3. Ibid., "Part 3: Development Strategy and Programs," 12.

4. Hernando de Soto, *The Mystery of Capital* (New York, 1990).

5. World Bank, *World Development Indicators, 2001* (Washington, D.C., 2002). During the same time period, Thailand and Korea averaged more than 8 percent growth, while Singapore, Chile, Malaysia, Botswana, and Indonesia averaged more than 7 percent. (This period was chosen for comparison in order to avoid the effects of the Asian financial crisis that began in 1997.) If one looks at the three decades from 1970 to 1999, Botswana averaged a growth rate of 10.3 percent, based largely on diamond exports and its very small population.

6. International Monetary Fund, "Islamic Republic of Afghanistan: Seventh Review under the Staff-Monitored Program and Discussions on a PRGF-Supported Program, Concluding Statement" (Washington, D.C., March 26, 2006).

7. United Nations Development Program–Afghanistan, "Overview of UNDP in Afghanistan" (Kabul, 2005),www.undp.org.af/about_us/overview_undp_afg/default.htm.

8. For a detailed examination of the problem of opium in Afghanistan, see Cindy Fazey, chapter 8 in this volume.

9. See Islamic Republic of Afghanistan, *Interim Afghanistan National Development Strategy*, volume I, "Part 3: Strategy" (Kabul, 2005), 95.

10. Center for International Private Enterprise, "Training Needs Assessment" (Washington, D.C., 2004). The three categories were lack of investment capital, unavailability of credit, and lack of modern machinery.

11. OTF Group, "Situation Analysis of Afghanistan's Finance Cluster" (Watertown, Mass., 2006), 10. The study cited information gathered from interviews and data provided by financial institutions. A draft of the report is available upon request by e-mailing: rhenning@otfgroup.com.

12. Afghanistan Central Statistical Office, "Afghanistan National Statistics" (Kabul, 2004).

13. Center for International Private Enterprise, "Training Needs Assessment."

14. World Bank, Asian Development Bank, and UN Development Program, "Afghanistan's Preliminary Needs Assessment for Reconstruction and Development" (Washington, D.C., 2002), table 1, www.adb.org/Documents/Reports/Afghanistan.

15. World Bank and Ministry of Construction, Japan, "Malaysia: Public-Private Partnerships in an Asian Way," in *Asian Toll Road Development Program* (Tokyo, 1999), III–84.

16. World Bank, Private Sector Development and Finance Unit, South Asia Region, "The Investment Climate Assessment of Afghanistan—Exploiting Opportunities in an Uncertain Environment" (Washington, D.C., 2005), siteresources.worldbank.org/INTAFGHANISTAN/Resources/AF_ICA_Report.pdf.

17. Noorullah Delawari, "Development of Microfinance and SME Lending in Afghanistan," South Asian Association for Regional Cooperation finance symposium (Dhaka, Bangladesh, February 15–16, 2006), 2.

18. World Bank, "Doing Business 2005" (Washington, D.C., 2005), www.doingbusiness.org.

19. World Bank, "The Investment Climate Assessment of Afghanistan," 20.

20. Afghanistan Competitiveness Project, "National Competitiveness Survey" (Kabul, 2005), 14. The Competitiveness Project is a two-year project in Afghanistan, funded by the U.S. Agency for International Development and implemented by OTF Group.) For further analysis of security in Afghanistan, see Hekmat Karzai, chapter 3 in this volume, and Ali A. Jalali, chapter 2 in this volume.

21. World Bank, "Doing Business 2005."

22. Islamic Republic of Afghanistan, *Interim Afghanistan National Development Strategy*, table 9.

23. See for example, World Bank, "The Investment Climate Assessment of Afghanistan," 26.

24. ANDS, "Summary Report," 24.

25. See also S. Frederick Starr, chapter 7 in this volume.

26. ANDS, "Summary Report," 23.

27. SAARC consists of Bangladesh, Bhutan, India, the Maldives, Nepal, Pakistan, and Sri Lanka. Afghanistan was invited to join SAARC as a full member during the Thirteenth SAARC Summit (Dhaka, Bangladesh, November 12–13, 2005).

7 Regional Development in Greater Central Asia: The Afghan Pivot

S. Frederick Starr

What are the likely benefits of greater regional cooperation in the region of which Afghanistan is the heart, and what are the prospects that such cooperation might actually be achieved? For more than a generation, the very question would have seemed quixotic and utopian. After all, during the decades of Afghanistan's crisis both major powers and neighboring states viewed that suffering land mainly as a source of problems to be avoided at all cost. Madeleine Albright's oft-quoted quip that the best approach to Afghanistan was to "build a fence around the country and forget about it" aptly, if cynically, reflected the prevailing view pre–September 11.

It is no surprise that the new Afghan government created by the Bonn process was preoccupied over the first years of its existence with building internal institutions and normalizing contacts with the UN, United States, and major donors. That process is far from complete, but it has advanced to the point that the new government can focus more directly on its relations with neighbors. Not that it ever avoided this topic, for relations with Pakistan in particular were always of first-order importance. But only since 2005 has the Karzai administration reached the point at which it can not only respond to problems involving neighbors but begin pursuing the benefits that might derive from closer interaction with them.

Impediments to Regional and Continental Trade Involving Afghanistan

Good intentions are necessary but not sufficient; Afghanistan must, as it turns outward, address the legacy of a quarter century of being justly viewed as a threat to states beyond its borders. In the case of its northern neighbors that were formerly part of the USSR, this notion of Afghanistan-as-threat was and, in all cases except Turkmenistan, still is enshrined in their military doctrine. Indeed, as recently as November 2005, the Russian foreign minister invoked it once more to justify his renewed effort to invigorate the common defense agreement that is part of the flagging Commonwealth of Independent States.[1]

The obvious justification for such talk is the flow of opium and cocaine from Afghanistan. Money from this trade is a significant factor in the GDP of both the Kyrgyz Republic and Tajikistan, while the associated criminality affects all regional states. Since traffickers pay their workers in kind, it has led to an appalling increase of addiction in all the neighboring countries, especially Iran. On this basis Russia prodded the Shanghai Cooperation Organization to establish an antinarcotics center in Bishkek, the capital of Kyrgyzstan, and, more recently, set up an office of its own antinarcotics agency in Kabul.

Yet there is a disingenuous element in this use of the narcotics issue to perpetuate the isolation of Afghanistan within the region. The entire industry is demand driven, with nine-tenths of the demand for Afghan heroin coming from Europe and Russia.[2] Moreover, nearly all the money from the trafficking goes to the consuming and trafficking countries, not to Afghanistan. Beneficiaries include not only the Balkan, Turkish, Nigerian, and Russian mafias but also prominent politicians in several countries neighboring Afghanistan.[3] As former Minister of the Interior Ali Jalali said, "Afghan farmers do not create traffickers; traffickers create opium farmers."[4] Given this fact, one might suggest that Afghans have as good a case against the consuming and trafficking countries as the latter have against the Afghans.

Beyond drugs, each regional state has had its own concrete and specific reasons for treating Afghanistan as a kind of pathology. The flow of arms and millions of immigrants during the Soviet invasion and civil war threatened to destabilize Pakistan, prompting it to support the Taliban as a means of pacifying its neighbor. The successes of the overwhelmingly Pashtun Taliban in turn marginalized Tajiks and Uzbeks in the north of Afghanistan.

The new states of Uzbekistan and Tajikistan had virtually no contact with their co-ethnic populations to the south since Stalin closed the border in 1936 and viewed them as backward, ignorant, and superstitious. Yet they could not ignore their fate, if only because of the danger of cross-border migration it created. No wonder, then, that Tajikistan hosted an early post–September 11 meeting at which Russian president Vladimir Putin and Russian general Anatoli Kvashnin anointed the largely Tajik Northern Alliance as the new rulers of Afghanistan. The Bonn Conference a few weeks later imprudently recognized this gross power play, and it took President Karzai two years to reverse its dangerous consequences and introduce ethnic balance into his administration.

Uzbekistan, meanwhile, knew well that the Islamic Movement of Uzbekistan had found refuge and financial support in Afghanistan both from the Taliban and from al Qaeda, and that people with close Afghan ties were responsible for the 1998 bombings in Tashkent. There is controversy over the degree of Uzbekistan's support for Abdul Rashid Dostum, the Afghan Uzbek warlord, but it is understandable that Uzbekistan was concerned over developments to its south. In 1998 it was the first country to raise concerns over terrorism to the U.S. government.[5] The Islamic Movement of Uzbekistan failed in 1999 and again in 2000 to enter Uzbekistan, but its forces found financial and material support in Afghanistan, wintered comfortably at the hot springs in the Jirgital District of Tajikistan, and were able to pass unopposed through parts of Kyrgyzstan's Batken province and the mountains east of Shimkent in Kazakhstan—confirming Tashkent's fears of Afghanistan as the main source of a radical Islamist contagion for Uzbekistan and its neighbors.

Iran had equally sound reasons to fear its neighbor, Afghanistan. Centuries earlier the Sunni Muslim army of Afghanistan had toppled the government of a newly Shia Safavid Persia, and Ayatollah Khomeini's Iran feared a repeat. Like several of Afghanistan's other neighbors, Iran sought out sympathetic warlords and parties inside Afghanistan whom it could back and generally worked to undermine Taliban power and contain Afghan energies.

Similar fears arose in Beijing regarding the easternmost zone of Central Asia, China's Xinjiang Uighur Autonomous Region. The Turkic independence movement had never been strong there, nor did radical Islam make much headway, in spite of the fact that trader-missionaries entered the area from Pakistan's Northwest Frontier province and a few Uighurs found their way into Afghanistan, where they fought with the Taliban.[6] But China's "Strike Hard—Maximum Pressure" program against local Turkic Muslims, launched in 1998, explicitly identified Afghanistan, and also the newly independent states of Kazakhstan, Kyrgyzstan, and Tajikistan, as the new threats to China's territorial integrity. In 2001 China convened the Shanghai Group (later the Shanghai Cooperation Organization) with the explicit purposes of neutralizing its three western neighbors as sources of separatist propaganda and Afghanistan as a source of Islamist proselytizing.[7] In the same year, China lent cautious support to Operation Enduring Freedom as a means of containing the Afghan threat.

Thus each of Afghanistan's neighbors before 2002 viewed that country as a serious, if not the most serious, threat to its national security. This threat was incorporated into their respective security doctrines and translated into practical programs of action. To contain that threat or hamper worse alternatives, they all supported forces within Afghanistan that they considered might moderate the threat to Afghanistan's neighbors. Most of these forces posed serious dangers of their own and contributed to internal division and centrifugal pressures within Afghanistan itself.

With the exception of Pakistan, none of Afghanistan's neighbors recognized any Afghan government between the Soviet invasion and 1992. As an important consequence, the elites in all the neighboring countries (with only the partial exception of Pakistan) until very recently had no real knowledge of the country beyond the particular warlord or faction their country was supporting.

Normal contact between Afghanistan and both Turkey and India was suspended for a generation. Turkish followers of the Kemalist Sufi leader Fethullah Gülen operated secular schools in several Afghan provinces until the Taliban closed them down, while India lent quiet support to whatever forces within Afghanistan opposed those backed by Pakistan. Beyond these token efforts, the mutual isolation of Afghanistan and these regional powers was complete.

The one exception to this prevailing fear, hostility, and lack of contact with Afghanistan was Turkmenistan. Besides being concerned over its conationals in Afghanistan, Ashgabat under President Saparmurat Niyazov and especially (former) foreign minister Boris Shikhmuradov was eager to free itself from Russian economic dominance by building a gas pipeline across Afghanistan to Multan in Pakistan.[8] This interest led to steadier and closer relations between Afghanistan and Turkmenistan than existed between Afghanistan and any other former Soviet state of Central Asia. Even these ties were modest and did not really affect the overall conclusion that Afghanistan's regional neighbors, at the time of September 11, had to reconstitute both their knowledge of and contacts with Afghanistan, beginning nearly from zero. What they did know was of little use to them as they struggled to make sense of the new conditions that emerged after the Taliban's fall and the start of the Bonn process. In short, legitimate suspicions and fears nurtured over a generation slowed the development of new relations with the Karzai government.

Today the Bonn process is complete, Afghan sovereignty is reestablished, and an impressive electoral process has put in place a government that enjoys legitimacy at home and abroad. What, then, are its prospects for the future? Security remains a serious concern, with Mullah Mohammed Omar, speaking from Peshawar as recently as late 2005, calling for an Afghan jihad against foreign forces. Killings by Taliban holdouts also continue. Even though these have been concentrated in areas adjoining the border with Pakistan, the number and effectiveness of attacks increased during 2005. Such concerns naturally fan all the old fears. Pakistan's President Pervez Musharraf's quip, much derided in Kabul, about building a security fence along Pakistan's border with Afghanistan, shows how insecurity within Afghanistan still has the potential to isolate the country within its neighborhood.

Trade's Potential and Reasons for Its Underdevelopment

Closely related to the problem of insecurity is Afghanistan's prevailing poverty, which economic growth since 2002 has barely touched. Besides perpetuating human misery, Afghanistan's pitifully low GDP leaves the government without a tax base sufficient to fund even the most rudimentary social and economic services, let alone provide for the nation's security. Until such a tax base exists, the government will remain dependent on foreign assistance, mainly from the United States, which is now approximately $10 billion a year for security and $2.4 billion a year for economic and social development, sums that are surely unsustainable.[9] Hence Afghanistan's future depends directly on future expansion of the economy to the point at which it is able, through taxes, to provide the government with a normal income stream.

It has often been pointed out that manufacturing is the quickest path to national prosperity, outstripping both agriculture and trade. But for Afghanistan, almost wholly lacking in modern skills and manufacturing infrastructures, this solution holds little immediate promise. Agriculture offers better prospects, but this sector requires both processing and storage capacities that do not now exist in Afghanistan, and also access to regional and international markets. Barring the discovery of large deposits of hydrocarbons or rare minerals, Afghanistan's best hope lies in the area of regional and especially continental trade, which is scarcely surprising, as such trade has defined the country's economy and culture for three millennia.

Trade has already begun to revive both within the borders of Afghanistan and with the country's immediate neighbors, especially Pakistan and Iran. Reconstruction in Kabul and projects elsewhere in the country have created a huge demand for everything from vehicles, machinery, and building materials to household supplies, tools, and manufactured clothing. Pashtun traders from Pakistan have tapped a seemingly limitless market for such goods in Afghanistan. The value of exports from Afghanistan to Pakistan is barely a sixth as large as the reverse trade, but it, too, is growing rapidly.

A similar situation exists with respect to Iran. The traditional eastern orientation of Iranian trade did not cease even during the Soviet occupation of Afghanistan and the subsequent civil war. To facilitate this trade, Iran has established consulates in various parts of Afghanistan, provided assistance for the construction of roads leading to its territory, and mounted trade fairs in Kabul and Herat.[10]

By comparison, Afghan trade with the formerly Soviet states to the north is minimal. Isolated from each other for generations, neither Afghan businessmen nor their counterparts to the north are accustomed to think in terms of the other's market. Poor infrastructure reinforces this pattern. Until the recent opening of three small bridges over the Pyandzh River in the Pamirs, there was no commercial intercourse between Tajik and Afghan parts of Badakhshan, even though they are linked by common Old Iranian languages and common Pamiri ethnicity. Trade between the rest of Tajikistan and Afghanistan has been constrained by the absence of a major Pyandzh bridge and feeder roads to the north. While the old Soviet-built "Friendship Bridge" still links Afghanistan with Uzbekistan, it is in precarious condition, and the border otherwise lacks all the customs and organizational infrastructure needed to sustain active trade. By comparison, the border with Turkmenistan is easily passable, although in this case trade is limited by the absence of major population centers and markets in the border areas of both countries.

A more serious constraint on trade between Afghanistan and its neighbors is the scarcity of obvious complementarities between their economies.[11]

Afghan agricultural products do not differ sharply in either type or quality from those of its neighbors, and the country has little to offer in exchange for imports other than raw materials. It could compete on the basis of the exceptionally low cost of labor inputs there, but to reap this benefit, Afghanistan would require efficient systems of communications and transport and secondary market centers, none of which now exist.

Revival of Regional and Continental Trade

The combination of old thinking, shortcomings of infrastructure, and the lack of complementarities between their economies has thwarted the development of trade between Afghanistan and its neighbors. These problems hold especially true for north-south exchange but affect east-west trade as well, notwithstanding the relatively greater volume of trade along this axis. Recently, however, there have been some signs of positive change. Thanks to help from the United States, cement manufacturers in the Kyrgyz Republic have gained a foothold in the Afghan market. Uzbek and Tajik suppliers of building materials have opened contacts in Afghanistan. Tajikistan and Turkmenistan are both selling electric energy to Afghanistan, and the first Kazakh bank is soon to open an office in Kabul.

Despite these promising beginnings, intraregional trade among the countries of what might be called Greater Central Asia is likely to remain limited. What are the prospects for continental trade crossing Afghanistan, that is, long-distance transfers by land between China and Northeast Asia and the Middle East, between Europe and the Middle East and the Indian subcontinent and beyond, and between Russia and India? These, after all, were the grand routes that defined the world's most lucrative land trade for millennia, the so-called Silk Road.

For the time being, such trade is all but nonexistent. A few major Turkish firms (such as Yuksel Construction Company) have transported volumes of building supplies by land across Iran to Afghanistan, but this activity is ad hoc and will not lead to sustained, two-way commerce. The United States has also engaged a couple of Chinese firms from Xinjiang in projects in Afghanistan, which necessitated their bringing materials across the Pamirs, but these transfers, too, were both limited and irregular.

Notwithstanding its present insignificance, continental trade through Afghanistan holds great potential for the future. Indian manufacturers from Mumbai and Gujarat could send products not only to Central Asian markets but beyond to Russia and Eastern Europe. China could transport products to Iran and the Middle East by routes crossing Afghanistan, while Iranian and Middle Eastern suppliers could send goods overland to South Asia. West Siberia and the Urals, presently dependent mainly on modest east-west traffic, could open up new prospects in the Middle East, Pakistan, India, and beyond, provided that they could convey goods by road or railroad through Afghanistan and the rest of Central Asia.

No less promising is the continental transport of energy from Central Asia and Afghanistan to the Indian subcontinent. Pipelines could send oil and gas from the Caspian basin across Central Asia and Afghanistan to energy-starved India or overland to Pakistani and Iranian ports and thence by tankers and liquefied natural gas ships to Southeast Asia. Electric power from Tajikistan and the Kyrgyz Republic could find ready markets in Pakistan, not to mention in Afghanistan itself.

The absence of essential infrastructure for this trade has already been noted. This deficit exists both with respect to physical installations—roads, bridges, pipelines, power transmission lines, gas and service stations, and the like—and to the critically important institutional support system, including reliable border security, common standards for weights and signage, mutual recognition of licenses, moderate tariffs and duties, and efficient systems for their collection.

Responsibility in all these areas inevitably falls to government. Indeed, development of these systems and processes is an essential element of state building. Yet the Afghan reconstruction effort has responded far more attentively to the need to develop a constitution and elective political institutions than to the equally important need to develop the normal institutions of state. Bonn's timetable pertains to political benchmarks, not statebuilding benchmarks.

Many efforts are under way to address this shortcoming. Japan, Saudi Arabia, and the United States are working to complete the essential but long delayed "ring road" that will connect Herat, Kabul, and Kandahar and serve as a kind of mixing bowl for truck traffic coming from east, west, and north. The United States recently proposed to double the $622 million a year now designated for this project.[12] The United States has also begun construction on a critically important Pyandzh bridge that will become a key element of north-south transit in and through the region.[13] China has engaged a Turkish construction firm to complete the road across the Kulma Pass from Xinjiang to Tajik Badakhshan, which in turn links to the new American bridge via the Khorog-Kulyab highway now being rebuilt with international assistance. Iran's 115 Construction Company meanwhile has already built a new road linking Herat with the Iranian border town of Islam Qala and is now engaged in rebuilding the internal road system of Herat province.

Even secondary roads are being rebuilt, although these projects are proceeding more slowly. Within Afghanistan, the United States is rebuilding the fifty-five-kilometer road linking the eastern towns of Sharana and Orgun, and also the sixty-four-kilometer road between Qalata and Shinkay. The latter projects have involved 600 Afghan contractors and laborers, many of them demobilized irregular fighters.[14]

Parallel with these efforts, Iran, with help from Russia and India, is rushing to complete a trunk highway and railroads that will lead south from Kazakhstan and Turkmenistan across Iranian Khorosan to its new port of Chabahar. It is also supporting the construction of a new road from Chabahar to Afghanistan's Helmand province, and China and Pakistan are hastening to complete construction of the major new port at Gwadar, east of Chabahar in Pakistani Baluchistan.[15] China and Pakistan are also collaborating in reconstructing the roadway of the Karakoram Highway south from Xinjiang to Islamabad and then extending it to Gwadar. Closely related is the critically important Kandahar-Gwadar road, which will link the Afghan ring road with the new port and thus provide a continuous road link between the Urals, West Siberia, Central Asia, and the Indian subcontinent. While engineering work on this project has been completed, actual construction has barely begun and may be delayed by persistent security problems along the route.

For the time being, all attention regarding oil and gas pipelines is focused on the Turkmenistan-Afghanistan-Pakistan (TAP) route. The Asia Development Bank in 2005 issued an encouraging report on the economic prospects of this project, and the participating countries have moved rapidly to assemble construction and management teams.[16] The three governments declared that work will begin by 2008 but qualified their timetable with a disconcerting warning that the project still awaited definitive commitments from investors.[17] Given its scale, said to reach 4.6 billion cubic meters a year from Turkmenistan's Dauletabad field alone, it is all but certain that funding will be found for the 1,600-kilometer project. The problem is that this capacity is more than can be consumed by Pakistan alone. This issue poses no problem if India and Pakistan settle their decades-long competition over Kashmir and other border areas. Should they fail, however, the entire project would doubtless be placed in jeopardy, at least until the Pakistani economy develops new demand.

In addition to the aforementioned issues, the international gas crisis of January 2006 also had an impact on the future of the TAP project. Russia pursued its political objective of dominating its neighbors by briefly withholding gas supplies from Ukraine, Moldova, and Georgia. Then, as the winter deepened and demand within Russia soared, it cut back deliveries to Western Europe was well. Russia's plan to build a "liberal empire" through the use of its gas weapon required that it control the export of all gas from Turkmenistan as well. To this end it vehemently opposed the TAP pipeline and proposed instead an alternative that would run from Iran directly to Pakistan and then to India, bypassing both Turkmenistan and Afghanistan.[18] In January 2006 Russia pushed this project forward to the point of announcing it publicly long before the funding was in place. It is by no means clear as of this writing that the Iranian alternative will in fact be constructed or that the construction of this rival line would kill the present momentum for the TAP project.

By their nature all these projects call for financial and organizational collaborations between two or even three countries. Without such cooperation it is unlikely that the project will be built. For example, no country will commit resources to road or bridge construction until it is convinced that its relevant neighbor will complete needed work on its side of the border. In the case of the TAP project, Turkmenistan and Afghanistan depend on Pakistan to find consumers for all the gas delivered (since gas, unlike oil, cannot be stored and must be used soon after it is delivered.)

Even if the relevant two or three countries approve in principle a given project, it can often die without the help of a major outside power for one simple reason: the absence of sustained prior contacts within the region has left a residue of misunderstanding that often requires a third party to mediate and guarantee the deal. Independent of its ability to finance projects, the United States is seen by many in the region as an "honest broker." In that role, it can use its convening power to bring the contending parties together in a productive relationship that might not otherwise exist. The United States has a vital role to play in the development of physical infrastructure across all of greater Central Asia and the Caucasus. The Pyandzh bridge between Tajikistan and Afghanistan is the most significant manifestation of this role to date. Up to now the tripartite consultative group consisting of Afghanistan, Pakistan, and the United States has been used mainly to address security issues, but trade is also on its agenda, and it could be a useful vehicle for coordinating infrastructure projects as well.

Unfortunately, many of the most promising prospects for regional and continental trade are hostage to bad relations among states at a distance from the main countries involved. Thus, for example, both the Kazakh-Uzbek and Kazakh-Kyrgyz border posts mainly process bilateral trade. The absence of continental trade at these crossing points traces to the fact that the distant Indian-Pakistani border remains closed to long-distance truck traffic. Similarly, poor relations between Uzbekistan and Turkmenistan (as well as indifference on the part of its sponsor, the European Union) have constrained the development of the entire east-west TRASECA network extending from the Mediterranean to China.[19]

Rarely do countries whose actions create these choke points accept responsibility for their negative impact on more distant countries, and it is equally rare that the affected countries wield sufficient influence to change the practices of distant nations that are hindering their commerce. The only way to resolve such problems is for a major state or international financial institution to involve itself as mediator.

The biggest impediments to continental trade across greater Central Asia are a very few highly specific political conflicts that have endured for decades. First among these are the simmering tensions between India and Pakistan over Kashmir, which effectively close all of Central Asia to commercial intercourse with South Asia. Also, since the only functioning north-south pass traversing the western Himalayas is via Pakistan, the same conflict bars direct commerce between Xinjiang and India. Finally, the closed border between Pakistan and India prevents Iran from regaining its age-old role as a leading link between the Middle East and the Indian subcontinent. Reopening that single border would quickly revitalize Iran as a commercial power and generate significant income for Afghanistan.

It is customary to speak of trade as a kind of reward that is conferred on countries that successfully resolve their cross-border political problems. In the same breath, however, it is often acknowledged that trade creates common interests and therefore improves relations. To the extent that the latter is true, regional and continental trade in the Greater Central Asia region should be viewed as an important tool that, deftly wielded, can soften cross-border political tensions. Unfortunately, not one state in the region has embraced this approach, even though a number of external powers and international financial institutions, as well as some multilateral groups, are encouraging them to do so.

A number of complex issues must be addressed if trade is to flow. Among these, the financing and construction of costly physical infrastructure may be the simplest to resolve. Far more vexing are the problems of establishing physical security in border zones, the development of tax and customs regimes that foster trade rather than inhibiting it, the creation of coordinated and simplified border control points for customs and duties, and reaching agreement on licensing and standards. Unfortunately, progress by one country in one or even several areas does not necessarily elicit progress from its neighbor. At 4 percent ad valorem, Afghanistan's tariffs are the lowest in the region (far less onerous, for example, than Pakistan's 120 percent), but this low rate has not triggered any general move toward tariff reduction.[20] Similarly, Kyrgyzstan rushed to join the World Trade Organization, but its accession brought about no changes in the border and tariff regimes of any of its neighbors except fellow World Trade Organization member China.[21]

Regional and International Groupings and Organizations Promoting Trade across Greater Central Asia

The best hope for progress lies in multilateral initiatives. Even though these are inevitably more complex than uni- or bilateral steps, they are more efficacious because they spread inconvenience and cost more or less equally among natural competitors. Thus, when members of the Economic Cooperation Organization decided in Kabul in late 2005 to reduce tariffs to 10 percent over a ten-year period, their initiative was immediately credible because its costs were equitably distributed.[22]

In light of this important principle, it is worth inquiring into the status of multilateral initiatives to promote regional and continental trade involving the countries of Greater Central Asia. What are the various multilateral groupings of regional states, and how has each of these performed in the area of trade and commerce?

The number of institutions vying in this arena is surprisingly large, as is the range of their aspirations and programs. Leaving aside the World Trade Organization, Organization of Islamic States, and other large international entities to which the regional states may belong, it is possible to speak of at least nine regional entities that are directly relevant to the region's commercial future.

First in terms of age is the Economic Cooperation Organization (ECO). Formed in 1985 by Turkey, Iran, and Pakistan on the foundation of an earlier entity dating to the 1960s, it was expanded in 1992 to include all five of the former Soviet republics of Central Asia, and in 2003 to include Afghanistan.[23] In late 2005 its ten members held a Trade and Investment

Conference in Kabul chaired by Hedayat Amin Arsala, minister of commerce of Afghanistan, and hosted by Omar Zakhilwal, head of Afghanistan's newly established Investment Support Agency. Even though 200 people attended this event, it is by no means clear, judging by ECO's past record, that it is capable of delivering on the expectations it has raised. Past ECO initiatives in the areas of regional banking, spearheaded by Turkey, and in common engineering standards for highways and tax standards for shipments by road have each begun with strong resolutions and have been followed up with competent research but then have stalled completely.

For a more eastern-oriented group of states, the much-discussed Shanghai Cooperation Organization (SCO), founded in 2001, has inherited many of the expectations raised by ECO. Unlike ECO, however, SCO arose from the security concerns of one power, China, which wanted to throttle Uighur activities among neighboring states to the west. It has now extended its ambitions into the fields of hydroelectric energy, oil prospecting, oil and gas pipeline construction, water use, and regional trade. However, SCO does not yet include Afghanistan. True, President Karzai attended the SCO summit in Tashkent in June 2005, and SCO in turn has set up a contact group to open relations with Kabul. But according to Zhang Deguang, the head of SCO's secretariat, the organization will not be ready to admit new members for some time. It therefore remains unclear to what extent SCO can foster regional and continental trade involving Afghanistan. And even when that occurs, will SCO become a force for the equitable development of trade involving regional states or, as Niklas Swanstrom recently argued, an instrument for creating new forms of vassalage in the region?[24]

Bureaucratic divisions that assign countries in the region to different divisions negatively affect the activities of other institutions as well. Both the World Bank and the European Bank for Reconstruction and Development continue to accept the southern border of the former USSR as the dividing line between bureaus, thus hindering regionwide programming. Happily, this division does not rule out interbureau cooperation in the area of research.[25]

The same problem of regional administrative divisions affects the otherwise commendable work of the Japanese government in Greater Central Asia. In 2004 Japan's prime minister inaugurated the "Six Plus One" consultative group involving Japan and the five former Soviet states of Central Asia and Azerbaijan.[26] Designed to coordinate Japanese development activities on a regionwide basis, the Six Plus One group does not include Afghanistan because Tokyo's Foreign Ministry assigns that country to a separate South

Asian bureau. Efforts are under way to correct this designation and draw Afghanistan into Six Plus One activity, but these have so far not borne fruit.

The Eurasian Economic Union (EEU), sponsored by the Russian Federation, suffers from the same organizational problem. This entity, which now includes Russia, all the former Soviet states of Central Asia except Turkmenistan, and Belarus has its origins in two very different initiatives, each of which in turn evolved from two other entities. The EEU is a lineal descendant of the Central Asia Union, founded by Kazakhstan, Kyrgyzstan, and Uzbekistan in 1993.[27] Prior to the addition of Uzbekistan and Tajikistan in 2005, the Eurasian Economic Union was intended as a kind of confederation that would lead eventually to a semiunion among its members. By contrast, the Commonwealth of Independent States (CIS) was to be a looser organization modeled vaguely on the postcolonial British Commonwealth or France's association of former African colonies. The EEU today stands somewhere between its old identity as a future union of states and the commonwealth notion that informed CIS, with Central Asian members (and Belarus as well) seeking somehow to preserve their sovereignty within it, and Russia's powerful nationalists pushing instead for a new multinational state.

As the CIS talked of expanding to include security interests, Russia sought and received observer status in 1996. The next year Tajikistan joined, and the CIS changed its name to the Central Asia Cooperation Organization, a name chosen explicitly to indicate that no merging of sovereignties was planned. In 2004 the group acceded to Russia's strong request for full membership, and by 2005 Russia dominated the group to such a degree that it could merge with the EEU. This step in turn elicited from Kazakhstan's president Nursultan Nazarbayev the proposal that a new, purely Central Asian entity be created to consist initially of Kazakhstan, the Kyrgyz Republic, and Tajikistan.

Such is the hold of Soviet thinking among Afghanistan's northern neighbors that at no time has it been suggested that Afghanistan be included either in the CIS, EEU, Central Asia Union, Central Asia Cooperation Organization, or Nazarbayev's as yet to be formed Central Asian group. Russia, and to a lesser extent the former Soviet states of Central Asia, continue to treat Afghanistan mainly as a security threat. In November 2005 Sergei Lavrov, Russia's foreign minister, forcefully reiterated this view, going so far as to propose the creation of a "security belt" around Afghanistan.[28] By implication he suggested the merging of the old CIS Collective Security agreement with the new EEU in a manner that would continue to isolate Afghanistan within the region of which it is the heart.

Even if Afghanistan were incorporated in any of the above groupings, it would remain isolated from countries that have the greatest untapped potential for expanding regional and continental trade across its territory, namely India and Pakistan. Far from "opening windows" to the south and southeast, these groupings would all reinforce Soviet-era trade patterns that led to the grotesque situation of products from Afghanistan and its Central Asian neighbors being sent to world markets via Baltic Sea ports. Nevertheless, routes north to Russia are important elements of any continental trade network involving Afghanistan, as are routes west to Europe and the Middle East via Central Asia or Iran, and routes to China via Tajikistan and the Kyrgyz Republic. The long-term expansion and viability of all three of these channels of trade will depend in large measure on whether goods being shipped to or from the Indian subcontinent and Southeast Asia are part of this overall commerce. Indeed, the single most important factor ensuring the return of Afghanistan to its central position in trade across the Eurasian landmass will be the opening of routes through Afghanistan to South and Southeast Asia.

Thanks to this reality, international groupings and organizations that link Afghanistan with its immediate and distant neighbors to the east are of particular importance to the overall revival of trade. ECO and the Organization of the Islamic Conference are both promising in this regard in that they include Pakistan, but their value is limited by the fact that they do not include India.[29] By contrast, the South Asian Association for Regional Cooperation (SAARC), comprising Bangladesh, Bhutan, India, the Maldives, Nepal, Pakistan, and Sri Lanka, has the potential to integrate commerce passing through Afghanistan from the north and west with the heretofore closed markets to the southeast.

SAARC, established in 1985, focuses on poverty reduction, emergency relief, antiterror activities, and trade, the last having steadily gained in importance among the grouping's priorities. In 2005 Foreign Minister Abdullah Abdullah of Afghanistan wrote to his counterpart in Islamabad asking for Afghanistan to be admitted to SAARC. Pakistan promptly proposed Afghanistan for membership, and at a meeting held in late 2005, the request was approved.[30] For the first time in a quarter century, Afghanistan has a venue for advancing its trade with the vast markets to its east.

The Asian Development Bank (ADB) is even more promising than SAARC as a tool for the integration of regionwide trade. ADB's territorial focus comprises not only the countries of South and East Asia but also the five former Soviet republics of Central Asia, as well as Azerbaijan. To a far greater degree than all the other international development banks, ADB has embraced the notion of continental trade as the key to economic development.[31] Working initially with the five former Soviet republics and Azerbaijan, ADB has promoted periodic ministerial meetings on issues pertinent to trade, as well as regular working group meetings of lower officials. Until 2005 its chief interest was the opening of east-west corridors extending from the Caucasus to China. Increasingly, however, it has recognized the importance of links to South and Southeast Asia, and for this reason it has included Afghanistan more actively in its counsels. ADB's internal administrative setup does not yet reflect this emerging interest, but it is clear that this is already changing and that in the future ADB will fully embrace this cause.

Role of the United States

Given the central role of the United States in the abolition of Taliban rule and the reestablishment of normal institutions of government in Afghanistan, it is relevant to ask what, if anything, the United States might do in the future to revive regional and continental trade not only across Afghanistan but in Greater Central Asia as a whole. Between 2001 and 2004, the United States focused its attention and resources on fighting terrorism and creating basic institutions of government in Afghanistan proper. As the post–September 11 agenda has been achieved, it is now possible, and indeed necessary, to adopt a "post-post–September 11" strategy.[32]

The need for such a strategy is urgent. From 1992 to 2001, the United States engaged intensely with the former Soviet states of Central Asia through a wide range of activities in many areas. Local governments, believing that the United States considered itself to have long-term interests in the region, made their plans accordingly. Foreign Minister Kassymzhomart Tokaev of Kazakhstan frequently articulated the strategy adopted eventually by all five states in the region, namely, to use China as a foil to Russia, and the United States as a counterweight to China and Russia. With September 11, however, the United States subordinated any long-term interests in the region to its short-term strategic goals of destroying al Qaeda and bringing down the Taliban government in Afghanistan. Going further, it declared to both the Kyrgyz Republic and

Uzbekistan that the presence of its military in the region would cease as soon as Afghanistan became secure, which was expected to be within a couple of years. This declaration alarmed the former Soviet states, which in the first half of 2005 hastened to solidify alternate security arrangements involving Russia and China. Thus, as of mid-2005, the United States had effectively written itself out of the region north of the Pyandzh River at precisely the moment that it needed to maximize cooperation with all of Afghanistan's neighbors in order to strengthen the fragile new government in Kabul. Rather than build on success in Afghanistan, the United States appeared headed toward regional retrenchment, in effect "cutting its gains."

Into this dangerous situation, this author introduced a series of proposals during the spring and summer of 2005 for the United States to reengage with all of Afghanistan's neighbors by focusing on the development of regional and continental trade. It was suggested that the United States establish regionwide consultative processes on the use of existing and future aid funds, and that these efforts be carried out through a new "partnership office" reporting to senior officials in the Department of State.

All the elements of this proposal had been in circulation for some time. ADB had long championed some sort of regional coordination of trade initiatives, and the Japanese Six Plus One initiative anticipated most features of the proposed United States partnership. More important, the Afghan government itself had already moved in this direction as it reached out to new regional groupings. Against this background it is not surprising that the Organization for Security and Cooperation in Europe (OSCE) took up the proposal, stripping it of its American focus but applying its main points to a renewed OSCE involvement with economic matters.

In spite of the fact that its founding charter identifies three areas or "baskets" for OSCE activity—security, economic development, and human rights–democracy—this organization had long concentrated most of its energies on the third group. Under the Belgian presidency, however, the "economic" basket has been coming again to the fore. Thus the idea of regional consultation on trade meshed with OSCE thinking, even though Afghanistan itself is not an OSCE member. Moving quickly, OSCE has held one conference on a Greater Central Asia initiative in Dushanbe, and is planning a regional meeting in Istanbul to prepare broader initiatives.[33] OSCE's involvement holds promise, although in the end OSCE activity may be limited by financial constraints.

For all its dynamism during the 1990s, American involvement with the states of Greater Central Asia was mainly bilateral and included little, if any, crosscutting regional programs that included Afghanistan. In the summer of 2005, however, the State Department paved the way for regionwide coordination and planning when it shifted the five former Soviet states of Central Asia and Afghanistan from its European bureau to the South Asian bureau. This important decision removed a chief impediment to a "Greater Central Asia partnership," although there as yet appears to be little interest within the State Department to proceed further along this line.

The Pentagon has always supported regionwide approaches and sees a U.S.-sponsored regional trade initiative as the logical extension of its own activities in the security area. The fact that several strongly nationalistic Russian authors have roundly criticized the idea only adds to its appeal within the Department of Defense.[34] The Department of Commerce, too, has long favored a regional approach while at the same time being constrained by the same organization problem that beset the State Department until summer 2005. But neither the Pentagon nor the Department of Commerce is in a position to propose a comprehensive policy reorientation along these lines. With the State Department apparently unwilling to do so, the initiative shifted inevitably to Congress.

Senator Sam Brownback was the author of the 1999 Silk Road Strategy Act that for the first time introduced an element of regional thinking into U.S. policy toward Central Asia and the Caucasus. That legislation, however, dated from the period of Taliban rule in Afghanistan and therefore excluded that country from its programs. Brownback changed course and proposed a Silk Road Strategy Act II that would include Afghanistan and concentrate on the same set of issues enumerated in the proposal for a Greater Central Asia partnership.[35] The focus on continental transit trade comes naturally to Senator Brownback, as it is a mainstay of the economy of his native state, Kansas.

In an effort to convince U.S. officials of the benefits to Afghanistan, its neighbors, and the United States itself of regional coordination of American initiatives to foster long-distance trade in the region, the Central Asia–Caucasus Institute, in conjunction with Afghanistan's Foreign Ministry and Ministry of Commerce, held a conference in Kabul in mid-2006 on a possible U.S.-Afghan–Central Asia partnership. Kazakhstan's influential minister of foreign affairs assumed a prominent role in this project, signaling Kazakhstan's intention to become a leader in regional affairs, including those involving continental trade.[36]

Alarm Bells: New Political Fragmentation in Greater Central Asia?

Reviewing recent discussions of regional and continental trade involving Afghanistan and its neighbors, one might be tempted to conclude that some kind of concrete actions in this direction are all but inevitable in the coming period. It is a logical "next step" not only for Afghanistan in its post-Bonn phase of development but also for its neighbors, all of whom have an interest in using trade to reinforce the new elements of stability that a transformed Afghanistan is introducing into the region. It would seem equally logical for the United States to use its programs to foster such a development as the keystone of a post-post–September 11 strategy for the region as a whole.

Unfortunately, the stabilization of Afghanistan has been accompanied by disturbing new trends among its neighbors, especially Uzbekistan, Iran, and Pakistan. Were they to continue, these trends could imperil Afghanistan's ability to reap financial benefit from its location at the potential hub of a new regional and continental cooperative trade network.

In Uzbekistan the modernizing and Westernizing party within the government that promoted the 2002 Agreement of Strategic Partnership has now fallen from power. Having enjoyed President Islam Karimov's full support from 1999 to 2002, this group, led by foreign minister Sodyq Safaev and minister of defense Kodyr Gulyamov, argued that close ties with the United States would strengthen Uzbekistan's geopolitical and economic security and were willing to promote democratization to secure such a relationship. When the Agreement of Strategic Partnership failed to evolve into a broader relationship (due mainly to the U.S. preoccupation with the war on terrorism), an opposing faction led by the Ministry of Internal Affairs (police), Security Services, and some key regional and industrial power brokers pushed aside the reformers and gained Karimov's support for an approach to Russia and China. The fact that these developments have been accompanied by unsettling social developments in Uzbekistan, including the now notorious events of May 2005 in Andijan, has created an environment in which the U.S. State Department is equally disinclined to engage constructively with that country, removing for the time being a key state from the proposed regional partnership.[37]

The election of Mahmoud Ahmadinejad to the presidency of Iran created an analogous problem with that country. Even though the United States would not have welcomed Iran into a trade partnership under any circumstances, prior to Ahmadinejad's election one could have imagined the United States setting conditions, however severe, that any new state (including Iran) would have to meet in order to gain entry to the group. Ahmadinejad's actions since coming into office have ruled out even this degree of cooperation, effectively leaving all east-west links across Afghanistan's western border to bilateral arrangements between Kabul and Teheran.

Finally, Pakistan's behavior vis-à-vis Afghanistan, as well as its activities in Kashmir, continues to put on the defensive all those in the United States favoring closer collaboration with that country. The fact that a high percentage of all instances of armed insurgency in Afghanistan occur in areas bordering Pakistan convinces many that Islamabad continues to pursue a two-track policy of close collaboration with the United States and Afghanistan at the official level and support for active measures to destabilize Afghanistan at the unofficial level.

While the facts in Iran seem not to be in doubt, there is controversy over the precise nature and meaning of developments in both Uzbekistan and Pakistan. Both turn on the degree to which presidents Karimov and Musharraf actively sponsor the developments that concern the United States as opposed to their being unable to control events and hence being forced to make concessions to powerful and retrograde forces within their governments.

Either way, the question eventually comes down to this: are international trade and commerce sufficiently powerful forces that they can generate common interests between Afghanistan and its neighbors that can, over time, reduce areas of conflict? Or should trade and commerce be treated as a reward to be conferred on Afghanistan's neighbors once they have addressed the issues to which the United States objects? The prevailing view in Washington as of this writing favors the latter approach. For many, it is a matter of simple common sense. Yet the alternative view may be closer to the truth and have the additional benefit of providing the basis for a more productive strategy in the long run. For if continental and regional trade involving Afghanistan and its neighbors is indeed the powerful engine for economic development that all the international financial institutions claim it to be, then trade should be encouraged as quickly as possible on the grounds that the countries will steadily build the shared interests that alone can overcome the conditions that still divide states in the region.

Notes

1. Ministry of Foreign Affairs of the Russian Federation, "Transcript of Speech by Russian Foreign Minister Sergey Lavrov at University of World Economy and Diplomacy, Uzbekistan" (Tashkent, October 21, 2005), www.mid.ru/brp_4.nsf/e78a48070f128a 7b43256999005bcbb3/a0135df4462b5db0c32570a50026241a?OpenDocument.

2. See Svante E. Cornell and Niklas L. P. Swanstrom, "Trafficking in Afghan Opiates: Impact on Transit Countries" (New York, 2006), 3–26.

3. Svante Cornell, "The Narcotics Threat in Greater Central Asia: From Crime Terror Nexus to State Infiltration," *China and Eurasia Forum Quarterly*, IV (2006), 37–68.

4. Ali Jalali, personal interview with the author, Washington, D.C., October 18, 2005.

5. John C. K. Daly and others, "Anatomy of a Crisis: U.S.-Uzbekistan Relations, 2001–2005," Silk Road Paper, Central Asia–Caucasus Institute (Washington, D.C., February 2006), 6.

6. S. Frederick Starr (ed.), *Xinjiang: China's Muslim Borderland* (New York and London, 2004), 144–145, 316–318.

7. Pan Guang, "Shanghai Cooperation Organization in the Context of International Antiterrorist Campaign," *Central Asia and the Caucasus* III (2003), 48–54; see also Starr, *Xinjiang*, 18.

8. "Consortium Formed to Build Central Asia Gas Pipeline," press release, Unocal Corporation (October 27, 1997).

9. S. Frederick Starr, "U.S. Policy in Afghanistan: It's Working," Central Asia–Caucasus Institute Policy Paper (Washington, D.C., 2004), 20.

10. Afzal Khan, "Trade between Afghanistan and Iran Reaches Record Levels," *Eurasia Daily Monitor* I (July 9, 2004), 48.

11. Johannes Linn, "Central Asia Human Development Report," United Nations Development Program (Bratislava, Slovakia, 2005), 192–193.

12. Ambassador Ronald Neumann, quoted in "Ambassador: U.S. Should Double Afghan Aid in Election's Wake. Nation Lacks Resources to Build a Centralized Government, He Says," *Dallas Morning News* (October 28, 2005).

13. U.S. Embassy to Tajikistan, "U.S. Ambassador to Tajikistan Richard Hoagland Joins Presidents Karzai and Rahmonov at Pyanzh River Bridge Groundbreaking Ceremony," press release (Dushanbe, Tajikistan, June 18, 2005), dushanbe.usembassy.gov/pr_06182005.html.

14. Combined Forces Command–Afghanistan Coalition Press Information Center, "Major Road Improvement Projects Near Completion," press release 051111-02 (Kabul, November 11, 2005).

15. Rizwan Zeb, "Gwadar and Chabahar: Competition or Complementarity?" *Central Asia–Caucasus Institute Analyst* (October 22, 2003), www.cacianalyst.org/view_article. php?articleid=1835.

16. Asian Development Bank, "Technical Assistance for the Feasibility Studies of the Turkmenistan-Afghanistan-Pakistan Natural Gas Pipeline Project," draft feasibility report TA 6066-REG (Manila, 2002).

17. "Afghan Gas Pipeline Project Likely in 2006," *News International* (Pakistan) (November 21, 2005).

18. "Gazprom Keen to Take Part in Iran-India Pipeline," *Iran News* (October 1, 2005).

19. Alexander Rahr, "Europe in the New Central Asia," in Trilateral Commission, *The New Central Asia: In Search of Stability*, Task Force Report LIV (Washington, D.C., 2000), 66–86. TRASECA stands for Transport Corridor Europe Caucasus Asia.

20. "Central Asian States Meet in Afghanistan to Revive Trade," Agence France-Presse (November 10, 2005).

21. S. Frederick Starr, "Tiny Kyrgyzstan Follows the West's Rules but Gets No Reward," *Boston Globe* (February 15, 1999).

22. "Central Asian Nations Meet in Afghanistan to Revive Trade," Agence France-Presse (November 9, 2005).

23. For more on ECO, see www.ecosecretariat.org.

24. Niklas Swanstrom, "China and Central Asia: A New Great Game or Traditional Vassal Relations," *Journal of Contemporary China* XIV (2005), 569–584.

25. See World Bank, "Prospects for Regional Development and Economic Cooperation in the Wider Central Asia Region," paper presented at the Kabul Conference on Regional Economic Development (December 4–5, 2005). This paper drew on the expertise of the World Bank's Europe–Central Asia group, Middle East–North Africa group, and South Asia group. This document is one of the most comprehensive studies to date of the prospects for regional and continental trade involving Afghanistan, but it remains to be seen whether, and how, its recommendations will be translated into practice.

26. S. Frederick Starr, "A Strong Japanese Initiative in Central Asia," *Central Asia–Caucasus Institute Analyst* (October 20, 2004), www.cacianalyst.org/view_article.php?articleid=2789.

27. S. Frederick Starr, "Central Asia in the Global Economy," *Foreign Policy* CXLIV (2004), special Asian Development Bank supplement.

28. "Afghan Territory Remains Source of Threat—Foreign Ministry," RIA Novosti (November 8, 2005), en.rian.ru/russia/20051108/42023190.html. The invocation of the CIS Collective Security Treaty in this context was also made explicit by Russia's deputy foreign minister Grigory Karasin.

29. On the Organization of the Islamic Conference, see www.oic-oci.org.

30. "Dhaka Declaration," Thirteenth SAARC Summit (Dhaka, Bangladesh, November 12–13 2005), www.saarc-sec.org/main.php?id=159&t=7.1.

31. Asian Development Bank, "Asian Development Outlook 2005" (Hong Kong, 2005), 20.

32. S. Frederick Starr, "A 'Greater Central Asia Partnership' for Afghanistan and Its Neighbors," Central Asia–Caucasus Institute Occasional Paper (Washington, D.C., 2005); S. Frederick Starr., "A Partnership for Central Asia," *Foreign Affairs*, LXXXIV (2005), 164–178.

33. OSCE, first preparatory conference for the Fourteenth Economic Forum (Dushanbe, Tajikistan, November 7–8, 2005).

34. Irina Zvyagelskaya, "Klyuchi ot schastia ili Bolshaya Tsentralnaya Aziya" (Keys to happiness or the Greater Central Asia), *Rossiia v global'noi politike* IV (2005), 88–94.

35. Starr, "A 'Greater Central Asia Partnership' for Afghanistan."

36. Central Asia–Caucasus Institute, International Conference on Partnership, Trade, and Development in Greater Central Asia (Kabul, Afghanistan, April 1–2, 2006), www.silkroadstudies.org/new/inside/forum/trade_kabul_description.html.

37. Daly and others, "Anatomy of a Crisis: U.S.-Uzbekistan Relations."

8 | Responding to the Opium Dilemma

Cindy Fazey

"The challenge of tackling the opium economy is central to the challenge of building a modern Afghan state and economy."[1] The estimate of opium production in Afghanistan for 2005 was 4,100 metric tons, down 2 percent from 2004.[2] The actual hectares under cultivation (104,000) apparently dropped by 21 percent from 2004, which was itself a record high. A 2006 assessment suggests that there will again be an increase in cultivation but that the amount produced will depend on eradication campaigns.[3] (These figures should be compared to 350 metric tons of opium and 29,000 hectares under cultivation in 1986.)

Some provinces that were previously major producers of opium, such as Nangarhar and Badakhshan, have greatly reduced their production; others, such as Kandahar, Nimroz, Balkh, and Farah, have greatly increased opium production.[4] The Afghan opium problem has become urgent, not only because of the effect illegal heroin has on Western societies but also because of the damage that the trade is doing to Afghanistan itself, which is well on the way to becoming a narcoeconomy, if it is not one already. The figures speak not only for themselves but also for the failure of the U.S., British, and Afghan governments to put a dent in the problem so far. International policy seems to be fracturing into three distinct propositions: eradication of the opium crop with or without aid to the farmers, eradication with conditional aid, or aid and the development of alternative livelihoods followed by eradication. Opium production is, nevertheless, a crucial problem affecting the whole of Afghan society and economy. "The opium economy—including its nexus with insecurity, warlords, state weakness, and poor governance—constitutes a central development problem for the country."[5]

The Afghan government is not short of suggestions for how to deal with this problem, but the majority of its recommendations fall short on the practicalities or have long-term unintended consequences, from entrenchment of opium production to countrywide uprising. This chapter seeks to examine the various suggestions for coping with the opium harvest and the consequent morphine and heroin production, and explores the rationale behind the many panaceas offered, with an analysis of what might happen if those policies were pursued. The main proposals examined are those put forward by the British government, the U.S. government (the State Department and International Narcotics and Law Enforcement Affairs), United Nations Office on Drugs and Crime (UNODC), the Senlis Council, the World Bank, and the Afghan government itself.

In October 2004, under pressure from the countries engaged in the reconstruction of the country, the Afghan government ordered its provincial governors to eradicate opium fields. In the previous year, they set specific targets of reducing poppy production by 70 percent in five years and total eradication in ten years. Many countries, not least the United States and Britain, have found this practice to be foolish because the targets are in reality unachievable and often proposed by politicians who know that they will not be in office when the deadline dates arrive. For example, targets for reduction in domestic drug consumption given by President Clinton during his last term were quietly dropped subsequently, not least because they were unachieved and unachievable. Similar targets in the British drug strategy of 1998 were also dropped by the next version in 2003. It is regrettable that the Afghan government has been pushed in this direction. But how can they be successful and what would be the effect if they were?

In these circumstances, U.S. and British determination to get tough on drugs seems a golden opportunity to turn what has so far been a mere failure into a full-blown disaster by giving large numbers of Afghan tribal leaders and their followers a reason to unite and defend their common interests. To understand why this might happen, one must remember the nature of the country, its location, its history, and its ethnic mix.

The West is reaping the whirlwind for encouraging the sowing of poppy seeds in Afghanistan during that country's war with the Soviet Union. Opium poppies are the best cash crop there is: cultivation is easy, prices are usually excellent, and there is a ready market. When records were broken in 2004, it was mainly because opium production had spread into all thirty-two Afghan provinces for the first time and, according to the UNODC, narcotics became firmly established as the main engine of economic growth.[6]

Many of the suggested policies and strategies target the farmers and are concerned with methods of eradicating the opium crop. Many suggestions are flawed by the failure to ask the fundamental question, *"Cui bono?"* Who benefits from the opium trade? They also often do not pay sufficient attention to the history of the country and to its diverse ethnic, cultural, language, and social heritage.

History

The history of the geographical area that we now call Afghanistan is one of invasion and fighting for more than the past 2,000 years, not just the two decades-plus cited by the World Bank.[7] The reasons for the problems of implementation are found within Afghanistan's long, troubled history and its makeup. Policy initiatives too often founder on the obstacle of the practical problems of implementation. There are a host of examples of policy failures elsewhere because of the failure of effective implementation, sometimes because of the opposition of those who are to accomplish the implementation and sometimes because of the absence of structures, organizations, or simply basic local administrative frameworks. Afghanistan is a nineteenth century colonialist's idea of a nation-state. There is no geographical or cultural rationale to the borders that clump its disparate tribes together and supposedly divide the country from Iran, Turkmenistan, Uzbekistan, Tajikistan, China, and Pakistan. There are nine different ethnic groups or tribes. Five of these straddle the borders, which therefore remain unrecognized locally by the indigenous tribes and are therefore porous.

The country's long mountainous border with Pakistan—known as the Durand Line—was drawn arbitrarily by the British Raj to follow the foothills and was named after Sir Mortimer Durand, the administrator who devised it, in 1893. The purpose was to divide the warrior-like Pathans.

Areas to the southeast of the mountains could be policed; those across the mountains could not. The 1919 Treaty of Rawalpindi accepted the border but did not assuage the aspirations of the Afghans to regain their previous territory. Apart from the Pathans, Afghanistan's borders also include people from the Aimaq, Baluch, Hazara, Kirghiz, Nuristani, Tajik, Turkmen, and Uzbek tribes. Only the Hazara and Nuristani are contained wholly within Afghanistan; all of the other tribes are located partially in Afghanistan and partially on the other side of their local section of the national border. The northern border was settled after decades of the "Great Game" between Britain and Russia, played because of Russia's desire to conquer India; Afghanistan was seen as a route for getting there.[8]

Nevertheless, because of the rigid USSR border, there was very little contact across the northern border with people of the same ethnic origin, which not only hindered the development of trade but also of drug trafficking, in contrast to the Baluchis in the west, who straddled the Iranian border, and the Pathans in the east, who regularly traveled across the Pakistani border.

To add to this natural propensity to disunity, there are three main languages and two branches of Islam. Understandably, there is a long history of intertribal antipathy at best, and war at worst, among these various peoples, allowing the colonial powers, who played the Great Game for control of the region in the days of empire, to divide what they could not rule.[9] These ethnic and regional differences contribute to the lack of what, in many Western countries, would be called a universal civil administration. There is no local administration dedicated to universal values of impartial implementation of central policy initiatives. What is also absent is the class of administrative clerks who can deal with the practicalities of implementation—one of the main reasons for the failure of the initial British policy of paying farmers not to grow opium.

When there was a common interest—such as repelling invaders—there has usually been some degree of cooperation among the different groups. The British were humiliated in the nineteenth century when an entire invading army and its baggage train were massacred, with one man left alive to tell the tale. The Russians in the 1980s were worn down by attrition and a collapse of morale. The latter defeat was aided greatly by CIA advisers and trainers funded by the CIA, and Pakistan's Interservices Intelligence Service, who encouraged the growing of opium poppies and cannabis to create a drug problem among the invaders, in the same way that U.S. troops were undermined by drug abuse in Vietnam in the 1960s and 1970s. Thus, the present massive production of opium in Afghanistan can be laid, to some extent, at the door of the United States, which may explain the adamant U.S. determination to eradicate it.[10] The crucial role of the Taliban, however, in escalating the production of opium, while at the same time stopping the production of cannabis, cannot be underestimated.[11]

The Role of Opium in the Afghan Economy

Opium has become an integral part of the economy. Overall production may involve over 2 million people (around 8 percent of the population). Some opium is grown in large plantations by wholesalers or by traffickers; however, most opium is grown in small patches, representing only about 25 percent of the farmers' cultivated fields but a disproportionate part of their income. It also satisfies the need for wage labor. "There is a large interpenetration of the opium economy with local and central political interests, and many millions of people participate in the profits, in a broad network of protection and pay-offs. Drug profits are clearly financing local warlords and the political elite but also sustain the livelihoods of many quite poor people."[12] The pauperization of rural farmers has also led to an elaborate system of debt for the farmers. They usually have to borrow money to start opium farming and as income against a future crop, while the landless sharecroppers might borrow money to buy food. In one study, 95 percent of the landless, 86 percent of the owner-cultivators, and 72 percent of the landlords had obtained credit in the previous twelve months.[13] The authors noted that "credit is an important part of the livelihood strategies amongst all socio-economic groups" and that "opium is an important source of credit, savings, and investment."[14] In the absence of a formal banking system, opium is also a form of savings. Therefore, a reliable formal banking system urgently needs to be introduced, not at the expense of but running in parallel with the *hawala* system, the informal, untraceable, unregulated Islamic system of money transfer that even the aid agencies must use. Only over time will the hawala system lose its dominance, but it is never likely to be totally supplanted.

Cultivation

It must be remembered that the opium poppy is grown both legally as well as illegally. In order for countries to have any morphine, heroin, codeine, or thebaine, they need to estimate their future requirements for medical and scientific purposes, and the International Narcotics Control Board (INCB) then authorizes the acreage that countries can use to grow the opium poppy each year. Traditional growing countries such as Turkey and India have been the main producers, and indeed the United States insists that 80 percent of imports of opium or its derivatives must come from traditional growers, but after a crackdown on the amount under cultivation in Turkey because of diversion and illegal cultivation, Tasmania began growing the poppy. The world estimates for the year 2000 were a total production of 440 metric tons of morphine equivalent. India was still the largest producer with 115.8 metric tons (but there are often wide fluctuations in India's production). Australia is the second largest producer with 91.6 metric tons. Other producers are France, with 64.2 metric tons; Turkey, with 50.5; and Spain, with 11.9; another 11.1 metric tons are produced by various other countries.[15] Australian production is highly mechanized and controlled, extracting the raw opium and then the natural alkaloids from poppy straw, which comprises the poppy seed capsule and some stalk. The poppy is harvested by a machine like a combine harvester, and the process is extremely efficient. Traditionally, however, the opium from the poppy is harvested by hand, which is extremely labor intensive. Indeed, the whole process of sowing, weeding, and collecting opium from the opium poppy is a labor-intensive exercise. For each hectare the labor intensity is eight or nine times greater than for black cumin and two to three times greater than for wheat. It is estimated that 350 person days are needed to cultivate one hectare of opium poppy (200 of which are for harvesting), whereas black cumin and wheat take 41 and 135 person days, respectively.[16]

The opium poppy, *Papaver somniferum*, is an annual plant, and therefore it must be sown each year. First the poppy fields have to be cleared, then sown. Next they have to be weeded, or else the crop will be overgrown. About fourteen days after the poppies have flowered and the petals have fallen—but before the seed head ripens, grows brown, and the bracts open to scatter the seed—the poppy head is scored. Opium is in fact only produced by the poppy in this short period of ripening; after the twelve to fourteen days, the alkaloids are no longer produced and in fact are broken down. This scoring of the poppy head must be done by hand, usually by young, male itinerant laborers. Some come from the refugee camps in Pakistan, others from different provinces in Afghanistan, but mainly, in Helmand at least, they are also cultivators of opium themselves from local districts.[17] A knife with multiple blades—usually three—is used to score the seed head; thus one pass of the hand produces three incisions. A milky, latex-type liquid oozes out and is left to dry overnight. As it dries, it turns brown, resulting in raw opium. This brown gum is then collected by hand by scraping a small crescent-shaped knife around the poppy head. Many countries have experimented with whether it is worth going through the whole process one or two times more to extract the last little bit of opium, but it has not proven productive given the increased labor involved. In the north and east of the country, women play a very important role in opium poppy cultivation, but this is not so in the south, which tends to be more conservative in its attitudes toward women. Normally they are not paid wages for their work, but because of the shortage of labor in Badakhshan and Takhar provinces, women are being paid for the very first time. Traditionally, in some provinces women are allowed to go through the fields after the harvest to collect what has been missed. Extra work for women, however, involves catering for the itinerant harvesters and, before harvesting, weeding the opium fields.

The opium may be transported in crude form, but more often it travels as "prepared" opium. Prepared opium for smoking or for subsequent delivery to laboratories for processing has the dross and impurities removed by boiling, filtering, and drying. With the gross impurities removed, the opium is more malleable, easier to transport, and can be stored almost indefinitely. The resultant gum is wrapped in plastic or large leaves for onward sale.

To extract morphine from opium, all that is needed is slaked lime (calcium hydroxide) or a fertilizer with a high lime content, a means of heating the opium in water, and, at its crudest, a flannel or sack filter. Morphine is one of the natural alkaloids in opium (together with codeine and thebaine, but over fifty different alkaloids have been identified). The opium is boiled up with slaked lime to produce calcium morphenate—morphine in solution. The morphine is precipitated out by heating again with ammonium chloride, which is filtered to produce morphine base. Sometimes it is further purified with hydrochloric acid or sulphuric acid and heated with activated charcoal, then again filtered to produce morphine hydrochlorate. Alternatively, it can also be washed with acetone to purify the morphine base. This product can then be stored or sent on to heroin laboratories. For the morphine base to become heroin, it needs to be heated to 185 degrees Fahrenheit with an equal amount of acetic anhydride in a two-stage process. The solution is allowed to cool, and then water and chloroform are added, along with activated charcoal and sodium bicarbonate. The heroin can be redissolved and filtered several times before adding ethyl alcohol, ether, and concentrated hydrochloric acid. Many of the chemicals can be substituted, and which particular ones are used depends on the country or even the region.

The advantage of at least getting to the morphine base stage is that this product weighs about 10 percent as much as the raw opium. With each step toward achieving a pure white heroin powder, the chemist must be more skilled and more chemicals are needed; but stopping at the first, prepared stage means that the drug is considerably less bulky, can be stored more easily, and does not entail sophisticated chemical processes.

Laboratories for processing morphine base into heroin existed as far back as the Russian occupation. It was realized that the troops needed heroin, not opium or morphine base. Chemists were recruited and heroin was produced. There has been, however, a greater move to process the morphine base inside Afghanistan rather than in neighboring countries such as Pakistan. The seizures in neighboring countries indicate a larger number of laboratories operating in Afghanistan and access to acetic anhydride in particular.

Opium is collected by itinerant farm gate buyers, who may have bought forward of the crop on commission. These buyers sell to shop owners in the regional opium bazaars, who in turn may sell to the laboratories, wholesale traders, or foreign traffickers. There are also a number of large-scale traders who operate throughout the year and organize the traffic of the drugs to the big bazaars, such as Landi Kotal in Pakistan, or to major traffickers.

Trafficking

The trafficking of opium, morphine base, and heroin from Afghanistan has been devastating for many of its neighbors. Afghanistan shares borders with Pakistan, Tajikistan, Iran, China, Turkmenistan, and Uzbekistan, and opiates cross all these borders. Virtually every neighboring country has seized opiates, and all have problems with use by the local population as well as the spread of drug-related HIV. Iran is a major transit country and claims to have 2 million addicts. The drug passes through Turkey, the Balkan route, and into Europe. From Turkmenistan the route goes through Iran or across the Caspian Sea to Azerbaijan and on to Georgia, then across the Black Sea. Chechnya, North Ossetia, and Ingushetia have also turned up as trafficking countries. Kazakhstan has borders with Uzbekistan and Kyrgyzstan to the south, and has suffered considerably from its role as a major transshipment country, en route to Russia.[18] There do not appear to be cartels but rather a myriad of organizations bound together by family ties and ethnicity. The Afghans themselves do not appear to be major traffickers, just major traders. In Europe the main traffickers are Turkish people and Kurds, the two often in bitter conflict; Albanians, when the route is through Kosovo; and Romanians, for a more northerly route. Even going back to the early 1970s, the Romanians were identified as major players in trafficking, as were the Turks, who were also major producers in the 1950s.[19] It is said that they still control the British heroin trade.

There are many countries, usually those adjacent to Afghanistan, that are both transit countries and also processing countries. The opium flows out of Afghanistan in all directions, each route resembling a river delta, and the routes change and multiply. The main routes, however, are through Pakistan and Iran.

Cui Bono? Who Benefits?

As the UNODC pointed out, farmers are easy targets for crop eradication, but they receive less than 30 percent of the total amount of the drug income.[20] As with all farming, it is the distributors, the wholesalers, and the retailers who make the money, a factor that must not be overlooked. The local warlords and commanders may derive their entire income from the drug trade and use it to support a militia that is armed from the profits. The farm gate value of this illegal 2005 crop was comparatively tiny at $560 million. But its export value was a whopping $2.7 billion, or 35 percent of Afghanistan's gross domestic product. The traffickers' income was a staggering $2.14 billion.

Part of this increasing efficiency includes adding as much value to the product as possible before it leaves for onward sale in foreign markets. So where Afghanistan once exported opium base for conversion elsewhere to heroin, it now does the processing itself. This processing in turn reduces the volume of the contraband as it is shipped out of the country, making it much easier to conceal as well as keeping more profit at home.

The 2005 figures were lower than those for 2004, but the harvest for 2006 increased again, so that opium's share of Afghanistan's GDP rose. Rather than representing a downward trend from the ominous increase in opium production since 2002, the 2005 figures may have been anomalous. The flow of illicit heroin continued almost unabated, and Afghan heroin and opium continue to be sold cheaply in most European cities.

These figures suggest the development of an increasingly efficient illicit drugs industry in Afghanistan, with ever stronger wholesale and distribution networks that can squeeze their growers and organize their exports on a massive, indeed, global scale. Those in charge could probably write a perfect case study for the training department of an international supermarketeer.

It is almost certainly impossible to organize an industry on this scale without connivance—or more probably wholehearted participation—within the top strata of Afghanistan's government and society. The government is not necessarily corrupt, but large sections of Afghanistan's ruling groups and their interlocking social and political networks must be. With no effective centralized control of the country, the Afghan government may promise its Western allies one thing, but the acid test is how effectively these promises are met. The record so far is of failure.

There are also vested interests beyond Afghanistan's borders. Many of its immediate neighbors either process opium or benefit from the trafficking or both, and might even be tempted to grow it themselves or support farmers against attempted eradication moves.

Proposals for Solving the Opium Problem

Several countries and international bodies are attempting to reduce the growth of opium poppies in Afghanistan.

Britain and the Price of Opium

Afghan farmers produced 3,400 metric tons of opium in 2002, when Britain offered Afghan farmers the princely sum of $500 an acre not to grow the poppies.[21] How effective this strategy was can be seen from the UN's Afghan opium surveys for 2003, when production went up to 3,600 tons and increased again to 4,200 tons in 2004.

Even though bad weather in 2004 reduced average yields per acre by 28 percent, there was still a record harvest of 4,200 metric tons, compared with 3,600 metric tons in 2003. In "normal" weather the figure would have been nearly 6,000 metric tons. Despite the relatively poor growing conditions, gross income per hectare for opium was still $4,600—well down from the $12,700 per hectare of 2003. But accepting the British offer of payment not to grow poppies would have produced only $1,235 for each hectare, though this income could have been supplemented by substituting wheat at $390 a hectare.

Small wonder then that these farmer incentives do not work. There is, in effect, no civil society and no banking or administrative infrastructure to deliver the money other than through the warlords, who would use it for their own purposes—such as buying more arms. It is difficult to understand why the British government embarked on such a policy. Clearly they had no knowledge or understanding of previous forays in this field, such as the United Nations Development Fund's efforts in the early 1970s in the Hindu Kush. The net result was an increase in the total opium production because farmers grew more in order to be paid not to grow it. Britain spent $70 million, but to little or no effect. Indeed, in some ways the policy might have been counterproductive. There were a large number of farmers who were promised money for not growing opium, did not grow it, but got nothing in return. "At the level of farmers and rural communities, the offer of compensation raised again the specter of perverse incentives to neighboring communities, but in reality the main damage was caused by the failure to honor offers of compensation, which pauperized smaller farmers (especially small farmers locked into opium denominated debt) and harmed the weak credibility both of the program and of the government that backed it."[22] Future promises may be viewed in a somewhat cynical light.

Britain has sought to target laboratories. The laboratories, however, can be very small and even mobile (like those used in Laos), and are more difficult to find. Also, heroin processing need not be a continuous process. Each laboratory can be easily concealed and used for only two weeks every six months (which is how the Corsicans of the French Connection operated to avoid capture). Britain also established the Afghan Narcotics Special Forces in 2004, under the control of the British Special Forces, the Special Air Service, and Special Boat Service which claim to have destroyed eighty laboratories and seized some seventy-five tons of opiates. It remains to be seen whether this rate of destruction will continue or whether the processing and markets will go underground. The fact that these forces also say that two opium bazaars were also disrupted testifies to the impunity with which bazaars operate and might indicate that in the future they will be more clandestine in their operations. One effect of this approach is to operate like the customs service and, in effect, impose a tax on the traffickers. It does not significantly affect the overall trade, but it makes them pay a price.

Other parts of the policy will probably include tighter controls to interdict the processing chemicals that the laboratories need, as well as a crackdown on money laundering to try to reduce profits. This scheme is made more difficult because the informal hawala system is Afghanistan's primary banking system.

Crop substitution programs will struggle on but, as has been shown, wheat produces less income than poppies. High-value crops such as apricots, for which Afghanistan was once famous, may look attractive, but it takes seven years to grow a fruit-bearing apricot tree capable of replacing one of those chopped down previously in the switch to opium cultivation or devastated during the Russian occupation.

The leaders of the growing opium industry and the farmers who supply them are hardly going to stand by and watch their lucrative businesses destroyed. They will certainly move their laboratories underground or onto difficult terrain where they can inflict casualties on Western troops, as well as convert more laboratories into smaller, mobile units, if they have not done so already. The stakes are so high that traffickers, warlords, tribal chiefs, and farmers would almost certainly fight to protect their incomes and common interests. Going on past British and Soviet experience, they would probably win, not least because of the political value to them of long-term attritional military stalemate and a steady drip of Western casualties.

According to Washington,

Afghans produce opium and heroin because there is an unquenchable demand for them in Europe, which gets 80–90 percent of its heroin from Afghanistan. It is pointless and cynical to beat up on Afghan farmers, for even if they cease production, farmers in some other backward land will step in to satisfy the demand. . . . Europe . . . does not acknowledge its culpability in the rise of Afghan drug production. . . . Serious progress against drug production in Afghanistan will begin only when the European Union admits that the problem traces directly to its own citizens' demand for heroin and that this places on Europe the obligation to provide the kind of massive help to the Afghans that the U.S. has extended to Colombia.[23]

The argument is that the United States accepts its responsibility for cocaine production in Colombia and therefore invests heavily in the eradication of coca production in that country because the United States is the major consumer. This argument is very naïve and lacks an understanding of history and opium poppy and coca production. The South Americans for many years argued that they should not be blamed for the coca production so long as the Americans were consuming cocaine. Eventually it was accepted that the responsibility was shared. One conclusion that could be drawn is that money should be invested in demand reduction and the treatment of heroin addicts rather than vainly trying to eradicate production.

The U.S. Approach

With the opium trade funding the buying of arms, small wonder that the United States is anxious to take a more belligerent tack. Since most of the Afghan opium goes to the ex-Soviet republics and Western Europe, the problem had not been of immediate concern to the United States, but it appears to be seen more and more as intertwined with arms and terrorism.

The United States was also getting rather annoyed with Britain for not being effective in ridding the country of opium. It appointed the former head of Drug Enforcement Administration operations to the U.S. embassy in Kabul, set up a parallel counterdrug command structure, and established the U.S.-controlled Central Poppy Eradication Force. This force was deployed in those provinces where the local governors did not do enough to enforce the ban.[24] As a consequence Britain established the Central Eradication Planning Cell in an attempt to influence where the Central Poppy Eradication Force went and to ensure that alternative incomes were available to the farmers affected.

It is possible to try to destroy poppy crops drastically with fungus or to spray them with herbicides. Regarding the former, research suggests that the opium fungus, *Pleospora papaveracea*, may well be effective but would also cause widespread damage to other crops.[25] The latter approach would be risky because of the potential for collateral damage: in spraying herbicides, the U.S. forces would want to operate from the safest height possible to avoid antiaircraft fire, which would lead to inaccuracy and the spread of the chemicals to nontarget vegetation, as has happened in Colombia.

It has been alleged that the United States did in fact try herbicide spraying in the first week of November 2004, an allegation that the U.S. government has always denied. Farmers from two districts of eastern Nangarhar province complained to the Afghan Islamic Press, and the Afghan Transitional Government sent a delegation to investigate. The minister of health confirmed that there had been aerial spraying. The chemical composition of the spray was not identified, but it was not glyphosate, the chemical used in Colombia. It caused serious damage to all other crops and also skin ailments and breathing problems. Both the United States and Britain denied involvement.[26]

Yet, irrespective of the facts and the possibly dire consequences, governments remain attracted to eradication. Democratically elected leaders usually need their successes in nothing longer than four-year cycles. Eradication offers political visibility and TV images of action, even though it has failed to influence global markets and often created disaster for those least able to defend themselves—the farmers.

United Nations Office on Drugs and Crime

The UNODC argues that drugs and poverty must be fought simultaneously. "Food security and income generation programmes must remain in place, to support both the farmers' decisions not to plant opium, and enforcement measures to eradicate the opium that is planted against the law . . . eradicated fields leave families in economic distress, trigger humanitarian disaster, and increase the temptation to join the insurgency."[27] It can be argued that this pattern is repeating what has happened in Colombia, where crop spraying has eradicated both coca plants and food plants, leading to the flight of peasant farmers to the slums of the cities. This kind of depopulation has already occurred in the Dir Valley in Pakistan, where opium growing was eventually eradicated, and alternative development did not prove to be feasible. To where will the 2.5 million Afghans estimated to be engaged in the opium industry migrate?

The extent of corruption associated with the narcodollar is acknowledged, but the goals set by the UNODC seem to be more expressions of aspiration rather than realistic and achievable ends. The six goals put forward are

—removal of corrupt governors where opium cultivation is not declining;

—removal of all government administration officials found to be involved or to benefit from the drug industry;

—commitment by members of the Afghan Parliament to abstain from direct or indirect involvement in the drug industry and to resign if found out;

—disarmament and reintegration of militias with zero tolerance for warlord involvement in refining and trafficking of drugs;

—extradition of major drug traffickers; and

—commitment from farming communities to refrain from drug cultivation as a qualifying condition to obtain future development assistance.[28]

How these goals will be implemented is beyond anyone's experience. Who will remove the governors—and on what evidence—and who will replace them? Who can guarantee that the new governors will not be as corrupt, if not more, than their predecessors? What will happen if after five years and five new governors, opium production continues unabated? Who is to extradite the major drugs traffickers and to where?

How will the fourth goal be realized? The militias are hardly likely to disarm without some incentive and guaranteed security for themselves and their families against those groups not yet disarmed. Nor are the warlords likely to give up a very lucrative trade. The warlords and their militias will need to be incorporated into the state, probably via some financial incentives. They need to be brought into the tent, as is the case with those people who are termed guerrilla leaders by their opponents and freedom fighters by their supporters. Unless the part that opium plays in the lives of all the people involved is understood (a role that will not only vary but also change according to location and social and cultural context), then it is unlikely that a successful strategy can be outlined.

The last goal on the list is one that has already conspicuously failed because compensation for not growing opium only reached one tenth of the farmers who eradicated crops, leaving most impoverished and in debt.[29] Farmers need development assistance before eradication, not after it.

Senlis Council

Another suggestion for "solving the opium problem" has been put forward by the Senlis Council.[30] In its 2005 study, the Council asserted that "there is a significant global shortage of opium based medicines such as morphine and codeine." It suggests that there is a pain relief crisis arising from HIV/AIDS and cancer cases, claiming that "high prices and stringent and inappropriate market regulation mean that too many people are dying in pain, particularly in the developing world." This study goes on to say that "an insufficient opium supply for medicine production . . . has led to a global pain crisis."[31]

While rejecting eradication and noting that the concept of alternative livelihoods is the right approach but would take too long before positive outcomes could be achieved, the Senlis Council suggests that a license to export opium would be a short-term solution. The council also points to Turkey and India as examples of illicit opium-producing countries that were turned into licit producers with outside aid. However, these cases bear no resemblance to that of Afghanistan.

The case of Turkey is an interesting one. President Nixon's "war on drugs" actually began against the Mexicans with Operation Intercept. Instead of stopping the drug trade, however, it caused a diplomatic disaster and was quietly dropped. Attention was then drawn to Turkey, which was not even the largest producer of illegal opium, accounting for less than 8 percent of world supply; however, it was, politically, a more manageable target than Mexico. It was a long way away from Washington and the U.S. media. The country was a NATO ally and needed U.S. arms, so pressure could be applied to stop the illicit opium trade. Turkey initially resisted, but a coup d'état in 1971 by the military determined that arms and aid mattered more than the opium farmers.

The farmers received $35 million in compensation, and Nixon got his decisive victory against the heroin trade. Two important points to note are that the army was in control of the country and that the country covered 300,000 square miles with a population of 58 million as opposed to Afghanistan's 250,000 square miles with a population of only 17 million. A more densely populated country is usually more easily surveilled and controlled.

Unfortunately, the Senlis group's whole edifice of suggested policies, which runs to 650 pages, is predicated on a false assumption. There is no global shortage of opiate-based medicines, as a reading of the reports of the International Narcotics Control Board demonstrates. Admittedly, it could be said that the board itself appeared to foster this illusion, if its reports of 1994 and 1999 are read in a cursory manner.[32]

The Senlis assumption is that there is a shortage of production, but the INCB argued that there was, in effect, a shortage of demand. At one time the INCB berated Turkey for not fulfilling its duty to produce more opium as one of the traditional suppliers but at the same time denied the Australians any chance of expanding their areas under licensed cultivation.

Indeed, in its 2004 report, the INCB noted that there was an overproduction both of morphine and thebaine and that there were increasing stocks. "Stocks of both types of opiate raw materials reached a record high at the end of 2003. Consequently, those stocks continue to be more than sufficient to cover the global demand for opiate raw materials for one year ... most governments have followed its advice and maintained the area to be cultivated with opium poppy well below the level of 2002 or 2003."[33] In 2003 the total legal production of morphine was 487 metric tons and that of thebaine, 80 metric tons. Contrast these figures with Afghanistan's production of 4,100 metric tons of opium, which represents 410 metric tons of morphine.

In the 1994 report, the INCB noted that only 20 percent of the twelve metric tons of morphine used worldwide to treat severe pain was used in the developing countries.[34] Countries, the INCB pointed out, had a duty to make sure that there was an "availability of an adequate amount of drugs for medical and scientific use." The same report noted that in some countries there was an "inadequacy of the licit distribution systems for pharmaceuticals." A 2001 report noted that "most developing countries lack the resources and expertise required for determining medical needs and adjusting supply to meet those needs."[35]

The INCB again took up the issue of "freedom from pain and suffering." In a joint board and WHO study, it was concluded that "while efforts to prevent oversupply should be maintained, more emphasis should be put on facilitating the supply of licit drugs to underdeveloped areas. . . . Outdated restrictive regulations and, more frequently, uninformed interpretations of otherwise correct regulations, misguided fears, and ingrained prejudices about using opioids for medical purposes continue to prevail."[36] Nevertheless, by the following year, the INCB was complaining of the overconsumption of internationally controlled drugs.[37]

The INCB seems to be saying that more painkilling drugs are needed but, for the reasons that it sets out, are not being used or prescribed. To change this culture will take years. Lack of a regulatory framework or even a secure distribution network would inevitably lead to diversion onto an illicit market. In so many medical schools, the use of any opiate is often regarded as a last resort—and by many not worth the hassle if some authority should think that they made a mistake. Even in Western countries, the fear of disciplinary procedures against doctors who prescribe morphine may be greater than the perception of the patients' need for it.

If opiates were made more easily available to many countries in Africa, the results could be disastrous. Outside of South Africa, Mauritius, and Namibia, there is no substantial heroin problem in Africa. The availability of opiates would add yet another burden to an overburdened continent. As the INCB notes, "New patterns of drug abuse can easily develop as a result of excessive availability and inadequate regulatory controls."[38]

It must also be understood that many African countries simply have higher priorities in health and medicines than buying cheap morphine. Buying antiretroviral medicines to treat HIV/AIDS as well as drugs to prevent and treat malaria are a much higher priority.

In Central Asia and Eastern Europe, the Senlis Council argued that the increasing prevalence of HIV/AIDS and cancer cases means that "the high prices charged for these medicines combined with stringent and inappropriate market regulations mean that too many people are needlessly dying in pain."[39] So here it is not the shortage of supply but the cost of it. The obvious answer is for those regions to grow and process their own drugs. Russia certainly has the knowledge and expertise if it wanted to do so.

The Senlis Council recommended that poppies with high thebaine content be developed. The Australians have already done so and supply the limited market, predominantly in Japan.

Senlis also suggested that the licensing of poppy growing could be limited to medicinal needs. This plan could be enacted if a control mechanism were put into place, but the amount of additional land under poppy cultivation would be a fraction of that already used for growing opium poppies. In fact, production in Afghanistan is at a level that could almost provide the world's licit requirement for morphine. What would happen to the Tasmanian, Turkish, and Indian farmers who have the legal right to grow now? Are they to be told that they must switch to another crop? How quickly could this be done? Alternatively, is the world morphine market going to double in one or two years? How should it be decided how much opium is needed? Who will grow it and who will not?

If paying farmers not to grow opium has not halted cultivation, then paying them to grow it certainly will result in even more cultivation. There will be an explosion in the amount of poppy cultivation that already takes place in every province of Afghanistan. Who will choose who can grow and who not, or what proportion of the crop will be allowed in the future? Inevitably, a parallel illicit market will spring up, supplied by those not incorporated into the licit market and encouraged by the warlords and traffickers who make most of the profits today.

How would licensing be policed? The UNODC surveyors would not be allowed in if eradication would be the result. The population would not cooperate. Therefore, satellite imaging alone would have to be used. Yet experience shows that a combination of both satellite surveillance and human observation is needed in order to achieve accuracy.

What about the warlords and traffickers? They would all lose income. But would they just sit down and accept it? It is not just the farmers who are dependent on the heroin trade. As noted earlier, the economics of the trade means that farmers receive less than 30 percent of the total value. This proposal does not take into account that it is not the farmers who make the profit but the wholesalers and traffickers.

The Senlis Council also suggested growing different types of poppies that do not contain morphine, such as *Papaver orientale* (formerly *bracteatum*). This option was researched in the 1960s, but the resultant product was found to contain the Bentley compounds, 1,000 times more powerful than morphine.

Whether the opium is distributed, causing new problems in countries with little or no opium problems at present, or whether it is destroyed, increasing the amount of licensed poppy grown would mean the final destruction of the Afghan economy and a never-ending burden on the donors to keep paying for the drug. The plan would destroy the Afghan economy because growing opium poppies would be the most lucrative crop, and food would have to be imported. Most of the economy would not be taxed, and thus the government would not have the revenue to develop infrastructure and services for the country.

The World Bank

There are two excellent World Bank papers written by Christopher Ward and William Byrd that examine the Afghan government's strategy in detail and assess all the alternatives that have been suggested.[40] They also emphasize the importance of alternative livelihoods—alternative, that is, to producing opium poppies. "A livelihood comprises all the capabilities, assets (including both material and social resources) and activities required for a means of living. It is more than just a job. The term alternative livelihoods was coined to describe the broader, sustainable approach to improving people's livelihoods, and to distinguish this approach from the failures of previous *alternative development* projects in drugs-producing countries."[41] The time scale of which they write is much longer than that used by other authors, for they point out that it took thirty years in Thailand and twenty years in Pakistan to eliminate poppy cultivation. (Others would argue that Burma [Myanmar] and Laos took over poppy cultivation from Thailand, and that in the Dir Valley in Pakistan, depopulation was the result, with opium growing again resurgent.) Ward and Byrd also argue strongly against conditional development, which closely links developmental assistance to the eradication of the opium poppy. They assert that the interdiction of opium processing and trafficking should go hand in hand with alternative livelihoods programs.

They look in detail at four options for implementing the counternarcotics strategy: an interdiction-led approach, an eradication approach, an alternative livelihoods-led approach, and alternative livelihoods programs accompanied by law enforcement. Looking at the rationale, direct effect, economic and incentive impacts, implementation issues, and their relative strengths and weaknesses, these researchers conclude that the last option holds out the most hope for a solution. They add several caveats, notably that donors would have to commit to the project for many years and that there must to be agreement on sequencing, with monitoring and evaluation.

It is argued that "the response to the drug economy must occur within a broader strategic framework of state building, improving security, and curbing warlords."[42] They also criticize the failure to control the financial flows and particularly the lack of control over the hawala system. Clearly there is a need to establish a government-controlled banking system that works and is trusted by the users. There are, however, considerable challenges to developing it. A new style of banking must be developed that has the advantages of the hawala system but includes transparency regarding the transfer of funds.

The Afghan Government

In 2002 the Counter Narcotics Directorate (CND) was created by the Afghan government to coordinate Afghanistan's counternarcotics struggle. The national strategy, which has received almost universal approval, is based on eight pillars: building institutions, public awareness and information campaigns, alternative livelihoods, interdiction and law enforcement, criminal justice, eradication, demand reduction and the treatment of addicts, and regional cooperation. The strategy starts with interdiction and alternative livelihoods. This policy is aimed at stopping the traffickers and at the same time providing alternative sources of income, but it also includes a whole package of support in terms of health, education, and organizational and administrative structure. Eradication is to follow. The government has also laid out action plans for implementing the strategy. A 2006 strategy document also includes the establishment of a banking system and the development of rural credit and microfinance institutions.[43] Later in 2006, President Karzai said that Afghanistan, despite the donors, was going to abandon eradication.[44]

Implementation is always one of the most critical areas of strategy and policy formation. A brilliant strategy that is bungled in its implementation is of no use, and it will often be assumed that it was the strategy that failed rather than the way in which it was executed. The CND is responsible for counternarcotics strategy development and coordination. It is not responsible for the implementation, which is handled by the relevant ministries and agencies. Herein lies a problem. Each ministry or agency is likely to demand the money that it feels should be allocated for the implementation of its part of the strategy. Many will then either redistribute the money to other projects or reinterpret the strategy according to their own beliefs about what is effective.

There is always a danger that even with the best will and good faith, different ministries and agencies will feel that they know their own area best and know what should be done. They may not set out deliberately to derail a strategy, but by not paying attention to their role in the whole scheme, they may nevertheless do so. Thus can a good strategy be undermined. The strategy will only be accepted by each of the implementing agencies if each is not only held accountable but also if the philosophy of the strategy is constantly reinforced by frequent joint meetings at a high level. Accountability is the key watchword. The whole of the timing and sequencing of the strategy needs to be controlled by the CND; otherwise the strategy could be sent off course. A strengthened role for the CND, with more power and authority, seems crucial for the strategy's success. There is always an additional danger that donors will cherry-pick the part of the strategy where they either have expertise or an ideological commitment. It is vitally important that the Afghans themselves retain control of the program, including its implementation, in an order and at a speed that they themselves deem reasonable.

Many donors object to Afghan control out of fear of corruption—within the government and among the governors in the country—and fear of failure. The Afghans themselves, however, are best placed to understand who is corrupt and who is not, who are the traffickers and who are not. In addition, the government insists that drug control objectives must be mainstreamed into all rural development programs. It might be a better long-term policy to grant Afghans the political maturity and knowledge to deal with this issue in their own way. They are fully cognizant of their problem. "In the absence of significant development and rule of law, no other economic activity provides competitive returns. The cash incomes produced by drug trafficking finance bribes that have corrupted significant portions of the administration."[45] If a few years down the line there has been negligible or no improvement, then the donors would be justified in insisting on a more proactive role, but encouragement rather than control would seem to be a more effective strategy.

Another problem of implementation is the power of the local warlords, who could undermine all of the central government's initiatives. Confronting them may not be the best policy in every case but rather incorporating them into the antidrug effort through economic support in return for aid in implementing the strategy. The idea of "cui bono" must not be forgotten.

To address this problem, in 2003 the government established the Counter Narcotics Police of Afghanistan. It has three sections: intelligence, investigation, and interdiction. This force has been supported by many donors, and its strength will be increased to 500 officers. Collusion between local police and the traffickers has limited the former's effectiveness. Perhaps in response to this problem, the Afghan Special Narcotics Force was created in January 2004. It is a rapid intervention force equipped with helicopters and able to make commando-style raids. This force will need to limit the profits of the traffickers and warlords if it is to have an impact, so it must be large enough to be effective but not so large or quickly developed that it is infiltrated by people reporting to the warlords. If members of this force are effective, they will become targets for the warlords and are likely to be in personal danger.

Can Eradication Ever Work?

Perhaps instead of digging ourselves into ever deeper holes, we should ask ourselves whether the principle of trying to stem the global problem of illicit drugs by attempting to eradicate supplies is the right one to follow in the first place. Some have argued that the achievement of the Taliban in enforcing a short production ban in 2000–2001 proves that the policy can be made to work.

But this argument ignores some uncomfortable realities. The Taliban, which had used drug profits to fund its war and build and sustain its power, already had a large stockpile of opium and heroin from previous overproduction. When the ban was in force, worldwide prices did not drop, as they should have done had the ban been effective in the marketplace. Indeed, some argue that the ban served the purpose of keeping prices stable, for they would have dropped had it not taken place.

The other uncomfortable reality is that such bans can only be enforced by draconian means. With the Taliban these measures included summary executions, severe violations of human rights, and starvation among poor farming families. The Taliban's purpose was hardly philanthropic; their aim was to use the ban to obtain Western recognition of their regime.

Supply eradication does not work. Where illicit drugs are concerned, history shows that shutting down one area of production simply displaces the volume elsewhere. This process is generated by market forces: where there is demand, supplies will emerge to meet it.

On a smaller scale, possibly successful attempts to eradicate opium production in the Dir Valley of the Northwest Frontier province of Pakistan commenced in 1985. For the next fifteen years, $35 million was spent, mainly in supply reduction. Between 1994 and 2002, a further $14 million went into the project. With no viable alternative crop, the valley was de-populated. Of the alternative crops of wheat, onions, and tomatoes, only wheat can be said to be marginally viable. The others reach the market so late because the territory is at such altitude that the crops mature too late to compete at anything but uneconomic prices. But this strategy represents one valley, not a country, and there are signs today that opium culti-vation is gradually resuming in Pakistan's remote tribal areas.

Another example occurred in 1991–1992 in Lebanon, when the Syrian army destroyed all opium and cannabis crops in the Bekaa Valley as part of a deal between then U.S. Secretary of State James Baker and Syrian Presi-dent Hafez al-Assad. The valley, seventy-five miles long and eight miles wide, was previously planted with 12,500 acres of opium poppies and 40,000 acres of cannabis to fund Hezbollah Islamic fundamentalists. The annual yield was about 50 tons of raw opium and 1,000 tons of hashish.[46]

The fields went unpoliced throughout Lebanon's civil war, but the Syr-ian army moved in after the Gulf War, when Baker suggested to Assad that he could improve relations with the United States and Europe by tackling Lebanon's role in supplying a significant part of the world's illegal drugs market. About 80 percent of the crops were eradicated in 1991 and the rest in 1992. As a result, the price of raw opium in Beirut rose from $70 a ton in 1990 to more than $500 a ton in 1992, and there was a shortage of cannabis on the illegal British market for several months. However, other producers soon filled the gaps in supply. It should be noted that the area where drug production was eliminated was small, easily policed, and under army control. In the end the world supply bounced back, just as it did in the 1970s when the Turkish suppression of production resulted in a rapid expansion of opium production in Laos, Vietnam, Burma, and Thailand.

Britain has taken the lead in NATO operations. Apart from consolidat-ing stability in Afghanistan, a key objective will be that of striking at the country's drug industry. The United States and Britain have decided to get tough on Afghan opium, the principal source of illegal heroin in Europe and the world's largest illicit supply. Britain is using special forces to target the secret, probably mobile laboratories where opium is converted into heroin. At the same time, Britain is offering incentives to farmers in the hope that they will voluntarily grow something else, such as the apricots and wheat that allowed the Afghanistan of old, before the Soviet invasion of 1979, to flourish. The preferred U.S. solution is somewhat less subtle: spray the fields with herbicide and hang the collateral damage.

It seems that the United States and Britain are trying to influence policy in totally different directions. The United States clearly favors eradication and believes that concern over the potential starvation of farmers and their families is totally misplaced. Establishment of the Central Poppy Eradication Force testifies to the U.S. commitment to this strategy; but unless the force can be controlled as to when and where it eradicates crops, the whole enterprise will fall apart. Instead of leaving different agencies and organizations to pursue their own agendas, it seems that a firm central control is needed to determine what actions are taken when and where. From all the evidence put forward by many analysts, there seems to be a consensus that a mainstreamed alternative livelihoods program needs to be the priority in conjunction with vigorous law enforcement. There is also an urgent need to set up a government-controlled banking system so that the farmers are not in debt to local opium traders and warlords. The whole strategy should be carefully evaluated as it is implemented so that any problems can be uncovered early, discussed, and addressed.

Little consideration seems to have been given to the "what if" scenario. In the Afghanistan case, what if the efforts at eradication were successful? There are two answers: opium production will move to another country or a newer class of opioids called fentanyl analogs will be manufactured. These entirely synthetic drugs are a thousand times more potent than heroin.

Another Afghanistan "what if" concerns the effects of a general uprising against the "invaders" to defend the drug trade. This outcome would hardly augur well for the proposed gas and oil pipelines from the Caspian Sea across Afghanistan, avoiding a route through Russia. Is this the new Great Game, with the United States taking over the role of the United Kingdom?[47] After all, it is one reason, perhaps even *the* reason, why the United States wants stability in Afghanistan.[48]

The harder course is to try to reduce demand for illicit drugs in the markets fed by the suppliers. This path is long term and difficult. It requires sustained spending on promoting the prevention of drug abuse that should rely on truthful education campaigns rather than patently false propaganda on the dangers of drugs, which young people ignore because it conflicts with their own experiences. Such campaigns must be tied to the general promotion of healthy lifestyles among young people in particular. At the same time, there has to be a policy to reduce the harm caused to society by drugs, for example, by controlling vectors for HIV/AIDS such as dirty users' needles, which would also reduce the harm drug users do to themselves. There has to be a realistic budget for treatment and rehabilitation, not only to help users to break their habits but also to try to break the link between drugs and crime. Putting addicts on long waiting lists for treatment, as happens now in many countries because of a shortage of places, is counterproductive. If governments want to be really radical, they would revert to what used to be British policy in the 1950s and 1960s and allow more doctors to prescribe drugs to addicts to help them stabilize their lives so that, ultimately, most of them would stop fueling demand.

Forcing such measures through would require great political bravery—certainly much more than giving orders for substantial military escalation of the fight against the illegal narcotics trade that clearly permeates the life and economy of Afghanistan.

Notes

1. Christopher Ward and William Byrd, "Afghanistan's Opium Drug Economy," World Bank Report SASPR-5 (Washington, D.C., 2004).

2. United Nations Office on Drugs and Crime (UNODC), *The Opium Situation in Afghanistan* (Vienna, 2005).

3. UNODC, *Afghanistan Opium Rapid Assessment Survey* (Vienna, 2006).

4. UNODC, *Afghanistan Opium Survey 2005* (Vienna, 2005).

5. William Byrd and Christopher Ward, "Drugs and Development in Afghanistan" (Washington, D.C., 2004), i.

6. UNODC, *Afghanistan Opium Survey 2004* (Vienna, 2004).

7. John C. Griffiths, *Afghanistan: A History of Conflict* (London, 2001); Byrd and Ward, "Drugs and Development in Afghanistan," 1.

8. Peter Hopkirk, *The Great Game: On Secret Service in High Asia* (Oxford, 1990).

9. Ibid.

10. Steve Coll, *Ghost Wars: The Secret History of the CIA, Afghanistan, and Bin Laden, from the Soviet Invasion to September 10, 2001* (New York, 2004); John K. Cooley, *Unholy Wars: Afghanistan, America and International Terrorism* (London, 1999).

11. Ahmed Rashid, *Taliban: Militant Islam, Oil and Fundamentalism in Central Asia* (New Haven, 2001).

12. Ward and Byrd, "Afghanistan's Opium Drug Economy," 3.

13. In 2004 the United Nations International Drug Control Program (UNDCP) changed its name to the United Nations Office on Drugs and Crime. See UNODC, *Strategic Study no. 3. The Role of Opium as a Source of Informal Credit* (Vienna, 1999).

14. Ibid., 3.

15. International Narcotics Control Board (INCB), *Report of the International Narcotics Board for 1999* (New York, 2000), 22.

16. UNODC, *Strategic Study no. 4. Access to Labour: The Role of Opium in the Livelihood Strategies of Itinerant Harvesters Working in Helmand Province, Afghanistan* (Vienna, 1999).

17. Ibid.

18. Stephane Allix, *La petite cuillère de Schéhérazade* (Paris, 1998).

19. Newsday staff, *The Heroin Trail* (New York, 1974).

20. UNODC, *Afghanistan Opium Survey 2005*, 1.

21. UNODC, *The Opium Economy in Afghanistan: An International Problem* (Vienna, 2003).

22. Ward and Byrd, "Afghanistan's Opium Drug Economy," 50.

23. S. Frederick Starr, "U.S. Policy in Afghanistan: It's Working," Central Asia–Caucasus Institute Policy Paper (Washington, D.C., 2004), 23–24.

24. Transnational Institute, "Downward Spiral. Banning Opium in Afghanistan and Burma," Drugs and Conflict Debate Paper no. 12 (Amsterdam, 2005).

25. This research was started by the Russians, then taken over with British funding in Uzbekistan at the Institute of Genetics and Experimental Biology and at Bristol University (Britain).

26. "Afghan Poppy Farmers Say Mystery Spraying Killed Crops," *New York Times* (December 5, 2004); "Poppy Crackdown Could Alienate Warlords and Imperil Afghan Poll, Say U.S. Generals," *Financial Times* (January 3, 2005); "Karzai Grills British Officials over 'Illegal' Poppy Crop Spraying," *The Independent* (December 1, 2004); "Afghan President Opposes Aerial Spraying of Opium Crop," Associated Press (November 19, 2004); "U.S. Backs Away from Afghan Aerial Spraying," *Los Angeles Times* (January 22, 2005); "British Troops Wage War on Afghan Drugs," *The Observer* (December 5, 2004).

27. UNODC, *Opium Situation in Afghanistan*, 5.

28. Ibid., 2.

29. Ward and Byrd, "Afghanistan's Opium Drug Economy."

30. The Senlis Council is an international policy think tank that focuses on foreign policy, security, development, and counternarcotics policies. See www.senliscouncil.net/modules/about_us.

31. Senlis Council, "Feasibility Study on Opium Licensing in Afghanistan for the Production of Morphine and Other Essential Medicines" (London, 2005).

32. INCB, *Report of the International Narcotics Control Board for 1994* (New York, 1995); idem, *Report of the International Narcotics Control Board for 1999*.

33. INCB, *Report of the International Narcotics Control Board for 2004* (Vienna, 2005), 24.

34. INCB, *Report of the International Narcotics Control Board for 1994*, paragraph 20.

35. INCB, *Report of the International Narcotics Control Board for 2000* (Vienna, 2001), paragraph 10.

36. INCB, *Report of the International Narcotics Control Board for 1999*, paragraph 42.

37. INCB, *Report of the International Narcotics Control Board for 2000*.

38. Ibid., 1.

39. Senlis Council, "Feasibility Study on Opium Licensing in Afghanistan."

40. Ward and Byrd, "Afghanistan's Opium Drug Economy"; idem, "Drugs and Development in Afghanistan."

41. Ward and Byrd, "Afghanistan's Opium Drug Economy," 51.

42. Ward and Byrd, "Drugs and Development in Afghanistan," 19.

43. Afghanistan National Development Strategy, "Summary Report: An Interim Strategy for Security, Governance, Economic Growth and Poverty Reduction" (Kabul, 2006).

44. See Robert I. Rotberg, chapter 1, in this volume, 17.

45. Afghanistan National Development Strategy, "Summary Report," 23.

46. Ian Hamilton Fazey, "Syria Destroys Lebanese Drug Crop," *Financial Times* (July 8, 1992).

47. Lutz Kleveman, *The New Great Game: Blood and Oil in Central Asia* (New York, 2003).

48. Other consequences of a ban on opium cultivation are addressed in a special issue of the *International Journal of Drug Policy* (2005).

9

The Place of the Province in Afghanistan's Subnational Governance

Sarah Lister and Hamish Nixon

A t the beginning of 2006, the government of Afghanistan presented its Interim Afghanistan National Development Strategy (ANDS) and agreed with international donors to the terms of the Afghanistan Compact. These two guiding documents of the "post-Bonn" period outline the mutual commitments of the government and the international community for achieving concrete advances in three broad areas: security; governance, human rights, and the rule of law; and economic and social development. They come on the heels of the 2005 election of an Afghan parliament and provincial councils, a period of increasing attention on governance at the provincial level, as well as changes to community governance by the introduction of community development councils in over half of the country's villages through the National Solidarity Program.[1] With

When this was written, Sarah Lister and Hamish Nixon were both at the Afghanistan Research and Evaluation Unit (AREU) in Kabul, where she was a senior researcher in political economy and governance, and he was a researcher in subnational governance. Some of the arguments presented in this chapter have previously appeared in two AREU briefing papers: Sarah Lister, "Caught in Confusion: Local Governance Structures in Afghanistan" (March 2005), and Sarah Lister and Hamish Nixon, "Provincial Governance Structures in Afghanistan: From Confusion to Vision?" (May 2006).

these activities has come an increased recognition by government and donors alike that improving subnational governance is critical for realizing the vision for the country set out in the ANDS.[2] This vision includes increased democracy, representativeness, accountability, and effectiveness at "all levels of government."[3] However, both detailed plans and the overall framework for achieving them are still unclear about many aspects of subnational governance, and addressing this shortcoming will require increased attention and strong political leadership.

The ANDS and the Afghanistan Compact explicitly recognize the weakness of public administration, especially at the subnational level, and highlight the importance of subnational governance for political and development goals. They make specific reference to the establishment and improvement of structures that are to contribute to development planning, coordination, and representation at the provincial level. These documents, and the complex processes through which they were agreed, have tried to encourage government "ownership" of the issues and focus donor attention on the problems. For the first time since the fall of the Taliban, there is not only a consensus between the government and the donors that the issues of subnational governance must be tackled but also a stated commitment to tackle them.

This chapter examines some of the confusion around subnational governance, highlighting the implications of the absence of an overall framework for subnational governance and the structures of provincial government within such a framework. It looks in detail at three actual or proposed provincial structures—elected councils, provincial development committees, and provincial public administration. It considers what issues affect the ability of these structures to contribute to improved governance, and how the development of such bodies is hindered by an overall lack of a comprehensive framework.

Subnational Governance: The Need for a Framework

The 1382 Constitution of 2004 affirms Afghanistan as a unitary state. Afghanistan, however, is not only politically centralized; it is also, in theory, fiscally and administratively one of the most centralized countries in the world. Budgets are determined centrally and sectorally in Kabul and distributed downward through their ministerial "silos," while approval of appointments and reporting, at least formally, travels upward along the same paths. In the budgeting process, staff in ministries in Kabul decide how much funding will be requested from the Ministry of Finance, how much will be allocated to the provinces, and how the funds will be divided among different provinces. There are few discretionary funds available to provincial level authorities and even fewer for district authorities.[4] This administrative and fiscal structure narrowly constrains the potential for local participation and responsiveness in planning, budgeting, and appointments.

Despite the reality of existing centralized structures, initiatives to reform subnational governance are often underpinned by implicit assumptions about where and by whom decisions should be made, and for what purpose. What levels of political, fiscal, and administrative decentralization ensure not only political stability and equality of treatment for all citizens but also responsive and accountable government? What are the appropriate relationships between political bodies and public administration at different levels? How can traditional forms of governance relate to formal structures of representative government? Answers to these questions vary according to context, history, and tradition.

Among Afghans there are widely differing answers to these questions, informed by opinions about the nature and history of the Afghan state—in particular the long-standing confrontations between a weak center and regional and local power holders of various types.[5] Some minority ethnic leaders, in particular, have tended to push for either power sharing within the central state or recognition of their identities through mechanisms of local self-government.[6] Regardless of ethnicity, however, many Afghan politicians and policymakers from across the country favor a strong central state in order to curb powerful regional figures who often receive support from outside the country, as well as to reduce the danger of criminal influence over structures of local government. Research has also consistently shown that many ordinary Afghans favor a strong central government as a means of undermining the power of local commanders, at whose hands they have suffered for so many years.[7]

Beyond the orientation among many Afghan politicians and people toward strong centralization, international assistance and political pressure from outside the country have focused on consolidating and strengthening central governmental institutions following the Bonn Conference. Concerns about political stabilization and counterterrorist action tended, particularly on the part of the United States, to trump the development of strong local institutions, in part due to justifiable fears of local capture. In some parts of the country, the counterterror and counternarcotics efforts also compounded the difficulty by engaging with and strengthening local power holders without embedding them in rule-based governance institutions.

The widespread and understandable concern about the dangers of "federalism," the lack of understanding about different types of decentralization, and the domestic and international focus on building a stronger central state have all tended to stifle informed and measured debate about what degree of decentralization might ensure efficient and accountable government at lower levels. In the vacuum created by the lack of open public discussion about these issues, donors and other international bodies have moved ahead with their activities—creating parallel structures and great confusion. Much of the fruitlessness of some of the policy processes and governance programs in recent years, as well as the contradictory approaches being taken by different ministries and actors, can be attributed to the lack of consensus on any overarching framework for local governance. As discussed below, the roles and responsibilities of different bodies are unclear, as are the relationships between them.

The lack of clarity about the role of different subnational institutions in this centralized context is particularly evident in discussions about "provincial planning." These discussions often draw on the theoretical benefits of increasing subnational input into planning or on the need for better provincial level coordination of activities. However, these views are often put forward in a contextual vacuum, without discussion of how different approaches to "planning" might fit into overall government structures, especially current or proposed budgetary processes. Even if proposals for increased provincial level planning input through provincial councils and provincial development committees are implemented, there is no clear mechanism through which provincial level authorities can present a consolidated development plan linked to budgets that distinguishes among sectoral priorities at the provincial level. For example, a provincial plan may choose between allocating resources to a school rather than a hospital, but the budgeting structure does not allow this kind of trade-off at the provincial level. It is unclear from what sources provincial (or district) plans might get funded or how these plans can feed into national planning processes with any transparency. The introduction of provincial planning without corresponding structural reform to ensure that plans are able to feed into decisionmaking processes with budgets attached is potentially a waste of time, money, and citizens' willingness to participate. It also risks reinforcing citizen perceptions of governmental ineffectiveness, an issue that has become increasingly salient among ordinary Afghans throughout 2006 and contributed, for example, to violent rioting in Kabul in May 2006.

Despite this situation of political, administrative, and fiscal centralism, the possibility of de-concentrating or devolving some fiscal and administrative powers to lower levels does not contradict the concept of a unitary state and is, in fact, explicitly allowed within the Afghan Constitution. Article 137 of the constitution states that "the government, while preserving the principle of centralism, shall delegate certain authorities to local administration units for the purpose of expediting and promoting economic, social, and cultural affairs, and increasing the participation of people in the development of the nation."[8]

The elaboration of a national strategy through the ANDS process and the Afghanistan Compact has begun to open some space for a renewed discussion of these issues. This disjuncture between lower-level planning structures and the centralized budgeting mechanisms has been explicitly recognized by the government. For example, the ANDS notes that "subnational budget and coordination responsibilities remain uncertain: Because many services are provided locally, there is a need to consult with provincial (and in the longer term, district) administrations on budget formulation and execution responsibilities, as well as reviewing both revenues and expenditure assignments."[9]

Going further, the ANDS acknowledges that there is a problem with "excessive centralization," noting "although discussion of decentralization of certain functions and assignments is at an early stage . . . over time it may be desirable to consider a degree of decentralization and/or de-concentration of some policy-making and budget responsibilities" to increase effectiveness as well as local ownership.[10] This cautious "pro-decentralization" stance may seem very moderate to outside observers, but in the Afghan context it implies a considerable break from the focus of the Bonn period. Despite this recognition and the inclusion of a number of important benchmarks relating to subnational governance in both the ANDS and the Afghanistan Compact, these plans do not offer concrete content about a future framework of responsibilities, resources, and relationships at different levels of government and among different bodies tasked with subnational governance functions. Instead they merely note that "government will review the functional assignments of central, provincial and district administration."[11] The process for such a review and clarification of the subnational governance framework is not specified.

It is not immediately clear where such a framework can be developed since there is no one clear "home" within the government for such activities.

The Ministry of Interior, Ministry of Economy, the Independent Administrative Reform and Civil Service Commission (IARCSC), and the Ministry of Finance, as well as other line ministries and government agencies, all have a stake in subnational governance, and there are no functioning mechanisms to bring open debate and discussion into one place.

On the donor side, the lack of a strategic framework has meant that the usual problems of coordination in complex postconflict environments have been exacerbated. In some cases there has been an unwillingness to share information and to work in a coherent manner toward agreed goals, even between programs funded by the same donor.[12] The lack of a focal point within government has also contributed to a tendency for the international community to engage with those ministries or agencies that have the greatest capacity to engage, not necessarily those with the strongest mandate for involvement. The ministries that are central to the debate are marginalized in many discussions and planning. The outcome is the development of proposals and processes that do not have broad political legitimacy and are therefore blocked, either in the approval process or in implementation. Without clear guidelines on how different structures fit together and relate to each other, different programs and ministries have gone ahead with planning according to their own vision. However, they meet resistance when they attempt to engage others in their plans, and on many occasions this result has led either to inertia or failed implementation.

It will be extremely important that the review of responsibilities of subnational levels of government called for in the ANDS be undertaken with the cooperation of different ministries and stakeholders. This review will need to tackle the following questions:

—What are the resources, responsibilities, and relationships of different levels of government in trying to meet the goals of improved subnational governance set out in the ANDS? These factors will relate not only to administration and planning but also to service delivery.

—What is the role of the provincial level in development planning? This answer should include an agreed-upon definition of provincial planning, its purpose, and its relationship to budget processes.

—What are the relationships between different subnational bodies? This answer should spell out the relationships between elected provincial councils and provincial administrations, and between provincial councils and provincial development committees.

To address these questions, the establishment of an interministerial commission to develop an overall vision of subnational governance would represent a good first step and would provide the necessary home for these debates. However, considerable effort must be applied to make such a commission an active and functioning body with wide political support encompassing both the legislative and executive branches of government. An opportunity for wider input is also presented through the process of provincial consultations on the full Afghanistan National Development Strategy, due to continue in 2007. It is also extremely important rapidly to develop and put into practice an appropriate mechanism for monitoring the governance-related provisions of the Compact and the ANDS.

These mechanisms for the development of an overall subnational governance framework would not work in a vacuum—particularly at the provincial level. Despite the structural constraints just outlined, there have been various attempts to introduce new representative bodies and planning or coordination mechanisms at the provincial level. Some, such as the election and establishment of provincial councils, follow the provisions of the constitution. Others are more piecemeal attempts to improve coordination at the provincial level or to introduce planning processes. Finally, efforts at public administration reform have been extended to provincial and, in a few cases, district levels.

Elected Provincial Councils in Afghanistan

On November 10, 2005, Afghanistan's thirty-four elected provincial councils (*Shura-e Welayati*) met to elect their officers. Two days later each elected two of their number to the *Meshrano Jirga*, the upper house of the National Assembly.[13] The establishment of Afghanistan's first elected subnational institutions fulfills part of the conditions of the Bonn agreement and represents a significant accomplishment in the state-building process. However, a number of issues need to be resolved before provincial councils form a functional and legitimate part of the emerging democratic order described in the ANDS.

Before the 2005 elections took place, extended consultations between Afghan and international governmental and nongovernmental actors considered the role of the provincial councils. Eventually the cabinet awarded them relatively weak advisory functions focused on provincial level development planning and oversight of provincial administration. While the Afghan Constitution, the Law on Provincial Councils approved by the cabinet on August 15, 2005, and its supporting regulations broadly reflect this outcome in defining the councils' purpose and functions, significant obstacles to the effective practice of these minimal functions exist.[14]

Functions of Provincial Councils

The functions envisioned for the provincial councils fall into three broad areas. The first is participation in provincial developmental planning. Provincial councils are to consult the population and participate in determining developmental objectives for the province and designing development plans. This function can be seen as the primary representative role of the councils and embodies the notion that consulting people and communities is not only intrinsically desirable but contributes to better developmental outcomes.

Even so, there are a number of issues related to the provincial councils' contribution to development planning. There is as yet no framework defining provincial planning and its relation to budgets. No clear planning framework exists to clarify the part each body, including the provincial council, is to play. In addition, the relationship between the councils and the proposed provincial development committees and other bodies also with responsibilities for provincial planning is unclear. How will elected councils' input be included in the provincial planning process and used, evaluated, and publicized? Without answers, provincial councils risk delegitimization in the eyes of both members and electors.

The consultative mechanisms available to provincial councils are also unclear. The law requires councils to consult with the residents of their province on a quarterly basis, but neither the law nor regulations specify the mechanisms to do so. One contributing factor is the unsuitability of a provincially based single nontransferable vote system of election, which means that a council may not have members from all districts in a province.[15] A ward-based system of election that focuses on districts might be more likely to ensure that the full range of provincial conditions is reflected in local developmental planning.[16] The as yet undetermined future district and village representative arrangements will also significantly affect the eventual shape of these consultative mechanisms, so they too must form part of a comprehensive and coherent subnational governance framework. The National Area Based Development Program, funded by the United Nations Development Program and operated by the Ministry of Rural Rehabilitation and Development, does consider the role of provincial councils in integrating priorities from the district level, but risks the problems of single ministerial ownership and lack of broader political buy-in that have plagued other initiatives.

The second function with which councils are tasked is monitoring and appraising other provincial governance institutions, including "law enforcement bodies." They are required to meet with provincial governors, acquire information on the activities of their administration, and communicate their findings to the population. In turn, provincial governors must "take actions" and "design, organize, and implement programs" in "cooperation" with provincial councils.[17] In addition, the law and rules of procedure allow for meetings between the governor or other members of the administration and the council. However, there are no corresponding legal obligations for the administration, and particularly "law enforcement bodies," to attend meetings or respond to questions or requests for information from the councils. Such legal instruments will eventually be required so that the oversight function of the provincial councils can be exercised properly. The reform of provincial administration discussed below could introduce such mechanisms.

Another concern is that budget and staffing arrangements for councils are not independent of the provincial administration. Article 17 of the law determines that "the administrative affairs and service needs of the Provincial Council shall be organized and provided by the concerned province," and support staff are to be seconded from the provincial governor's office.[18] In effect, provincial councils are made dependent in their day-to-day functioning on the very provincial administration that they are charged with monitoring, with obvious implications for independence. The provincial councils have expressed a desire for a budget separate from provincial administrations, but the source of such budgets is not yet clear.

Finally, the councils' third function is to participate in the three interrelated activities of conflict resolution, elimination of customs "contrary to the law and shari'a" or human rights standards, and reduction of illicit drug activity. This category of responsibility includes functions of a quasi-judicial nature that require further clarification of relationships among judicial, law enforcement, and customary dispute resolution institutions, in particular in relation to the provincial councils' mandated "conflict resolution" roles. Consideration of the involvement of provincial councils and their relationships with other actors should form part of ongoing discussions of judicial reform and the place of customary institutions in dispute resolution, the promotion of human rights, and other goals. Provincial councils may, for example, be valuable as a liaison body between customary institutions and the formal structures of the state, and their role in this respect could further be legitimized.

In addition to their specific functions, there are issues of resources, capacity, and public perception that will affect the work of the councils. While venues and some resources were found for the inauguration of the councils in almost all provinces, these efforts occurred on an ad hoc basis and may not be sustainable. In 2006, all thirty-four councils noted inadequate working space and finances among their main problems. Even if the 2006 financial allocation levels are maintained, these resources remain limited in relation to the tasks of the councils.[19]

Orientation sessions have introduced the new members to their roles, but members will require ongoing training to help them navigate changing administrative structures at the provincial level as well as to learn about the drafting of resolutions, amendments, and recommendations, and about committee work. Such training should continue to emphasize Afghan ownership, norms, and participation. It should also be progressively based on increased legal specification of the councils' role and relationships to other bodies as well as specific capacity needs. It is also clear that during the election both voters and candidates had little awareness and held widely varying expectations of the roles of these bodies.[20] There is the risk of a mismatch between the relatively weak formal powers of the councils and the desire for representation, service, and patronage on the part of communities and individuals. This problem may be compounded by the presence of some council members with considerable informal networks of influence alongside others without them.

While these observations focus on the mandated roles of the provincial councils, it is important to note that the councils themselves have proven assertive, meeting and articulating demands for different funding arrangements and increased powers and resources through a resolution collectively adopted in 2006.[21] These requests form a useful basis for compromise and remediation.

Provincial Development Committees and Subnational Planning

In 2005–2006, Afghanistan saw considerable, if inconclusive, activity in the area of provincial coordination and planning. First, there was a desire, especially on the part of many donors, for more effective provincial level reconstruction and development planning. Second, the availability of large amounts of money to be spent at the provincial level, particularly related to the counternarcotics agenda and planning for "alternative livelihoods," helped to create new provincial coordination structures. The political weight behind counternarcotics activities, as well as timing issues related to crop cycles, meant that the establishment of provincial entities was pushed forward at breakneck speed, often ignoring existing or planned structures and other government-supported initiatives.

Recognizing the need for improved coordination of activities at the provincial level, a number of different agencies began parallel initiatives to establish coordination mechanisms. Different bodies with different names emerged across the country. Some had their roots in the previously established United Nations Assistance Mission in Afghanistan (UNAMA)–supported provincial coordination bodies, others were initiated by donors or provincial reconstruction teams (PRTs), and some were begun on the initiative of governors. The desire by many actors for better coordination is understandable, and there have been some notable successes in donor-driven coordination activities in some provinces. In Bamian, for example, the UNAMA office and the PRT have been instrumental in ensuring appropriate provincial level coordination. However, many acting in this area tended to pay only token attention to the structures of subnational administration. Moreover, they failed to understand, or perhaps chose to ignore, the limited legal, fiscal, and political mandate for subnational planning.

When the duplication of activities and structures became clear in summer 2005, a working group was established in Kabul, initially with representation from the Ministries of Interior, Finance, and Rural Rehabilitation and Development, and later expanded to include the IARCSC, Ministry of Economy, and a number of donors. A jointly agreed document outlining the structure and functions of provincial development committees (PDCs) arising from this working group was presented to the cabinet. However, the Ministry of Economy was subsequently asked to prepare a new plan and to implement it. The resulting written agreement was prepared and approved by the cabinet.[22]

As far as can be understood, tasks assigned to the PDCs are

—coordination, including between government departments and national and provincial levels of government, and between government, nongovernmental organizations, international organizations, and PRTs;

—communication between public administration, provincial councils, and "the people";

—provincial planning responsibilities, including budgeting and the approval of provincial strategies;

—advising on public and private investment strategies; and

—supervision of counternarcotics work.

However, the resulting approach to PDCs is unsatisfactory for a number of reasons, including a lack of clarity in general and in the following particular areas:

—It proposes powers for the PDC, such as supervision of sectoral projects and supervision of counternarcotics activities, that should not lie with a coordination body but rather with line ministries.

—It gives responsibility to the PDC to draft the provincial development budget when no such budget exists.

—It proposes both a secretariat and a "central office of the development committee" within the Ministry of Economy, which will be costly, unsustainable, and duplicative. The proposed budget suggests that $3 million will be required to set up the committees, and an annual operational budget of $2.7 million will be needed.

—The proposed allocation of duties between the PDC and the Ministry of Economy is not clear.

—Despite potential duplication of functions, no detail is given about the division of responsibilities and relationships with elected provincial councils.

—It is not obvious whether representatives of donors, PRTs, other international organizations, nongovernmental organizations, the private sector, and civil society are all equal members with heads of departments or whether they are supposed to contribute to sectoral working groups.

The cabinet did, however, specify that PDCs should be established without increasing the number of staff or the budget, and that provincial economy departments were responsible for forming the secretariat and making PDCs operational, using existing staff in their present structure.[23]

For a number of months there was no movement on the establishment of PDCs, with senior officials stating that they expected that the cabinet would be reshuffled, so they were not going to push the process forward.[24] Even after the approval of the relevant ministers by parliament, nothing changed. Nonetheless, despite confusion regarding membership, function, and relationships, the Ministry of Rural Rehabilitation and Development is pushing ahead with training PDCs through the National Area Based Development Program. In 2006, the training consisted of "training of trainers" in so-called "generic skills."[25] However, without clarification of these broader questions on the place of PDCs in an overall framework and absent cross-ministerial support, the value of such training may be seriously undermined.

Meanwhile, without a formal and agreed process for improved provincial coordination, diverse initiatives continue to proliferate, creating further confusion. In the southeast for example, the governors of Paktia, Paktika, Laghman, and Khost, with the facilitation of a contractor funded by the United States Agency for International Development, generated "provincial development strategies," establishing Strategic Policy Groups and Responsive Working Groups in a model that they intend to roll out across the country.[26] In Balkh the Civil Service Commission and the rest of the provincial administration turned the provincial coordination board into a "provincial planning and development council." They developed guidelines on the functions and relationships of this body and produced a useful manual that they thought could be shared nationwide. Learning that it was not in step with the Ministry of Economy's approach, they ceased their initiative and withdrew this manual but became increasingly frustrated that no progress was being made.[27] Elsewhere, ad hoc arrangements continue to function (or not), some of which have been renamed PDCs in recognition of the central government's stated commitment to creating these bodies.

Some donors and other stakeholders involved in the protracted planning efforts around PDCs privately say that it does not much matter whether a standardized structure is created in every province, and that it is more important that coordination mechanisms work than that they fit an agreed "model." For this reason these donors and stakeholders continue to support the ad hoc arrangements established in some provinces, and others support the new mechanisms that are springing up. While it is obviously necessary that there is functioning coordination in the short term, as the emphasis on the provincial level grows, it is also important that there is some measure of standardization. Standardization will ensure appropriate input from relevant provincial actors (such as the provincial councils) according to the law and will clarify roles and responsibilities. Standardization may also help institutionalize coordination rather than allowing it to be shaped by the strengths and interest of individuals, such as provincial governors. It may be that the processes of provincial consultation around the ANDS can provide some momentum to the stalled process of establishing PDCs, and donors should use the opportunity presented by this high-profile activity to encourage that outcome.

The activity around PDCs, the attempts to create a proposal that was acceptable to a number of different ministries, and the ultimate failure to produce a workable solution highlight several aspects of the "higher level" questions emphasized in this chapter. Some of the difficulties encountered in the process of trying to develop an agreed proposal for PDCs can be attributed to the lack of an overall framework for subnational governance, with agreement on roles and responsibilities of different bodies. There were, for example, different views as to how PDCs might contribute to provincial governance, with different implications for their roles, membership, and relationships. Moreover, the lack of an overall institutional "home" for issues of provincial governance meant that until the president made a decision, it was not clear who should be responsible for developing the proposal and then implementing it. There was also a certain amount of conflict between ministries on this issue. The experience around PDCs illustrates that a lack of clear political ownership and answers to these broader questions will continue to hamper progress, not only in the establishment of PDCs but also regarding broader reform of provincial level governance and administration.

Reform of Provincial Administration

Early attempts to reform subnational administration took place through the Afghanistan Stabilization Program (ASP). This National Priority Program was tasked with administrative reform at the provincial and district levels, the rebuilding of district level infrastructure, and the disbursement of a block grant of $1 million to each province though the Provincial Stabilization Fund. Indeed, the ASP also attempted to develop provincial coordinating mechanisms, especially around the use of the Stabilization Fund. However, numerous political and administrative difficulties assailed the program, rendering it unable to play an overall coordinating role at a provincial level. It has been largely sidelined, having made some infrastructural investments but no lasting changes to administrative functioning, governance, or planning.

The government channeled its efforts through its public administration reform (PAR) strategy, which has five pillars: administrative reform, including subnational administrative reform; salaries and incentives; civil service management; merit-based appointments; and capacity enhancement. The subnational administration reform element has three key components: strengthening the offices of the governors, building provincial level IARCSC capacity, and deepening reforms in subnational units of key ministries.

The restructuring of departments and changing of recruitment practices was initially piloted under the priority reform and restructuring (PRR) process. In return for specifying objectives and functions, some measure of restructuring, and merit-based recruitment, PRR allowed participating ministries and departments to pay higher salaries to qualified staff in selected positions. Although PRR showed some success in some areas, at a national level, the program proved problematic, with concerns raised about limited genuine organizational restructuring, the extent to which unqualified staff members were simply moved into higher-paid positions, and inequities across and within ministries.[28] The broader PAR program was revised, and activities formerly carried out under PRR have been subsumed into different components of the PAR program, including a more comprehensive reform of pay and grading.[29]

By 2006 there was some progress in establishing reform and capacity-building processes at the subnational level but with mixed results. In particular, a review conducted by the Afghanistan Research and Evaluation Unit in 2004–2005 found that there had been significant improvements in financial management at the provincial level.[30] Additionally, in the PRR pilot province of Balkh, there were encouraging signs of genuine reform—for example, the reform process created a 60 percent change in staff, and the number of graduates working in the governor's office increased from two to twenty-one.[31]

Some areas of reform have proven much harder and slower, however. In general, restructuring of departments, the changing of recruitment practices, and the development of sustainable training programs have been more difficult to achieve. Within ministerial departments at the provincial level, progress has been limited, with only the Ministry of Rural Rehabilitation and Development and the Ministry of Public Health undertaking significant reforms. In most provincial departments, the process only resulted in the movement of a few key posts (particularly directors) to the new salary scale and did not involve significant reform to the structure or function of the departments. In some cases, it also generated resistance among long-standing civil servants, for example, hospital administrators.[32]

Although PAR at the provincial level is new and there are limited evaluation data available, the initial experience of the pilot participants suggested that the PRR process tended to focus on salary change without corresponding attention to the structural and functional reform of the offices involved. Additionally, some disagreements have emerged over the definition of political and administrative appointments. Finally, most, if not all, provincial applicants for restructuring have had difficulty meeting the application requirements without substantial assistance, bringing into question the demand-led basis for the reforms. This difficulty seems to center on defining the appropriate structural and functional reforms, understandable in the context of the unclear provincial framework discussed in this chapter.

It thus seems likely that administrative reform in the provinces will encounter two sets of mutually reinforcing problems. The first set consists of the problems encountered by PAR generally but potentially heightened because of distance from Kabul, the diverse nature and complexity of local patronage systems, and even lower levels of capacity. The second set of problems relates to the lack of an overall framework for subnational governance and political commitment to reform processes. For example, PRR was seen as another "program" to be implemented but without linkages to a holistic process of reform. As a recent Afghanistan Research and Evaluation Unit study concluded, "PRR can be a positive tool if used to help shift the provincial administrations toward a more unified and coordinated entity. But if simply overlaid on the existing structures, in a piecemeal fashion reflecting current vertical lines of authority, PRR is more likely to be counterproductive."[33]

The two key multilateral institutions supporting public administration reform, the World Bank and the Asian Development Bank, agree that the lack of integration into a broader strategy of subnational governance reform is hampering change at the provincial level. A recent review of PRR conducted for the Asian Development Bank commented that "in the absence of agreed political, administrative and fiscal arrangements between provinces and central governments, it is very high risk to be pressing for PRR at the provincial government level. . . . Roll out of PRR into the provinces should be evaluated to reflect its effectiveness without formal government policies in place regarding provincial governments."[34] These concerns are equally relevant for the broader PAR process, as the new program still operates within the confused institutional environment outlined in this chapter.

A critical and related concern is that of capacity building and training at the subnational level. Although there has also been increasing activity in this area, efforts to date have been uncoordinated and piecemeal, and the vast majority of efforts have been centrally directed. Various international agencies and nongovernmental bodies have worked with different governmental institutions, including the IARCSC, to provide a variety of training. Initiatives have included the ASP; the Capacity Building Group training program, funded largely by the European Union; and a number of programs funded by UNAMA and the UN Development Program. However, a recent review of training needs at the subnational level concluded that "although some provinces and districts have benefited from limited amounts of training provided by a variety of governmental and non-governmental organizations, exposure to training was found to be low. . . . The training that has been supplied has been ad hoc in nature and uncoordinated in planning and delivery. Presently there is no culture of training or human resource development within the civil service."[35]

While there are clearly a number of issues related to the difficulty of developing capacity in Afghanistan, it is worth noting that the uncoordinated approach toward subnational governance has also contributed to the difficulties. The success of capacity-building initiatives is intimately linked to the overall success of the public administrative reform process, so that civil servants are trained for their new responsibilities within revised organizational structures. This critique does not suggest that all training must wait for such reforms to take place, but it is important that capacity building is integrated into a structured approach to subnational administration reform, which is in turn linked into an overall framework for subnational governance in general and provincial reform in particular.

Conclusions

Afghanistan has elected provincial councils, established provincial development committees, and begun public administration reform at subnational levels. Even so, there has been continuing ambiguity about the relative responsibilities, resources, and relationships of these new or proposed structures, potentially hampering their ability to perform the roles set out for them. More seriously, there has been no overall framework for how provincial structures fit within the vision of governance set out by the ANDS and the Afghanistan Compact. It is still not known who makes which decisions about what happens in the provinces, how planning is linked to budgets, and how different bodies work together.

The problematic results of a lack of common answers to these questions can be seen clearly. First, it is unclear how different provincial structures should be involved in planning developmental activities. PDCs and provincial councils are mandated to contribute to planning, but there is no administrative and fiscal structure that can make provincial "planning" meaningful in the sense of determining government spending. Until this lack of structure is rectified, it will work against the effectiveness and potentially the legitimacy of these arrangements in the longer term.

Second, since there is no consensus on the roles that different provincial structures play, it is proving hard to reform them and train staff. Subnational administrative reform efforts and the establishment and equipping of provincial councils are expected to improve the effectiveness and accountability of government, yet it is not always clear where such efforts are aimed. Both of these problems derive from the absence of an ongoing political process that can bring questions about the future shape of the Afghan state into the open and begin to provide answers that are shared among the ministries, parliament, donors, and other stakeholders.

Despite this lack of a detailed framework, an opportunity is presented by the elaboration of a general vision for subnational governance in the ANDS and Afghanistan Compact. While acknowledging the complexity, difficulties, and long-term nature of the processes required, including that of reaching consensus on complex long-term budgetary issues, we believe there are three specific actions that can be taken by the government and the international community to begin to resolve these issues and contribute to improved subnational governance:

First, the government should establish a high-level interministerial body to provide a focal point and clear leadership on issues relating to subnational governance and administration. This body must have the political support to bring questions about the overall framework of subnational governance into the open, in coordination with the ongoing National Development Strategy process.

Second, the Consultative Group focusing on governance should actively advise on the implementation and monitoring of the governance pillar in the ANDS and Afghanistan Compact, perhaps with a dedicated provincial or subnational governance working group. The terms of reference for these bodies must be clear, and every effort should be made to ensure, through the proposed reform of the Consultative Group system, that this group is working and active.

Third, donor initiatives to coordinate better support to subnational governance should be encouraged and extended. Donors need to recognize that apparently laudable efforts in one arena and a desire to ensure development, reconstruction, or other activities may actually undermine longer-term and more sustainable efforts in another arena. In developing capacity-building approaches and programs, donors should ensure that parallel or duplicative structures are not established and that their proposals fit easily into agreed governmental structures. Capacity building and the development of a clear framework for provincial governance must go hand in hand to answer the question, "Capacity to do what?"

Beyond these questions of vision, framework, and strategy, this chapter has also raised some specific issues confronting the new and reforming provincial structures. The following are key recommendations regarding provincial councils:

—Elaborate the bases of representation and consultation for provincial councils. This step will involve creating mechanisms for consulting the population, which will also entail decisions about the shape of other levels of subnational representation. It may also involve reconsidering the electoral system for provincial councils as well as that for future district and village elected bodies.

—Clarify the relationship—through reserved membership or otherwise—of provincial councils to PDCs and other planning bodies in the context of efforts to define provincial planning and its relationship to budgets.

—Laws governing provincial administrations and other bodies should include mechanisms to ensure the cooperation of those bodies in monitoring by provincial councils.

—Measures need to be taken to ensure that provincial councils have sufficient resources independent of governors' offices and receive capacity-building support.

—The role of provincial councils should be considered in future discussions of informal and formal justice sector activity.

Similarly, efforts to establish effective PDCs may benefit from considering the following recommendations:

—A revised plan should be prepared that more clearly defines the responsibilities and relationships of the PDCs.

—The process of establishing a PDC in every province should be resumed. It is important that a consistent structure be established in each province, even if the precise details and relationships have to be confirmed as the broader vision emerges.

Finally, the gradual extension of public administrative reform efforts to the provincial level should take into consideration two issues. First, there is a need for increased focus on true reform and restructuring rather than just salary increases. Second, donors and other actors must commit to an integrated approach to capacity building at the subnational level, with a focus on strengthening the IARCSC as implementer of the PAR agenda.

The reform of Afghanistan's subnational governance arrangements has reached a new and critical phase, exemplified by the attention given to it in the guiding documents of the post-Bonn era, the ANDS and the Afghanistan Compact. In the past, stabilization and the establishment of a few key functioning central government institutions have taken priority. While these issues remain important, the spread of reform and state building to the provincial level and beyond is critical. These attempts to bring representation, development, and sound governance closer to the people present new challenges to reformers. The focus on subnational governance provides an opportunity for change but will require strong political leadership, strategic thinking, new levels of cooperation and coordination, openness, and a willingness to engage with the issues holistically rather than on a piecemeal basis.

Notes

1. The National Solidarity Program is a community-driven development initiative funded by international donors including the World Bank, managed by the Ministry of Rural Rehabilitation and Development, and implemented by nongovernmental organization facilitating partners. It calls for elected community development councils to be formed that contribute to planning projects funded by a block grant and are intended to improve community governance generally. Controversially, many see them as forming the basis for future permanent structures of local representative governance.

2. Here the term "subnational governance" refers to the institutions and processes (both formal and informal) through which decisions affecting citizens (including allocation of resources and service delivery) are made below the national level. "Provincial government" refers to formal state structures, including formally elected bodies. "Subnational administration" refers to the governors' offices, provincial and district departments of line ministries, and other government agencies and commissions such as the Independent Afghanistan Reform and Civil Service Commission.

3. See Afghanistan National Development Strategy, "Interim Afghanistan National Development Strategy" and "The Afghanistan Compact," www.ands.gov.af.

4. See Anne Evans and others, *A Guide to Government in Afghanistan* (Kabul, 2004), and *Subnational Administration in Afghanistan: Assessment and Recommendations for Action* (Kabul, 2004); Anne Evans and Yasin Osmani, "Assessing Progress: Update Report on Subnational Administration in Afghanistan" (Kabul, 2005).

5. See Barnett Rubin and Helena Malikyar, "The Politics of Center-Periphery Relations in Afghanistan" (New York, 2003), www.cic.nyu.edu/archive/pdf/WBCPAfgh.pdf.

6. These different positions played themselves out in debates at the Constitutional Loya Jirga. See Barnett Rubin, "Crafting a Constitution for Afghanistan," *Journal of Democracy* V (2004), 5–19.

7. See, for example, Evans and others, *A Guide to Government in Afghanistan*.

8. Islamic Republic of Afghanistan, "The Constitution of Afghanistan, Year 1382," unofficial English translation (Kabul, 2003), 38, www.af/resources/aaca/constitution/FinalDraft ConstitutionEnglish.pdf.

9. Islamic Republic of Afghanistan, *Interim Afghanistan National Development Strategy* I (Kabul, 2005), 158.

10. Ibid., 59, 158.

11. Ibid., 71.

12. Personal communication to authors, bilateral donor, February 21, 2006.

13. Second-place candidates were elected to a temporary seat to allow for their replacement should district councils be established and elect their own Meshrano Jirga representatives, as required by article 84 of the Constitution of Afghanistan.

14. Islamic Republic of Afghanistan, "Law on Provincial Councils," August 15, 2005.

15. On the single nontransferable vote system in the Afghan context, see Andrew Reynolds and Andrew Wilder, "Free, Fair or Flawed: Challenges for Legitimate Elections in Afghanistan," Afghanistan Research and Evaluation Unit Briefing Paper Series (Kabul, 2004), 12; Andrew Wilder, *A House Divided? Analysing the 2005 Afghan Elections* (Kabul, 2005). Evidence suggests that many candidates ran with support bases on smaller than provincial scales.

16. One further issue with the election of provincial councils is the continuing presence of article 15 in the Law on Provincial Councils. This so-called assassination clause determines that deceased members be replaced by the next highest vote winner. The problematic incentives created by this clause have been removed from parliamentary election procedures and should be reconsidered for provincial councils.

17. Hamid Karzai, Presidential Decree 4116.

18. Islamic Republic of Afghanistan, "Law on Provincial Councils."

19. Personal communication, February 2006.

20. For an example of the lack of information among voters and candidates, see an editorial in the daily *Hewad* (August 22, 2005/31 Asad 1384). For an analysis of the parliamentary and provincial election campaign, including voter and candidate perceptions, see Wilder, *A House Divided?*

21. For example, council members have expressed interest in having a budget independent of any ministry, the power to approve provincial level appointments and budgets (were they to exist), and stronger mechanisms for cooperation by provincial authorities. See Provincial Councils Working Group, *Report of Provincial Councils National Conference* (Kabul, 2006).

22. Ministry of Economy, "Proposal for Establishing Provincial Development Committee," undated document, circulated October 2005. Discussed in the cabinet, November 7, 2005.

23. Extract of minutes of cabinet meeting, November 7, 2005.

24. Personal communication to authors, UNAMA official, February 2006.

25. Personal communication to authors, Ministry of Rural Rehabilitation and Development officials, May 4, 2006.

26. See "Provincial Development Strategy," undated anonymous document circulated in March 2006; see also Al-Haj Mohammad Gulab Mangal, Governor of Laghman Province, "Provincial Development Strategy," presentation at the Open Forum, Agency Coordinating Body for Afghan Relief (Kabul, March 29, 2006).

27. Personal communication to authors, officials at the Civil Service Commission, Balkh, April 23, 2006.

28. For a useful review of these broader problems, see Islamic Republic of Afghanistan and IARCSC, "Review: Priority Reform and Restructuring Initiatives" (Kabul, August 2005).

29. See Afghanistan National Development Strategy, "Government of Afghanistan's PAR Strategy and Program, 1385-9," draft (Kabul, 2005), www.ands.gov.af/admin/ands/goa/upload/UploadFolder/PAR%20Strategy%20-%2016%20Oct%20-%20English.pdf.

30. Sarah Lister and Hamish Nixon, "Provincial Governance Structures in Afghanistan: From Confusion to Vision?" (May 2006).

31. Governor Mohammed Atta, Ministry of Interior, and IARCSC, presentation at the IARCSC (Kabul, May 2, 2006).

32. Author interviews, Ministry of Public Health officials, July 2005.

33. Evans and Osmani, *Assessing Progress*, 28.

34. Islamic Republic of Afghanistan and IARCSC, "Priority Reform," 5, 10. See also World Bank, "Afghanistan. Public Administration Reform. Key Issues for Discussion," unpublished (May 9, 2005).

35. Islamic Republic of Afghanistan, IARCSC, and UN Development Program, "Subnational Training Needs Assessment Report" (Kabul, 2005).

Contributors

HEDAYAT AMIN ARSALA was appointed as the senior adviser to the president of Afghanistan and Minister of Commerce in 2004. In the latter capacity he also served as the chairman of the High Commission on Investment. Arsala worked at the World Bank in various economic and senior operational positions between 1969 and 1987. He left the World Bank to join the Afghan resistance movement, where he served as a minister of finance in the government in exile. After the change in regime, he became minister of foreign affairs of Afghanistan in the early 1990s. In 2001, he played an active role in the Bonn Conference and was appointed vice chairman and minister of finance under the interim administration. He was appointed vice president of Afghanistan in 2002. At the same time, he chaired the Independent Administrative Reform and Civil Service Commission, the National Economic Coordination Council, and the National Census Committee.

CINDY FAZEY is a criminologist. She was appointed Visiting Professor of International Drug Policy at the University of Liverpool in 1998, after eight years with the United Nations Drug Control Program in Vienna. She was the organization's first chief of demand reduction and later interregional adviser to member states on the subject. She drafted the UN Declaration on the Guiding Principles of Demand Reduction and steered it through the General Assembly drug summit in 1998.

ALI A. JALALI, formerly Minister of the Interior of Afghanistan (2003–2005), currently serves as a professor at the Near East South Asia Center for Strategic Studies, National Defense University. Jalali served as the director of the Afghanistan National Radio Network Initiative and chief of the Pashto Service at the Voice of America. A former officer in the Afghan army, Colonel Jalali served as a top military planner with the Afghan resistance after the Soviet invasion of Afghanistan. He is a graduate of high command and staff colleges in Afghanistan, Britain, and the United States. Jalali is the author of numerous books and articles on political, military, and security issues, including *Afghanistan Guerilla Warfare: In the Words of the Mujahideen Fighters* (2002) and *The Other Side of the Mountain: Mujahideen Tactics in the Soviet-Afghan War* (1994).

HEKMAT KARZAI is the head of the Centre for Conflict and Peace Studies, Kabul, Afghanistan. He currently serves as a Risk Management Solutions Fellow at the International Centre for Political Violence and Terrorism Research, Institute of Defense and Strategic Studies, Singapore. Earlier, Karzai was first secretary to the Embassy of Afghanistan in Washington, D.C.

SARAH LISTER was senior researcher, political economy and governance, at the Afghanistan Research and Evaluation Unit in Kabul (2003–2006). She has also worked at the Institute of Development Studies, Sussex. She holds a Ph.D. in social policy from the London School of Economics.

ALASTAIR J. MCKECHNIE is the World Bank's country director for Afghanistan, Bhutan, Maldives, and regional programs. He coordinated the regional response to the Asian tsunami disaster. Formerly, he was operations director for the South Asia region, where in addition to his Afghanistan work, he assisted the vice president for the region and oversaw the Bank's operations in South Asia. Earlier, he was the energy sector director for the South Asia region, responsible for the Bank's energy operations in Bangladesh, India, Nepal, Pakistan, and Sri Lanka. McKechnie was formerly the World Bank division chief for Energy, Infrastructure, and Private-Sector Development in the Maghreb, Egypt, and Iran Department in the Middle East–North Africa region from 1991 to 1997. From 1987 to 1991 he was a manager in a UN Development Program–World Bank energy sector technical assistance program.

PAULA R. NEWBERG was Dean of Special Programs at Skidmore College. Newberg has spent most of the past decade working overseas, first as Peace Corps country director for the Kyrgyz Republic, and then as an adviser to the United Nations and its partner organizations in countries undergoing crisis and transition in Europe, Africa, and Asia. A specialist in democracy and governance, she has also helped to establish, finance, and manage an array of nongovernmental organizations in the United States, Europe, and Asia. Newberg was a senior associate at the Carnegie Endowment for International Peace. Newberg has taught at the Columbia University Graduate School of International and Public Affairs, the Rutgers University Graduate School of Management, and the Nitze School of International Affairs at Johns Hopkins University. She is the author of books and monographs including *Judging the State: Courts and Constitutional Politics in Pakistan* (1995), *Double Betrayal: Human Rights and Insurgency in Kashmir* (1995), and "Politics at the Heart: The Architecture of Humanitarian Assistance to Afghanistan" (1999).

HAMISH NIXON was the subnational governance researcher at the Afghanistan Research and Evaluation Unit in Kabul (2005–2006). He has researched and advised on postconflict governance issues in Cambodia, El Salvador, and Afghanistan, and has supervised or monitored numerous postconflict and transitional elections in Afghanistan, the Balkans, Russia, the Middle East, Central America, and Southeast Asia. He completed his Ph.D. on peace processes and postconflict political development at St. Antony's College, University of Oxford.

ROBERT I. ROTBERG is President, World Peace Foundation, and Director of the Belfer Center's Program on Intrastate Conflict and Conflict Resolution in the Kennedy School of Government, Harvard University. He was professor of Political Science and History, MIT; academic vice president, Tufts University; and president, Lafayette College. He is the author and editor of numerous books and articles on U.S. foreign policy, Africa, Asia, and the Caribbean, most recently *Battling Terrorism in the Horn of Africa* (2005), *Crafting the New Nigeria: Confronting the Challenges* (2004), *When States Fail: Causes and Consequences* (2004), *State Failure and State Weakness in a Time of Terror* (2003), *Ending Autocracy, Enabling Democracy: The Tribulations of Southern Africa*

1960–2000 (2002), *Peacekeeping and Peace Enforcement in Africa: Methods of Conflict Prevention* (2000), and *Truth v. Justice: The Morality of Truth Commissions* (2000).

S. FREDERICK STARR is chairman of the Central Asia–Caucasus Institute and research professor at the School of Advanced International Studies, Johns Hopkins University. Starr is the former president of Oberlin College and of the Aspen Institute, founding director of the Kennan Institute for Advanced Russian Studies, the first non-Russian laureate of the Literary Gazette in Moscow, a former associate professor of history at Princeton University, and past vice president for Academic Affairs at Tulane University, where he also taught in the School of Architecture. He was rector pro tem of the University of Central Asia. He holds a Ph.D. in history from Princeton University and is the author or editor of twenty books and more than 200 articles on Russian and Eurasian affairs, including *Xinjiang: China's Muslim Borderland* (2004).

Index

United Nations Assistance Mission to
  Afghanistan (UNAMA), 124, 215, 221
United Nations Development Fund, 188
United Nations Development Program, 124,
  142, 212, 221
United Nations Human Development Index,
  6, 140
United Nations Office on Drugs and Crime
  (UNODC), 18, 113, 140, 180, 186,
  191–92
United States: antinarcotics strategies, 16,
  192–93; relations with central Asian
  countries, 170–71, 172, 173; relations
  with Iran, 173–74; relations with
  Pakistan, 174; September *11, 2001*,
  attacks, 22, 27; strategic partnership with
  Afghanistan, 44, 51; support of anti-
  Soviet mujahideen, 26
U.S.-Afghan-Pakistani Commission, 41
U.S. Agency for International Development,
  115, 217
U.S. Army, cultural blunders, 71–72. *See also*
  United States forces
U.S. Defense Intelligence Agency, 2
United States forces: cultural blunders,
  71–73; detainees, 62, 72; negative impact,
  43–44; number of, 4, 43, 57; status of
  forces agreement, 44; support of Karzai
  government, 2. *See also* Coalition forces;
  Operation Enduring Freedom
UNODC. *See* United Nations Office on
  Drugs and Crime
Urbanization, 15
Uruzgan province, 2, 16
Uzbekistan: foreign policy, 173, 174; Islamic
  Movement of, 157; relations with Afghan-
  istan, 157; relations with United States,
  170–71, 173; road links to Afghanistan,
  160; trade impediments, 165; trade with
  Afghanistan, 161

Uzbeks, 10, 26, 157, 181. *See also* Northern
  Alliance

Villages. *See* Local government

Wahhabis, 28, 60
Walsh, Declan, 7–8
War crimes, 93
Ward, Christopher, 196–97
Warlords: conflicts among, 31–32; drug
  profits, 16, 182, 198; foreign support,
  157; in government, 45; militias, 30, 32,
  44; power, 30, 31, 44–45; relations with
  Karzai government, 16
Water: irrigation, 113, 114, 116; regional
  resource management, 128
Websites, 65, 67
Wheat production, 15, 17–19, 113, 114
Women, role in opium poppy cultivation, 184
World Bank: on administrative reform, 220;
  Afghanistan Reconstruction Trust Fund,
  124; bureaucratic organization, 167;
  business registration system study, 146;
  economic statistics, 12; on institutional
  capacity, 101; needs assessment for
  Afghanistan, 38; property rights system
  reports, 13, 109–10, 144; revenue
  mobilization scenarios, 123; studies of
  anti-drug strategies, 196–97; view of
  Afghan banking system, 14
World Trade Organization (WTO), 147,
  148–49, 166

Xinjiang Uighur Autonomous Region,
  China, 157–58, 161, 162

Zabul province, 2
Zadran, Bacha Khan, 31
Zakhilwal, Omar, 167
Zhang Deguang, 167
Zubaydah, Abu, 73